ROBIN
RESCUES
DINNER

ROBIN
RESCUES
DINNER

52 Weeks of Quick-Fix
Meals, **350 Recipes**,
and a Realistic Plan
to Get Weeknight
Dinners on the Table

ROBIN MILLER

Clarkson Potter/Publishers
New York

For Kyle and Luke, my superstar, ever-amazing, precious little boys

Published in the United States by Clarkson Potter/Publishers, an imprint of the Crown Publishing Group,
a division of Random House, Inc., New York.
www.crownpublishing.com
www.clarksonpotter.com

CLARKSON POTTER is a trademark and POTTER with colophon is a registered trademark of Random House, Inc.

Library of Congress Cataloging-in-Publication Data
Miller, Robin, 1964–
    Robin rescues dinner / Robin Miller.
        p.   cm.
    Includes index.
    1. Quick and easy cookery. 2. Dinners and Dining. I. Title.
    TX833.5.M5453   2009
    641.5'55—dc22   2008036066

ISBN 978-0-307-45140-8

Printed in the United States of America

Design by Elizabeth Van Itallie

10   9   8   7   6   5   4   3   2   1

First Edition

Contents

Introduction

Imagine this: It's Tuesday night. The baseball game just went into extra innings. It's already getting dark and everyone's starved. Wouldn't you feel great knowing that you don't have to rush home to start dinner? Wouldn't you want to have a stash of meals ready for whatever the week throws at you?

Welcome to a year's worth of quick and delicious weeknight meals! That's right, you can sit down to 52 weeks of home-cooked meals, dishes that are flavorful, healthful, and varied enough to keep everyone satisfied. It's possible—even for time-strapped households (and whose isn't?!)—I promise!

It's one thing to have an ambitious plan to cook a healthy dinner from scratch for your family every single weeknight; it's an entirely different thing to execute it. I am not superwoman—and this book won't turn you into her, either; but it will share my bag of tricks for taking the stress out of weeknight cooking. It's no big secret how I get it done. It's all about the planning.

On the weekend, I map out my week ahead. First and foremost, I am realistic about what that week looks like: hectic! Between after-school activities for my boys, work for my husband and me, school functions, play dates, and everything else, it's invariably going to be another fun, busy week! But if I have three meals planned out and ready to go before Monday rolls around, I feel better prepared already. I don't set the bar so high that I can't meet it.

Cooking three school-night meals a week is completely doable, especially when you make "planned" leftovers from one meal to use on another night. If you're already cooking chicken breasts, cook extra to reinvent into a completely new meal. A great way to plan extras from a pork dish, for example, is to turn the Bacon-Wrapped Pork Tenderloin with Roasted Pineapple into the Alsatian Tart. Also, you can use extra steak from the Seared Teriyaki Beef Roll with Gingered Vegetables to make the Chimichangas Ranchero with Steak and Pink Beans. I also have dozens of fast meals-in-minutes ideas up my sleeve for whipping up something from pantry ingredients. Having three weeknight meals in the bag still leaves room for a little spontaneity—and for take-out night, aka the cook's night off!

So that's what *Robin Rescues Dinner* is all about: stress-free weeknight meals. Between these covers, you'll find 156 recipes for those dinners, along with heaps of optional sides and desserts; a bunch of ideas for almost instantaneous homemade meals; and a whole lot of room for flexibility. All told I have outlined more than 350 dishes in this book! The weeks run from the beginning of the year in January to the end, roughly following the seasons. So if you pick up this book during the summer, look someplace in the middle to find recipes perfect for warm weather and an abundance of fresh summer produce, such as Chicken Burgers with Guacamole, Cheddar, and Charred Tomatoes; Grilled Tuna with Parsley-Parmesan Vinaigrette; Grilled Moroccan Steak with Charred Zucchini-Mint Salsa; and Peach Tiramisù Parfaits. In colder weather, head for the extremes (the front and back of the book) for meals to warm you up from the inside out, such as Hearts of Palm Bake with Chicken and Gorgonzola; Beef and Noodles in Whiskey Cream Sauce; Pork Stew with Poblano Chiles and Hominy; and Potato Galette with Ham, Rosemary, and Goat Cheese.

You might also note a number of grilled dishes that give instructions for cooking on a stovetop grill pan or griddle. I chose this indoor method because this is what's real for weeknights when you're pressed for time. Any of the grilled dishes can go on a gas or charcoal grill on the weekend when you have time to fire it up.

Pick Your Prep Day (or Not)

At the beginning of each chapter, you'll find a Prep List of things you *can* do in advance, *if you want,* to make the week's dishes come together with even greater ease. You can choose to do just a couple of things ahead, such as chop an onion for a soup or cook pasta for a chicken casserole, or you can do slightly more, such as cook that soup in its entirety or assemble that casserole. Or you can do absolutely *nothing* ahead. You decide when you spend the time, whether it's on a prep day or on the day you enjoy the meal. It's all about giving you options. Even if you decide not to prep ahead *one single thing* for the week, the recipes are still simple enough for any weeknight preparation, from start to finish. Each recipe has a prep time and cook time listed, so you know how much time you'll invest before you begin. For weeks when you know you are going to be super busy, opt for dishes with minimal prep and cook times.

Additionally, each Prep List maps out the game plan for the week, including cooking an extra quantity of some ingredient on night one to have planned leftovers for another recipe that week.

For me, my prep time is often Saturday morning, right when I get back from the grocery store. For others, it might be Friday afternoon. It doesn't matter when you carve out a little time; the payoff is worthwhile during an especially busy week. Don't worry, I don't expect you to spend all Saturday morning chopping carrots and boiling pasta (I wouldn't do that, so I wouldn't assume anyone else would want to!). Just give yourself about 30 extra minutes each week (like when you're already in the kitchen preparing a meal), and you can enjoy the benefits all week long. Again, if you decide not to prep ahead, don't sweat it! All the recipes in this book are so easy, you can still get dinner on the table without a huge time investment.

Double It Up; Bank a Batch

Almost all of these recipes double easily. Use this to your advantage when you are planning a meal to serve eight instead of four. Additionally, many of the dishes freeze beautifully, meaning you can make a double batch (which is usually just as easy as making a single one) and freeze half to enjoy at a later date. In general, most foods can be frozen for up to three months in airtight containers or well-sealed freezer bags with the air pushed out and then can be defrosted in the microwave. But there are exceptions. Foods like salsa and guacamole, for example, do not freeze well. Some foods, including shrimp and casseroles, should not be defrosted in the microwave. I've noted these in the Prep Lists for specific recipes to take the guesswork out of the freezing issue.

Morph It

To give you even more options, I've included thoughts on using leftovers or extras from one meal to make another. Notes called "Morph *to* Another Meal" let you know when you can turn leftovers from the recipe at hand into something else. "Morph *from* Another Meal" notes indicate when you can use leftovers from a different recipe to make the one on that page. I'm also a big fan of cooking a little extra chicken or steak, for example, to have on hand to get a jump start on a whole new meal. Look for Versatile Recipes boxes of morph *to* ideas on pages 23 and 115 and a Plan Ahead box of morph *from* ideas on page 169.

And, keep this in mind: not all dishes can morph to or from one another. When I plan a recipe with leftovers, I pay particular attention to the ingredients. I want not only to create a fabulous first meal, I want a great second one, too! To achieve this, I make sure the seasonings aren't so intense that I can't transform the leftovers into another amazing dish. For example, the extra chicken from Chicken with Sweet Tomato–Pine Nut Sauce makes a terrific addition to the Corn Tortilla Soup with Chicken and Lime, without over-powering the dish. I also pick complementary flavors: Shanghai Chicken Strips with Spicy Citrus-Ginger Glaze and Wasabi–Blue Cheese Dip pack a palate punch, but you'll thoroughly enjoy the extra chicken in the Southwest Egg Rolls with Chipotle Ranch Dip. Again, it's all about the planning. But don't worry, I've taken the guesswork out of it and you can rest assured that my morphing recipes are flavorful and fun!

Instant Meals

Throughout this book you'll find boxes with ideas for preplanned fast dinners that can be made with pantry ingredients or even a rotisserie chicken picked up from the market. So if it's Thursday night—and you've already run through your preplanned meals, there's nothing in the fridge to morph, a night out isn't in the cards, and you're just not in the mood for takeout—look to these boxes for suggestions to get you through the rest of the work week.

Optional Sides and Desserts

Many recipes contain sidebars that provide side dishes and/or desserts that go well with the meal. Make them if you'd like; they're also a great way to extend a meal to serve five instead of four when you suddenly have an unexpected guest joining you (I know I'm not the only mom whose sons' friends often show up around dinner time!). And since I'd hate to see you miss out on a fabulous side dish while focusing on a single meal, be sure to check out the index headings Quick Side Dishes and Quick Desserts so you can mix and match these to suit your menu.

Holidays and Beyond: Great Meals when Company Drops By

Not only will you find incredible meals for "regular" weeks (what week is really regular?!), I've given you several weeks that boast fare worthy of a holiday celebration. It doesn't matter what you celebrate, or what season it falls in, you'll find a weekly menu that suits your needs.

Great examples of recipes to double when you've got company or sleepover guests include Bloody Mary Chili, Roast Beef Empanadas with Two Cheeses and Cilantro Sour Cream, Southwest Chicken Pot Pie, Manhattan Fish Chowder, Vegetable Lasagna with Pesto Cream Sauce, and Thai Chicken in Puff Pastry. These are also perfect recipes to turn to during the holidays, when guests drop by frequently and you have less time to cook (what with all the shopping!).

Week 1

Plum-Marinated Chicken with Balsamic Roasted Carrots and Baked Potatoes with Chipotle Butter

Nutty Asian Chicken over Noodles
Quick Side Dish: Mixed Bell Pepper Salad

Baked Potato Soup with Cheddar and Bacon
Quick Side Dish: Stuffed Endive Leaves

PREP LIST

* Cook extra chicken for the Asian chicken dish and extra potatoes for the soup when you prepare the plum-marinated chicken. (Refrigerate for up to 3 days or freeze for up to 3 months. Thaw overnight in the refrigerator or in the microwave on the defrost setting before using.)

* Cook the bacon for the soup. (Refrigerate for up to 3 days.)

Plum-Marinated Chicken with Balsamic Roasted Carrots and Baked Potatoes with Chipotle Butter

PREP TIME: **10 to 15 minutes** • COOK TIME: **45 minutes to 1 hour**

7 large baking potatoes

Cooking spray

8 boneless skinless chicken breast halves (about 5 ounces each)

Salt and freshly ground black pepper

1 cup plum preserves, blueberry preserves, or seedless blackberry preserves

2 tablespoons reduced-sodium soy sauce

1 tablespoon rice wine (mirin)

2 teaspoons finely minced peeled fresh ginger

2 garlic cloves, minced

3 tablespoons balsamic vinegar

2 tablespoons honey

3 cups (1 8-ounce bag) baby carrots

4 tablespoons (½ stick) butter, softened

1 teaspoon minced chipotle chiles in adobo sauce

Sweet plum preserves get a jolt of Asian-inspired flavor from soy sauce, rice wine, ginger, and garlic. The sweet and savory sauce is the perfect partner for chicken. Plus, as the chicken cooks, the sugar in the preserves caramelizes, creating a superb sweet crust.

> **Tip** Start the meal preparation by putting the potatoes in the oven; give them a head start while you prepare the chicken (since the potatoes take 45 minutes to 1 hour and the chicken takes just 25 to 30 minutes).

1. Preheat the oven to 400°F.

2. Prick the potatoes all over with a fork and place directly on the oven baking rack. Bake for 45 minutes to 1 hour, until fork tender.

3. Meanwhile, coat a shallow roasting pan with cooking spray. Arrange the chicken in the pan and season with salt and pepper.

4. In a small bowl, whisk together the plum preserves, soy sauce, rice wine, ginger, and garlic. Brush the mixture all over the chicken in the pan.

5. In a medium bowl, whisk together the balsamic vinegar and honey until blended. Add the carrots and toss to coat. Arrange the carrots alongside the chicken in the pan.

6. Roast the chicken and carrots for 25 to 30 minutes, until the chicken is cooked through and no longer pink on the inside and the carrots are tender.

7. In a small bowl, combine the butter and chipotle chiles. Mix until blended.

8. Serve 4 of the chicken breast halves with all of the carrots and 4 of the potatoes. Top the potatoes with the chipotle butter. (Reserve the remaining 4 chicken breast halves for the Asian chicken dish and the remaining 3 potatoes for the soup.)

Serves 4 (with leftovers for the Asian chicken dish and the soup)

Morph to Another Meal ▶ ▶ ▶ Instead of using the extra chicken in the noodle dish, use it in one of the recipes listed in the box below.

Versatile Recipes for Leftover Chicken

If you have leftover cooked chicken (about four chicken breasts)—or even a rotisserie chicken picked up from the supermarket on the way home—you are well on your way to a great meal. Try out any of the recipes below, which work well with mildly flavored cooked chicken as a start. In no time, you'll have a delicious and satisfying dinner for your family!

Southwest Chicken Pot Pie (page 67)
Miso-Marinated Chicken Paninis with Ginger Mayo (page 206)
Hearts of Palm Bake with Chicken and Gorgonzola (page 29)
Nutty Asian Chicken over Noodles (page 24)
Baja Chicken Soft Tacos (page 147)
Corn Tortilla Soup with Chicken and Lime (page 142)
Chicken Fra Diavolo (page 87)
Curried Cashew Chicken Salad with Toasted Raisin Bread (page 169)
Chicken Salad with Grilled Prosciutto and Creamy Balsamic Dressing (page 72)
Chicken Caesar Sandwich with Shaved Parmesan and Olive Tapenade (page 212)
Pan-Fried Chicken Enchiladas with Spinach and Cheese (page 130)

Nutty Asian Chicken over Noodles

PREP TIME: 10 to 15 minutes • COOK TIME: **2 to 5 minutes**

8 ounces cellophane noodles

1 cup frozen green peas

1½ cups reduced-sodium chicken broth

⅓ cup peanut butter

2 tablespoons ponzu sauce or reduced-sodium soy sauce

2 teaspoons toasted sesame oil

4 reserved cooked chicken breast halves, cut into thin strips (or 4 cups cooked chicken pieces or strips)

¼ cup chopped fresh cilantro

⅓ cup roasted cashews, whole or chopped

⅓ cup roasted macadamia nuts, chopped

You'll go nuts for this dish because it's got cashews, macadamia nuts, and peanut butter. Each nut variety lends its unique flavor to the chicken, as do ponzu sauce (a citrus–soy sauce blend) and toasted sesame oil. The clear cellophane noodles (also called bean thread or glass noodles) take the dish over the top.

1. Soak the cellophane noodles and green peas in enough hot water to cover for 10 minutes, until the noodles soften and become transparent and the peas have thawed. Drain, transfer both to a large bowl, and set aside.

2. Meanwhile, in a medium saucepan, whisk together the chicken broth, peanut butter, ponzu sauce, and sesame oil. Set the pan over medium heat and bring to a simmer. Add the chicken and simmer for 1 to 2 minutes to heat through.

3. Remove from the heat, pour the mixture over the noodles and peas, and toss to combine. Top the noodles with the cilantro, cashews, and macadamia nuts just before serving.

Serves 4

Quick Side Dish: Mixed Bell Pepper Salad

In a large bowl, combine 1 cup chopped roasted red bell peppers, 1 each seeded and chopped green and yellow bell peppers, 2 tablespoons each drained capers and chopped fresh flat-leaf parsley, 1 tablespoon each olive oil and balsamic vinegar, and 1 teaspoon each minced garlic and dried oregano. Toss to combine and season to taste with salt and freshly ground black pepper.

Baked Potato Soup with Cheddar and Bacon

PREP TIME: 10 to 15 minutes • COOK TIME: 8 to 10 minutes

3 tablespoons butter

3 tablespoons all-purpose flour

5 cups milk

3 reserved baked potatoes, peeled and cubed (about 3 cups)

4 scallions, chopped (green and white parts)

¾ cup shredded cheddar cheese

½ cup sour cream

4 slices bacon (regular or turkey bacon), cooked until crisp and crumbled

Salt and freshly ground black pepper

All the brilliant flavors of stuffed potato skins (bacon, sour cream, cheddar cheese, scallions) in a bowl!

1. Melt the butter in a large saucepan over medium-high heat. Whisk in the flour and cook for 2 to 3 minutes, until the mixture is blended and smooth. Whisk in the milk until blended. Stir in the potatoes and scallions and bring to a simmer, stirring frequently. Simmer for 5 minutes.

2. Reduce the heat to low, add the cheese, sour cream, and bacon, and simmer for 1 to 2 minutes, until the cheese melts. Season to taste with salt and pepper.

Serves 4

Quick Side Dish: Stuffed Endive Leaves

In a bowl, combine ½ cup plain yogurt, ½ cup diced roasted red bell peppers, and 1 tablespoon chopped fresh basil. Season to taste with salt and freshly ground black pepper. Spoon the mixture into 8 endive leaves just before serving.

Week 2

Voodoo Chicken with Sweet-and-Sour Onions
Quick Side Dish: Cumin-Roasted Yukon Gold Potatoes

Hearts of Palm Bake with Chicken and Gorgonzola
Quick Side Dish: Nutty Cashew Rice with Parsley

Zuppa di Pesce
Quick Side Dish: Three-Olive Tapenade on Bruschetta

PREP LIST

* Make the sweet and sour onions. (Refrigerate for up to 3 days.)

* Cook extra chicken for the hearts of palm bake when you prepare the voodoo chicken. (Refrigerate for up to 3 days or freeze for up to 3 months. Thaw overnight in the refrigerator or in the microwave on the defrost setting before using.)

* Assemble the hearts of palm bake. (Refrigerate for up to 3 days or freeze for up to 3 months. Thaw overnight in the refrigerator before baking. I don't recommend thawing in the microwave.)

Voodoo Chicken with Sweet-and-Sour Onions

PREP TIME: **10 to 15 minutes** • COOK TIME: **25 to 30 minutes**

Cooking spray

8 boneless skinless chicken breast halves (about 5 ounces each)

Salt and freshly ground black pepper

2 teaspoons Creole or Cajun seasoning

1 tablespoon olive or vegetable oil

1 cup thinly sliced red onion

2 tablespoons light brown sugar

½ cup light or dark rum (or ½ cup pineapple juice and ⅛ teaspoon almond extract)

1 tablespoon cider vinegar

Why "voodoo"? I discovered this fabulous dish in Memphis, where they call it voodoo for its spellbinding combination of Creole seasoning, brown sugar, spiced rum, and tangy vinegar.

1. Preheat the oven to 400°F. Coat a large, rimmed baking sheet with cooking spray.

2. Season both sides of the chicken breast halves with salt and pepper and arrange on the prepared baking sheet. Top 4 of the chicken breast halves with all of the Creole seasoning. Bake for 25 to 30 minutes, until the chicken is cooked through and no longer pink on the inside.

3. Meanwhile, to make the sweet-and-sour onions, heat the oil in a large skillet over medium-high heat. Add the onions and brown sugar and cook until the onions are soft and golden brown, about 7 minutes. Add the rum and vinegar and simmer for 3 to 5 minutes, until the liquid is absorbed.

4. Serve the Creole-topped chicken with the onions spooned over top. (Reserve the remaining 4 chicken breast halves for the hearts of palm bake.)

Serves 4 (with leftovers for the hearts of palm bake)

Quick Side Dish: Cumin-Roasted Yukon Gold Potatoes

Cut 2 pounds Yukon Gold potatoes (2 to 3 medium) into 2-inch cubes and toss with 1 tablespoon olive oil, 2 teaspoons each ground cumin and sugar, ½ teaspoon salt, and ¼ teaspoon freshly ground black pepper. Transfer to a rimmed baking sheet, in a single layer, and roast at 400°F for 25 to 30 minutes, until golden brown and tender.

Hearts of Palm Bake with Chicken and Gorgonzola

PREP TIME: **10 minutes** • COOK TIME: **45 minutes**

4 reserved cooked chicken breast halves, chopped (or 4 cups cubed cooked chicken)

1 14.5-ounce can hearts of palm, drained and chopped

1 10-ounce package frozen chopped spinach, thawed and well drained

1 15-ounce container sour cream

½ cup crumbled Gorgonzola cheese or any blue-veined cheese

½ cup grated Parmesan cheese

2 tablespoons chopped fresh flat-leaf parsley

1 tablespoon Dijon mustard

¼ cup seasoned dry bread crumbs

I love the addition of hearts of palm in baked dishes like this. They add a mild salty, briny flavor, which pairs nicely with sweet Gorgonzola, tangy sour cream, and Parmesan cheese.

1. Preheat the oven to 375°F.

2. In a large bowl, combine the chicken, hearts of palm, spinach, sour cream, Gorgonzola, ¼ cup of the Parmesan cheese, the parsley, and Dijon mustard. Mix well and transfer to a shallow baking dish.

3. In a small bowl, combine the bread crumbs and remaining ¼ cup Parmesan cheese. Sprinkle the mixture over the casserole. Cover with foil and bake for 30 minutes. Uncover and bake for 15 more minutes, or until the top is golden brown.

Serves 4

Quick Side Dish: Nutty Cashew Rice with Parsley

Combine in a medium saucepan 2 cups reduced-sodium chicken broth, 2 cups quick-cooking white or brown rice, and 1 teaspoon dried thyme. Set the pan over high heat and bring to a boil. Cover, remove from the heat, and let stand for 5 minutes. Stir in ½ cup chopped cashews and ⅓ cup chopped fresh flat-leaf parsley. Season to taste with salt and freshly ground black pepper.

Zuppa di Pesce

PREP TIME: 5 to 10 minutes • COOK TIME: **10 to 15 minutes**

1 28-ounce can tomato
puree

2 cups reduced-sodium
chicken broth

2 bay leaves

1 teaspoon dried
oregano

1 to 2 teaspoons hot
sauce, to taste

8 ounces peeled and
deveined fresh or
thawed, frozen medium
shrimp

1 11-ounce can (or
2 6-ounce cans) whole
baby clams, undrained

1 fresh or thawed,
frozen cod fillet (about
8 ounces), cut into 3- to
4-inch pieces

2 tablespoons chopped
fresh basil

Salt and freshly ground
black pepper

A classic tomato-based Italian seafood soup—what's not to love? Feel free to substitute frozen calamari rings for any of the seafood listed (no need to thaw first). I like to serve this with a warm baguette, garlic bread, or Three Olive Tapenade on Bruschetta.

1. In a large Dutch oven or stock pot, combine the tomato puree, broth, bay leaves, oregano, and hot sauce. Set the pot over medium-high heat and bring the mixture to a simmer. Add the shrimp, clams and their liquid, and cod and return to a simmer. Simmer for 5 minutes, until the cod pulls apart when tested with a fork and the shrimp are opaque and cooked through. Remove from the heat, remove the bay leaves, and stir in the basil. Season to taste with salt and pepper.

Serves 4

Quick Side Dish: Three-Olive Tapenade on Bruschetta

In a food processor, combine ½ cup pitted kalamata olives, ½ cup pitted green olives, ¼ cup pitted oil-cured olives, 1 tablespoon each fresh flat-leaf parsley leaves and drained capers, 3 anchovy fillets, 1 teaspoon fresh thyme, 1 chopped garlic clove, and a pinch of freshly ground black pepper. Puree until finely chopped. Spoon the mixture onto toasted thin baguette slices (preferably sourdough).

Week 3

Mango-Habanero Pork over Cuban Guacamole
Quick Side Dish: Chipotle Rice with Black Beans

Beef Curry with Mushrooms, Snow Peas, and Water Chestnuts
Quick Side Dish: Parsley-Spiked Egg Noodles with Butter

Lasagna Rolls with Herbed Cheese
Quick Side Dish: Oven-Roasted Green Beans

PREP LIST

* Cook the lasagna noodles for the lasagna rolls. (Refrigerate for up to 3 days.)

* Assemble the lasagna rolls. (Refrigerate for up to 3 days or freeze for up to 3 months. Thaw overnight in the refrigerator before baking. I don't recommend thawing in the microwave.)

Mango-Habanero Pork over Cuban Guacamole

PREP TIME: 10 to 15 minutes • COOK TIME: 25 minutes

Cooking spray

1 pork tenderloin (about 1¼ pounds)

Salt and freshly ground black pepper

½ cup prepared mango chutney

1 habanero chile pepper, seeded and minced

1 ripe avocado, peeled, pitted, and cut into 1-inch pieces

½ cup diced fresh pineapple (or canned in juice, drained)

2 tablespoons chopped fresh cilantro

1 tablespoon fresh lime juice

1 teaspoon ground cumin

Sweet heat. Mango chutney takes just enough fire from the habanero to create a perfect balance of sweet and hot for the pork, which gets nestled into a blend of creamy avocado and tart pineapple.

1. Preheat the oven to 400°F. Coat a shallow roasting pan with cooking spray.

2. Season the pork all over with salt and pepper and put it in the prepared pan. In a small bowl, combine the chutney and habanero. Mix well and then spoon the mixture all over the pork.

3. Roast for 25 minutes, or until a meat thermometer inserted into the center of the pork reads 160°F. Let stand for 5 minutes before slicing into ½-inch-thick slices.

4. Meanwhile, to make the guacamole, in a medium bowl, combine the avocado, pineapple, cilantro, lime juice, and cumin. Mix well and season with salt and pepper.

5. Transfer the guacamole to a serving platter. Nestle the pork slices into the guacamole and serve.

Serves 4

Morph to Another Meal ▶ ▶ ▶ Double the recipe for the pork portion and use the extra pork in Pork Fried Rice with Cashews and Raisins (page 216), Black Bean–Mandarin Salad with Sliced Pork and Cilantro (page 109), or Alsatian Tart (page 44).

Quick Side Dish: Chipotle Rice with Black Beans

In a medium saucepan, combine 2 cups reduced-sodium chicken broth, 2 cups quick-cooking white or brown rice, one 15-ounce can (rinsed and drained) black beans, and 1 to 2 tablespoons minced chipotle chiles in adobo sauce. Set the pan over high heat and bring to a boil. Cover, remove from the heat, and let stand for 5 minutes. Fluff with a fork and season to taste with salt and freshly ground black pepper.

Beef Curry with Mushrooms, Snow Peas, and Water Chestnuts

PREP TIME: 10 to 15 minutes • **COOK TIME: 15 minutes**

1 tablespoon
vegetable oil

2 garlic cloves, minced

1¼ pounds beef sirloin,
cut into 2-inch pieces

1 cup sliced cremini or
button mushrooms

1 tablespoon all-purpose
flour

1½ teaspoons curry
powder

1½ cups reduced-sodium
beef broth

1 cup fresh or frozen
snow peas

1 cup drained, canned
sliced water chestnuts

Salt and freshly ground
black pepper

Curried dishes have a reputation for t-a-k-i-n-g a l-o-n-g t-i-m-e. Fact is, you can enjoy the long-simmered flavor of traditional curry dishes in thirty minutes or less. In this meal, steak is simmered with mushrooms, snow peas, and water chestnuts in a delightfully rich and deep curry gravy. I typically serve this dish over rice or couscous or with the egg noodles in the sidebar.

1. Heat the oil in a large, deep skillet over medium-high heat. Add the garlic and cook for 1 minute. Add the steak and cook for 5 minutes, until golden brown on all sides. Add the mushrooms and cook for 3 minutes, until the mushrooms soften and release their juice.

2. Add the flour and curry powder and stir to coat the steak and mushrooms. Cook for 1 minute, until the curry is fragrant. Add the beef broth and bring to a simmer. Simmer for 2 minutes. Add the snow peas and water chestnuts and simmer for 2 minutes, until the sauce thickens and the snow peas are crisp-tender. Season to taste with salt and pepper.

Serves 4

Quick Side Dish: Parsley-Spiked Egg Noodles with Butter

Cook 8 ounces egg noodles according to the package directions. Drain and transfer to a large bowl. While still warm, stir in 1 to 2 tablespoons butter and 2 tablespoons chopped fresh flat-leaf parsley. Season to taste with salt and freshly ground black pepper.

Lasagna Rolls with Herbed Cheese

PREP TIME: 15 to 20 minutes • **COOK TIME: 20 to 25 minutes**

Cooking spray

12 lasagna noodles

1 cup soft herbed cheese (such as Boursin or Alouette)

½ cup shredded mozzarella cheese

2 tablespoons chopped fresh basil

1½ cups prepared tomato sauce

¼ cup grated Parmesan cheese

I think lasagna rolls might be cooler than regular lasagna. Why? Because they're easier to serve and they look better on your plate! I like to make tons of the rolls so I can have them handy in the freezer. As for the prepared sauce, use your favorite bottled tomato sauce.

1. Preheat the oven to 375ºF. Coat a shallow baking pan with cooking spray.

2. Cook the lasagna noodles according to package directions. Drain and set aside.

3. Meanwhile, in a small bowl, combine the herbed cheese, mozzarella, and basil. Mix well.

4. Arrange the lasagna noodles on a flat surface. Spoon a thin layer (about ¼ inch thick) of the cheese mixture onto each noodle. Starting from one of the shorter sides, roll up the noodles and secure with wooden picks. Place the rolls side-by-side in the prepared pan. Pour the tomato sauce on top and then sprinkle with the Parmesan cheese.

5. Bake for 20 to 25 minutes, until the cheese filling melts and the top is golden brown.

Serves 4

Quick Side Dish: Oven-Roasted Green Beans

In a large bowl, combine 1 pound trimmed green beans, 1 tablespoon olive oil, and 2 teaspoons dried minced garlic. Toss to combine. Transfer the green beans to a large, rimmed baking sheet, in a single layer, and season with salt and freshly ground black pepper. Roast at 425ºF for 8 minutes, until crisp-tender.

Week 4

Bloody Mary Chili

Scallops with Brown Butter, Lemon, and Capers
Quick Side Dish: Garlic Knots

Potato Galette with Ham, Rosemary, and Goat Cheese
Quick Side Dish: Butter Lettuce with Pistachios and Mint Vinaigrette

PREP LIST

* Chop the onion, carrots, bell pepper, and celery for the chili. (Refrigerate for up to 3 days.)

* Make the chili. (Refrigerate for up to 3 days or freeze for up to 3 months. Reheat—from frozen or thawed—in a large saucepan or in the microwave.)

* Slice the potatoes for the galette. (Refrigerate submerged in water for up to 24 hours.)

* Slice the onion for the galette. (Refrigerate for up to 3 days.)

Bloody Mary Chili

PREP TIME: 15 to 20 minutes • **COOK TIME: 25 minutes**

2 teaspoons olive oil

½ cup chopped onion

½ cup chopped carrots

1 green bell pepper, seeded and chopped

2 celery stalks, chopped

2 garlic cloves, minced

1 jalapeño pepper, seeded and minced

1¼ pounds ground beef

1 tablespoon chili powder

2 teaspoons ground cumin

1 teaspoon dried oregano

1 teaspoon crushed red pepper flakes

2 cups reduced-sodium beef broth

2 cups prepared Bloody Mary mix

Salt and freshly ground black pepper

Sour cream, for serving (optional)

Chopped scallions, for serving (optional)

Grated cheddar cheese, for serving (optional)

Using Bloody Mary mix instead of tomatoes in chili adds a unique peppery-lime flavor. I like to serve this chili in hollowed-out bread bowls or taco salad shells for Super Bowl Sunday or for a hearty dinner during those cold winter months.

1. Heat the oil in a large Dutch oven or pot over medium-high heat. Add the onion, carrots, bell pepper, celery, garlic, and jalapeño and cook for 3 to 5 minutes, until the vegetables are soft. Add the beef and cook, breaking up the meat as it cooks, for 5 minutes, until browned. Add the chili powder, cumin, oregano, and red pepper flakes and cook for 1 minute, until the spices are fragrant.

2. Add the broth and Bloody Mary mix and bring to a simmer. Simmer for 10 minutes, stirring frequently. Season to taste with salt and pepper.

3. Ladle the chili into bowls and top with sour cream, scallions, and cheddar cheese if desired.

Serves 4 to 6

Scallops with Brown Butter, Lemon, and Capers

PREP TIME: **10 to 15 minutes** • COOK TIME: **10 minutes**

1 cup reduced-sodium chicken broth

2 tablespoons fresh lemon juice

1 tablespoon honey

2 teaspoons cornstarch

1 tablespoon drained capers

1 tablespoon butter, preferably unsalted

1½ to 2 pounds sea scallops, patted dry

2 tablespoons chopped fresh flat-leaf parsley

Salt and freshly ground black pepper

Scallops are so sweet, I love to partner them with tangy lemon and salty capers. The three flavors come together in your mouth just beautifully.

1. In a small bowl, whisk together the broth, lemon juice, honey, and cornstarch. Whisk until the cornstarch dissolves. Stir in the capers and set aside.

2. Melt the butter in a large skillet over medium-high heat. When the butter just begins to brown, add the scallops and cook for 2 to 3 minutes per side, until opaque and cooked through. Remove the scallops from the pan and set them aside.

3. To the same skillet over medium-high heat, add the broth mixture and bring to a simmer. Simmer, stirring frequently, for 1 to 2 minutes, until the mixture thickens. Return the scallops to the pan and cook for 1 minute to heat through. Remove from the heat, stir in the parsley, and season to taste with salt and pepper.

Serves 4

Quick Side Dish: Garlic Knots

Separate one 7-ounce can refrigerated breadsticks into 6 breadsticks. Roll each breadstick until 6 inches long and loosely tie a knot in the center. Transfer the breadsticks to a baking sheet that's been coated with cooking spray and brush the surface of each breadstick with olive oil. Sprinkle the tops of the breadsticks with salt and dried minced garlic. Bake at 375°F for 12 to 15 minutes, until golden brown.

Potato Galette with Ham, Rosemary, and Goat Cheese

PREP TIME: 15 minutes • COOK TIME: 20 to 25 minutes

Cooking spray

2 large Yukon Gold potatoes (about 1 pound total), cut into ⅛-inch-thick slices

Salt and freshly ground black pepper

½ cup thinly sliced red onion

1 cup diced cooked ham

½ cup crumbled fresh goat cheese

1 tablespoon chopped fresh rosemary

1 teaspoon dried oregano

2 tablespoons grated Parmesan cheese

A galette is typically a rustic free-form pie that's flatter than one baked in a pie pan. But since I try to find variations on every dish, I created a galette using thinly sliced potatoes as the crust and ham, goat cheese, and rosemary as the topping. It's outrageously good, if I do say so myself! If you can, use a mandoline or food processor to get paper-thin potato slices and use a pizza slicer for easier serving.

1. Preheat the oven to 375°F. Coat a large baking sheet with cooking spray.

2. Arrange the potato slices in slightly overlapping rows on the prepared baking sheet, making a 10-inch square or slightly larger circle. Spray the potatoes with cooking spray and season with salt and pepper. Arrange the onion slices, ham, and goat cheese over the potatoes and sprinkle the top with rosemary, oregano, and Parmesan cheese.

3. Bake for 20 to 25 minutes, until the potatoes are golden brown and tender. Cut the galette into pieces and serve.

Serves 4

Quick Side Dish: Butter Lettuce with Pistachios and Mint Vinaigrette

Top 6 cups chopped butter lettuce leaves with 1 chopped orange or yellow bell pepper and ½ cup shelled pistachio nuts. In a blender, combine ½ cup reduced-sodium chicken broth, ¼ cup fresh mint leaves, 1 tablespoon fresh lemon juice, and 2 teaspoons Dijon mustard. Puree until smooth. Season to taste with salt and freshly ground black pepper. Drizzle the vinaigrette over the salad just before serving.

Week 5

Bacon-Wrapped Pork Tenderloin with Roasted Pineapple
Quick Side Dish: Mango Chutney–Brie Toasts
Quick Side Dish: Green Beans with Anchovies

Alsatian Tart
Quick Side Dish: Orange-Glazed Beets
Quick Side Dish: Spinach-Endive Salad with Lemon Vinaigrette

Stovetop Tex-Mex Mac and Cheese with Toasted Cornbread Crumbs
Quick Side Dish: Broccoli Rabe with Orange Sauce

PREP LIST

* Cook extra pork for the Alsatian tart when you prepare the bacon-wrapped tenderloin. (Refrigerate for up to 3 days or freeze for up to 3 months. Thaw overnight in the refrigerator or in the microwave on the defrost setting before using.)

* Slice the onion for the tart. (Refrigerate for up to 3 days.)

* Cook the macaroni for the mac and cheese. (Refrigerate for up to 3 days.)

* Assemble the Alsatian tart. (Refrigerate for up to 3 days or freeze for up to 3 months; thaw overnight in the refrigerator before baking. I don't recommend thawing in the microwave.)

Bacon-Wrapped Pork Tenderloin with Roasted Pineapple

PREP TIME: **10 minutes** • COOK TIME: **25 minutes**

Cooking spray

2 pork tenderloins (1 to 1¼ pounds each)

Salt and freshly ground black pepper

12 slices center-cut (lean) bacon

8 cored and peeled fresh pineapple rounds (or canned in juice, drained)

Bacon not only adds a fantastic salty smokiness to pork tenderloin, it keeps this lean piece of meat moist during cooking. Roasted pineapple lends a great sweet-and-sour flavor to the dish.

1. Preheat the oven to 400°F. Coat a large roasting pan with cooking spray.

2. Season both sides of the pork with salt and pepper. Wrap 6 slices of bacon around each pork tenderloin and transfer to the prepared roasting pan (secure the bacon with wooden picks if necessary). Arrange the pineapple slices around the pork in the pan.

3. Roast for 25 minutes, or until a meat thermometer inserted into the center of the pork reads 160°F. Let stand for 5 minutes before slicing crosswise into ½-inch-thick slices. Serve all but 6 slices of pork with all of the pineapple. (Reserve the remaining 6 slices of pork for the tart.)

Serves 4 (with leftovers for the Alsatian tart)

Quick Side Dish: Mango Chutney–Brie Toasts

Spread prepared mango chutney on slices of toasted sourdough bread. Top with sliced Brie cheese. Place the bread under the broiler and broil for 2 to 3 minutes, until the cheese begins to melt. Sprinkle the top with chopped fresh chives or flat-leaf parsley. Serve warm.

Quick Side Dish: Green Beans with Anchovies

Heat 2 teaspoons olive oil in a large skillet over medium-high heat. Add ¼ cup diced anchovy fillets and cook for 2 minutes. Add 1 pound trimmed green beans and ¼ cup water, cover, and cook for 4 to 6 minutes, until the green beans are crisp-tender. Uncover and cook until the liquid evaporates. Season to taste with salt and freshly ground black pepper.

Alsatian Tart

PREP TIME: 10 minutes • **COOK TIME: 30 to 35 minutes**

1 sheet frozen puff pastry, thawed according to package directions

1 cup mascarpone cheese or cream cheese (room temperature)

6 reserved bacon-wrapped pork slices, diced (or 2 cups diced cooked pork, chicken, or steak and ¼ cup crumbled cooked bacon)

1 cup thinly sliced red onion

1 teaspoon dried oregano

¼ cup grated Parmesan cheese

If you think a tart is strictly a sweet dessert, think again. An Alsatian tart typically boasts cheese, bacon, onion, and herbs. Thanks to the bacon-wrapped pork from the previous meal, we've got a head start on this dish, and worlds of flavor.

1. Preheat the oven to 375°F.

2. Unroll the puff pastry onto a baking sheet and fold over the edges slightly, making a ½-inch edge. Spread the cheese all over the pastry, making an even layer. Top with the pork and red onion. Sprinkle with the oregano and then the Parmesan cheese.

3. Bake for 30 to 35 minutes, until the pastry is golden brown. Cut into slices and serve hot.

Serves 4

Quick Side Dish: Orange-Glazed Beets

In a large saucepan, combine 4 cups (2 16-ounce cans or jars, drained) sliced cooked beets (not pickled), ½ cup orange juice, 1 tablespoon fresh lemon juice, and 2 tablespoons sugar. Set the pan over medium-high heat and bring to a simmer. Simmer for 5 to 7 minutes, until the liquid is almost completely absorbed. Season to taste with salt and freshly ground black pepper. Serve.

Quick Side Dish: Spinach-Endive Salad with Lemon Vinaigrette

In a large bowl, combine 3 cups baby spinach leaves and 3 cups sliced Belgian endive. In a small bowl, whisk together 2 tablespoons fresh lemon juice, 2 tablespoons olive oil, 1 tablespoon minced shallot, and 2 teaspoons honey mustard. Pour the mixture over the greens and toss to coat. Season to taste with salt and freshly ground black pepper.

Stovetop Tex-Mex Mac and Cheese with Toasted Cornbread Crumbs

PREP TIME: 10 to 15 minutes • **COOK TIME: 10 to 15 minutes**

12 ounces elbow macaroni

2 cups crumbled cornbread or corn muffins

2 tablespoons butter

2 tablespoons all-purpose flour

2 cups milk

3 cups shredded Monterey Jack cheese or pepper Jack cheese

1 teaspoon ground cumin

1 cup diced roasted red peppers

1 4-ounce can diced green chiles, drained

Salt and freshly ground black pepper

What makes this "Tex-Mex"? I use Monterey Jack cheese instead of cheddar and I add cumin, red bell peppers, and diced green chiles. As if that's not enough, I top the whole thing with toasted cornbread crumbs instead of bread crumbs for crunch! Yum!

1. Cook the macaroni according to the package directions. Drain and set aside.

2. Put the cornbread in a large dry skillet and set the pan over medium-high heat. Cook, shaking the pan frequently to prevent burning, for 5 minutes, until the cornbread crumbs are golden brown. Set aside.

3. Meanwhile, melt the butter in a large saucepan over medium heat. Whisk in the flour and cook for 2 to 3 minutes, until the mixture is blended and smooth. Whisk in the milk, cheese, and cumin and cook until the cheese melts. Fold in the macaroni, red peppers, and green chiles and season to taste with salt and pepper.

4. Spoon the mixture into shallow bowls and top with the toasted cornbread crumbs.

Serves 4

Quick Side Dish: Broccoli Rabe with Orange Sauce

Heat 1 tablespoon olive oil in a large skillet over medium-high heat. Add 2 bunches (1 pound) trimmed broccoli rabe and cook for 3 minutes. Add ½ cup orange juice and 1 tablespoon reduced-sodium soy sauce, cover, and cook for 5 minutes, until the broccoli rabe is tender. Season to taste with salt and freshly ground black pepper.

Week 6

Grilled Steak with Shiitake Mushrooms, Wilted Arugula, and Shaved Parmesan

Beef and Noodles in Whiskey Cream Sauce
Quick Side Dish: Caesar Salad with Dried Cherries

Butternut Squash Soup with Dried Apples
Quick Side Dish: Mixed Greens with Blue Cheese, Pine Nuts, and Apple Cider Vinaigrette

PREP LIST

* Cook extra steak for the noodle dish when you prepare the grilled steak. (Refrigerate for up to 3 days or freeze for up to 3 months. Thaw overnight in the refrigerator or in the microwave on the defrost setting before using.)

* Cook the egg noodles for the noodle dish. (Refrigerate for up to 3 days.)

* Bake the apple slices for the soup. (Store at room temperature for up to 3 days.)

* Chop the leeks and squash for the soup. (Refrigerate for up to 3 days.)

* Make the soup. (Refrigerate for up to 3 days or freeze for up to 3 months. Reheat—from frozen or thawed—in a saucepan or in the microwave.)

Grilled Steak with Shiitake Mushrooms, Wilted Arugula, and Shaved Parmesan

PREP TIME: 10 to 15 minutes • COOK TIME: 10 minutes

Cooking spray

1 flank or skirt steak
(1¾ to 2 pounds)

Salt and freshly ground
black pepper

2 teaspoons
Worcestershire sauce

1 tablespoon olive oil

¼ cup minced shallots

2 garlic cloves, minced

1 cup sliced shiitake
mushroom caps

2 cups arugula leaves

1 2-inch chunk
Parmesan cheese

Wild mushrooms and steak have a natural affinity—they play well together. Add a little peppery arugula and fruity/nutty Parmesan and you've got a virtual party on your plate.

1. Coat a stovetop grill pan or griddle with cooking spray and heat over medium-high heat. Season both sides of the steak with salt and pepper and brush with the Worcestershire sauce. Grill the steak for 5 minutes per side for medium-rare. Remove the steak from the pan and let stand for 5 minutes.

2. Meanwhile, heat the oil in a large skillet over medium-high heat. Add the shallots and garlic and cook for 3 minutes, or until soft. Add the mushrooms and cook for 5 minutes, until the mushrooms soften and release their juice. Add the arugula leaves and cook for 1 minute, or until the leaves wilt.

3. Slice the steaks crosswise, against the grain, into thin strips. Spoon the mushroom mixture over all but 1½ cups of sliced steak. Using a vegetable peeler, shave Parmesan cheese over the mushroom mixture and serve. (Reserve the remaining steak for the noodle dish.)

Serves 4 (with leftovers for the noodle dish)

Morph to Another Meal ▶ ▶ ▶ Instead of using the extra steak in the noodle dish, use it in one of the recipes listed in the box on page 115.

Roast Beef Empanadas with Cilantro Sour Cream, page 174.

Above: **Plum-Marinated Chicken with Balsamic Roasted Carrots and Baked Potatoes with Chipotle Butter**, page 22. Opposite: **Pork Stew with Poblano Chiles and Hominy**, page 282.

Above: **Steak Quesadillas with Spinach and Caramelized Onions and Chunky Ranch Guacamole,** page 196. Opposite: **Grilled Flank Steak with Blue Cheese–Crumb Topping,** page 195.

Mango-Habanero Pork over Cuban Guacamole, page 33.

Left: **Raspberry-Dijon Baked Ham,** page 270. Below: **"Ham Sandwich" Penne with Pumpernickel-Parmesan Bread Crumbs,** page 271. Opposite: **Alsatian Tart,** page 44.

Above: **Black Bean–Mandarin Salad with Sliced Pork and Cilantro**, page 109.
Opposite: **Chicken with Citrus-Soy BBQ Sauce over Pickled Ginger Noodles**, page 175.

Below: **Miso-Marinated Chicken Paninis with Ginger Mayo,** page 206. Right: **Shanghai Chicken Strips with Spicy Citrus-Ginger Glaze and Wasabi–Blue Cheese Dip,** page 247. Opposite: **Steak with Cognac Cream and Baked Brie Tartlets with Pear Relish,** page 296.

Above: **Kyle's Cedar-Plank Tilapia with Tomato-Caper Relish and Roasted Asparagus,** page 76.
Opposite: **Fish Soft Tacos with Black Beans,** page 137.

Panzanella and Shrimp Salad, page 293.

Beef and Noodles in Whiskey Cream Sauce

PREP TIME: 10 to 15 minutes • COOK TIME: 6 to 8 minutes

12 ounces egg noodles

2 tablespoons butter

2 tablespoons all-purpose flour

2 cups milk

2 tablespoons whiskey

1 teaspoon dried thyme

1½ cups sliced reserved cooked flank steak, cut into 1-inch pieces (or 1½ cups cooked cubed steak)

¼ cup chopped fresh flat-leaf parsley

Salt and freshly ground black pepper

Whiskey imparts a wonderful flavor to this cream sauce for steak and noodles, while also adding to the meal's richness—though if you're making this for a family dinner, you can leave the whiskey out and still have great results.

1. Cook the egg noodles according to the package directions. Drain and set aside.

2. Meanwhile, melt the butter in a large saucepan over medium heat. Whisk in the flour and cook for 2 to 3 minutes, until the mixture is blended and smooth. Whisk in the milk, whiskey, and thyme and bring to a simmer. Simmer for 3 minutes, or until the sauce thickens.

3. Fold in the egg noodles and steak and simmer for 1 minute to heat through. Remove from the heat, stir in the parsley, and season to taste with salt and pepper.

Serves 4

Quick Side Dish: Caesar Salad with Dried Cherries

Toss 6 cups chopped romaine lettuce with ⅓ cup prepared Caesar salad dressing. Top with ½ cup dried cherries. If desired, using a vegetable peeler, shave Parmesan or Romano cheese over the top just before serving.

Butternut Squash Soup with Dried Apples

PREP TIME: 10 minutes • **COOK TIME: 18 to 20 minutes**

½ cup dried apple slices, cut into 1-inch pieces

2 tablespoons butter

2 leeks, chopped and rinsed well

1 large butternut squash (about 3 pounds), peeled, seeded, and cut into 1-inch chunks

6 cups reduced-sodium chicken broth

Pinch of ground nutmeg

Salt and freshly ground black pepper

Cold days and even colder nights need warm soup. Butternut squash makes the perfect belly-warmer because it's comforting and slightly sweet, but not too rich. It also pairs nicely with apple "croutons."

1. Preheat the oven to 400°F.

2. Arrange the apple pieces on a large baking sheet and bake for 5 to 7 minutes, until golden brown. Set aside.

3. Melt the butter in a Dutch oven or large stockpot over medium-high heat. Add the leeks and cook for 5 minutes, or until soft. Add the squash and broth, increase the heat to high, and bring to a boil. Reduce the heat to medium-high and cook for 8 minutes, or until the squash is tender.

4. Remove the squash from the pan with a slotted spoon and, working in batches, puree in a blender, adding a little of the broth from the pan if necessary to get a fine puree. Return the puree to the pot and add the nutmeg. Season to taste with salt and pepper.

5. Ladle the soup into bowls and top with apple pieces.

Serves 4

Quick Side Dish: Mixed Greens with Blue Cheese, Pine Nuts, and Apple Cider Vinaigrette

Top 6 cups mixed baby greens with 1 cup chopped celery, ½ cup crumbled blue cheese, and ⅓ cup toasted pine nuts. In a small bowl, whisk together ⅓ cup apple cider, 1 tablespoon olive oil, 1 tablespoon cider vinegar, and 2 teaspoons each Dijon mustard and chopped chives. Season to taste with salt and freshly ground black pepper. Drizzle the vinaigrette over the salad just before serving.

Week 7

Tandoori Steak Kebabs

Toasted Wonton Ravioli with
Goat Cheese
Quick Side Dish: Roasted Brussels Sprouts with Prosciutto

Beef Tart with Sun-Dried Tomatoes
and Basil Vinaigrette
Quick Side Dish: Roasted Red Peppers with Mozzarella and Basil

PREP LIST

* Make the yogurt mixture. (Refrigerate for up to 2 days.)

* Marinate the beef for the kebabs. (Refrigerate for up to 24 hours.)

* Cook extra steak for the tart when you make the kebabs by skewering only beef (not vegetables) on two skewers. (Refrigerate for up to 3 days or freeze for up to 3 months. Thaw overnight in the refrigerator or in the microwave on the defrost setting before using.)

* Assemble the ravioli. (Refrigerate for up to 3 days or freeze for up to 3 months. No need to thaw before cooking; just add 5 minutes to the baking time.)

* Assemble the tart. (Refrigerate for up to 2 days or freeze for up to 3 months. Thaw overnight in the refrigerator before baking. I don't recommend thawing in the microwave.)

Tandoori Steak Kebabs

PREP TIME: 15 minutes • COOK TIME: 5 to 7 minutes

⅓ cup plain yogurt

2 tablespoons fresh lemon juice

1 teaspoon chili powder

1 teaspoon ground ginger

1 teaspoon garlic powder

1 teaspoon ground cumin

1 teaspoon garam masala or curry powder

½ teaspoon saffron, optional

2 pounds beef sirloin, cut into 2-inch cubes

1 red onion, cut into 2-inch pieces

1 yellow or orange bell pepper, seeded and cut into 2-inch pieces

1 cup button mushrooms

Salt and freshly ground black pepper

Cooking spray

Marinate steak in a yogurt-based sauce that's brimming with lemon, chili powder, ginger, garlic, cumin, garam masala, and saffron before skewering it alongside onion, bell peppers, and mushrooms, and you'll be taken instantly to your favorite Indian restaurant.

Note: When using wooden skewers, soak them in water for at least 20 minutes prior to using to prevent burning.

1. In a medium bowl, combine the yogurt, lemon juice, chili powder, ginger, garlic powder, cumin, garam masala, and saffron. Mix well. Add the beef cubes and toss to coat. Marinate for at least 5 minutes.

2. Skewer alternating pieces of steak, onion, bell pepper, and whole mushrooms on metal or wooden skewers. (Two skewers should only have beef on them for use in the tart.) Season the beef and vegetables with salt and pepper.

3. Coat a stovetop grill pan or griddle with cooking spray and heat over medium-high heat. Grill the skewers, turning frequently, for 5 to 7 minutes, until the steak is cooked to medium-rare or medium and the vegetables are tender.

4. Serve the steak and vegetable skewers. (Reserve the remaining steak-only skewers for the tart.)

Serves 4 (with leftovers for the tart)

Morph to Another Meal ▶ ▶ ▶ Instead of using the extra steak in the tart, use it in one of the recipes listed in the box on page 115.

Toasted Wonton Ravioli with Goat Cheese

PREP TIME: 15 minutes • COOK TIME: 15 to 20 minutes

Cooking spray

24 wonton wrappers

⅓ cup soft herbed goat cheese (such as Boursin or Alouette)

¼ cup grated Parmesan cheese

2 cups prepared tomato sauce, warmed

I love getting toasted "ravioli" as an appetizer in restaurants. You can eat them with your hands while sitting at the bar. This is my version—still eaten with your hands, but dunked in tomato sauce and turned into dinner!

1. Preheat the oven to 400°F. Coat a large baking sheet with cooking spray.

2. Arrange 12 wonton wrappers on a flat surface. Spoon a small amount (about 1 heaping teaspoon) of herbed cheese onto each wonton. Top each with a second wonton wrapper. Dip your fingers in water and wet the edges of the bottom wrappers, then press the top wontons into them, sealing the edges.

3. Transfer the wontons to the prepared baking sheet and spray them with cooking spray. Sprinkle the Parmesan cheese over the top. Bake for 15 to 20 minutes, until the wontons are golden brown and toasted.

4. Serve with tomato sauce on the side for dunking.

Serves 4

Quick Side Dish: Roasted Brussels Sprouts with Prosciutto

In a large bowl, combine 1 pound fresh or thawed, frozen Brussels sprouts, ⅓ cup diced prosciutto or bacon, and 1 tablespoon each olive oil and balsamic vinegar. Toss to combine. Transfer the mixture to a rimmed baking sheet and roast at 425°F for 15 to 20 minutes, until golden brown and tender. Season to taste with salt and freshly ground black pepper.

Beef Tart with Sun-Dried Tomatoes and Basil Vinaigrette

PREP TIME: 15 minutes • COOK TIME: 15 to 20 minutes

1 9-inch refrigerated pie crust

1 15-ounce container ricotta cheese

1 to 1½ cups reserved cooked steak, diced

1 large egg, lightly beaten

½ cup diced drained oil-packed sun-dried tomatoes

¼ cup crumbled feta cheese

1 teaspoon dried oregano

½ cup fresh basil leaves

¼ cup olive oil

2 tablespoons red wine vinegar

2 teaspoons Dijon mustard

Salt and freshly ground black pepper

Tarts look super fancy, but if you think about it, they're basically one-dish meals. Throw everything in a premade tart shell and bake—couldn't be easier. In this case, it couldn't be *tastier* because I combine reserved flavorful steak, sun-dried tomatoes, and feta cheese in the tart and then I drizzle over a fresh and tangy basil vinaigrette. Great for brunch or for a lunch party, too!

1. Preheat the oven to 375°F.

2. Press the pie crust into a 9-inch tart pan with a removable bottom.

3. In a medium bowl, combine the ricotta cheese, steak, egg, sun-dried tomatoes, feta cheese, and oregano. Mix well and then spoon the mixture into the prepared tart shell. Bake for 15 to 20 minutes, until the tart is set.

3. Meanwhile, to make the vinaigrette, in a blender, combine the basil leaves, olive oil, vinegar, and Dijon mustard. Puree until smooth, adding a little water if necessary to make a thin paste. Season to taste with salt and pepper.

5. Let the tart cool slightly before slicing into wedges. Spoon the basil vinaigrette over the tart just before serving.

Serves 4 to 6

Quick Side Dish: Roasted Red Peppers with Mozzarella and Basil

Layer on a serving dish sliced roasted red bell peppers, thinly sliced mozzarella cheese, and fresh basil leaves. Drizzle with olive oil and balsamic vinegar and sprinkle with salt and freshly ground black pepper.

20 Fast Meals from a Rotisserie Chicken

You've seen (and perhaps even smelled!) the wonderful roasted chickens now available at markets everywhere. Buy them hot, add rice and a salad, and you've got a hearty meal in minutes. And when you're ready to transform that tender bird into something truly fantastic, try the innovative recipe suggestions below!

1. Chicken and Swiss Panini with Thousand Island Dressing: Top 1 slice of sourdough bread with Thousand Island dressing, shredded cooked chicken, Swiss cheese, and prepared coleslaw. Top the filling with a second slice of bread. Brush the outside of the sandwich with olive oil. Press the sandwich in a panini press or cook in a large skillet until the cheese melts and the bread is golden brown (when cooking in a skillet or on a stovetop griddle, weigh the sandwiches down with a heavy skillet).

2. Mediterranean Pasta Salad with Smoked Mozzarella, Chicken, and Olives: Combine cooked orecchiette pasta, diced smoked mozzarella cheese, shredded or cubed cooked chicken, pitted kalamata or niçoise olives, chopped fresh basil, minced red onion, balsamic vinegar, and extra-virgin olive oil. Season to taste with salt and freshly ground black pepper, and serve.

3. Chicken and Rice Frittata: In a heavy skillet, combine shredded or cubed cooked chicken, cooked white or brown rice, chopped scallions, chopped fresh flat-leaf parsley, and salt-free garlic and herb seasoning. Whisk together about 4 eggs and 1 cup milk and pour over the chicken mixture (make enough egg mixture to cover the filling). Set the pan over medium heat and cook, without stirring, until almost cooked through to the top. Sprinkle the top with grated Parmesan cheese and place the pan under the broiler. Broil for a few minutes, until the eggs are cooked through and the top is golden brown.

4. Super-Fast Burritos with Pepper Jack and Salsa: In a bowl, combine shredded cooked chicken, sour cream, prepared salsa, shredded pepper Jack cheese, and a little ground cumin. Spoon the mixture onto the center of regular or whole-wheat flour tortillas and roll up. Place the burritos side by side in a shallow baking pan and top with more salsa and shredded pepper Jack or regular Monterey Jack cheese. Bake at 350°F for 15 minutes, or until the cheese melts and the tortillas are golden brown.

5. Cedar Plank Barbecued Chicken Pizzettes: Place 6-inch flour tortillas or prepared pizza crusts (such as Boboli) on a cedar plank and top with barbecue sauce, shredded cooked chicken, chopped red onion, and shredded mozzarella cheese. Bake at 400°F for 8 to 10 minutes, until the cheese melts.

6. Creamy Weeknight Pesto Penne: Combine cooked penne pasta, shredded or cubed cooked chicken, canned diced tomatoes (drained), prepared pesto sauce, and heavy cream or milk (enough cream or milk to make a nice sauce). Heat the mixture in the microwave or in a large saucepan until hot. Top with grated Parmesan cheese before serving.

7. Chicken Soup with Vegetables and Rice: In a stockpot, combine chicken broth, shredded or cubed cooked chicken, chopped celery and carrots, frozen peas, cooked white or brown rice, canned diced tomatoes (undrained), a piece of a Parmesan cheese rind (the part you would typically discard), 2 bay leaves, a little dried thyme and dried oregano, and salt and freshly ground black pepper to taste. Set the pan over high heat, and bring to a boil. Reduce the heat to low and simmer for 5 to 10 minutes. Remove the bay leaves and Parmesan cheese rind, stir in chopped fresh flat-leaf parsley, and sprinkle with Parmesan cheese before serving.

8. Hearty Chicken Chili: In a stockpot, combine canned pureed tomatoes, shredded or cubed cooked chicken, canned kidney beans (drained), chopped celery, frozen corn, chili powder, ground cumin, and hot sauce. Set the pan over high heat, and bring to a boil. Reduce the heat to low and simmer for 5 to 10 minutes. Stir in chopped fresh cilantro, and serve with a dollop of sour cream and shredded cheddar cheese on top.

9. South Philly Chicken Cheese Steaks with Fried Onions and Peppers: Sauté a sliced yellow onion and a sliced green bell pepper in olive oil until golden brown and tender. Top long sandwich rolls with shredded cooked chicken, the sautéed onion and pepper, shredded cheese (either cheddar or provolone), and pickled sliced jalapeño peppers. Serve with ketchup on the side.

10. Chicken Fried Rice with Egg: Heat peanut oil in a large skillet over medium heat. Add cooked white or brown rice, shredded or diced cooked chicken, diced carrots, chopped scallions, minced garlic, minced peeled ginger, and soy sauce and cook until heated through. Top with chopped cooked egg and season to taste with salt and freshly ground black pepper before serving.

11. Chicken Gyros with Tzatziki Sauce: In a bowl, combine yogurt, shredded cucumber, chopped fresh dill, garlic powder, and freshly ground black pepper. Spread the yogurt mixture on pocket-less pita rounds and top with shredded cooked chicken and diced tomatoes.

12. Chicken Cacciatore: In a large, deep skillet, combine canned diced tomatoes (undrained), chopped green bell pepper, sliced mushrooms, shredded or cubed cooked chicken, curry powder, ground cumin, and dried oregano. Set the pan over medium heat, and bring to a simmer. Simmer for 5 to 10 minutes. Stir in chopped fresh flat-leaf parsley and season to taste with salt and freshly ground black pepper before serving.

13. Sizzlin' Chicken Fajitas: Sauté a sliced yellow onion and sliced red and green bell peppers in olive oil until golden brown and tender. Add shredded cooked chicken, soy sauce, red wine vinegar, liquid smoke, hot sauce, and salt and freshly ground black pepper to taste, and cook for a few minutes to heat through. Serve the chicken mixture in flour tortillas with sour cream, guacamole, salsa, shredded lettuce, and shredded cheddar cheese on the side.

14. Chicken Pot Pie: In a deep-dish pie plate or shallow casserole dish, combine canned diced tomatoes (undrained), shredded or cubed cooked chicken, diced canned potatoes or leftover baked potatoes, frozen succotash, a little dried thyme and dried oregano, and salt and freshly ground black pepper to taste. Top the filling with a refrigerated pie crust and press down around the rim. Crimp the crust to make a decorative edge. Cut a few slits in the top of the crust, and bake at 375° for 15 to 20 minutes, until the crust is golden brown and the filling is bubbly.

15. Chicken Gumbo with Okra and Clams:
In a stockpot, combine canned diced tomatoes (undrained), chicken broth, shredded or cubed cooked chicken, frozen chopped okra, chopped carrots and celery, canned baby clams (undrained), 2 bay leaves, and a little dried thyme and dried oregano. Set the pan over high heat and bring to a boil. Reduce the heat to low and simmer for 5 to 10 minutes. Remove the bay leaves, stir in chopped fresh flat-leaf parsley, and season to taste with salt and freshly ground black pepper before serving.

16. Chicken Sloppy Joes:
In a large skillet, combine shredded cooked chicken, canned tomato sauce, ketchup, Dijon mustard, brown sugar, garlic powder, and onion powder. Set the pan over medium heat and bring to a simmer. Simmer for 5 to 10 minutes, until heated through. Serve the mixture on kaiser rolls or hamburger buns.

17. Chicken Spring Rolls with Shredded Cabbage and Carrots:
In a bowl, combine shredded cooked chicken, shredded coleslaw mix (cabbage and carrots), chopped scallions, chopped fresh cilantro, soy sauce, and sesame oil. Place the mixture on the center of spring roll wrappers. Roll halfway up, covering filling. Fold in the sides and finish rolling up. Transfer the rolls to a rimmed baking sheet and spray them with cooking spray. Bake at 375°F for 8 to 10 minutes, until golden brown. Serve with duck sauce or soy sauce on the side for dunking.

18. Curried Chicken with Vegetables and Cashews:
In a large skillet, combine canned petite-diced tomatoes (undrained), shredded or cubed cooked chicken, chopped green bell pepper, chopped onion, canned chickpeas (drained), frozen snap peas, frozen corn, curry powder, and salt and freshly ground black pepper to taste. Set the pan over medium heat and bring to a simmer. Simmer for 5 to 10 minutes, until heated through. Stir in sour cream or plain yogurt and cook for 1 minute to heat through. Top with dry-roasted cashews and chopped fresh cilantro before serving.

19. Buffalo Chicken Stew with Crunchy Tortillas:
In a stockpot, combine chicken broth, barbecue sauce, hot sauce, shredded or cubed cooked chicken, frozen corn, and salt and freshly ground black pepper to taste. Set the pan over medium heat and bring to a simmer. Simmer for 5 to 10 minutes, until heated through. Ladle the stew into bowls and top with crumbled tortilla chips.

20. Chicken Salad with Strawberries, Cucumber, and Mint:
In a bowl, combine shredded or cubed cooked chicken, mayonnaise, Dijon mustard, rice wine vinegar, honey, sliced strawberries, diced seedless cucumber, and chopped fresh mint. Stir gently to combine.

Week 8

5-Ingredient Asian Chicken Sausage
with Oranges and Cilantro
Quick Side Dish: Ginger-Soy Bok Choy

4-Ingredient Filo-Crusted Salmon
with Olives and Goat Cheese
Quick Side Dish: Broccoli Rabe with Sun-Dried Tomatoes and Cumin

Seared Pork with Warm Sherry-
Shallot Vinaigrette
Quick Side Dish: Parmesan-Seared Polenta Rounds

PREP LIST

* Shred the filo for the salmon. (Refrigerate for up to 2 days.)

* Assemble the salmon dish. (Refrigerate for up to 2 days before baking.)

* Make the vinaigrette for the pork dish. (Refrigerate for up to 2 days. Reheat in the microwave just before serving.)

5-Ingredient Asian Chicken Sausage with Oranges and Cilantro

PREP TIME: 10 minutes • COOK TIME: 15 minutes

1 tablespoon toasted sesame oil

1 pound chicken sausage links, cut into 2-inch pieces

½ cup seasoned rice wine (mirin) or reduced-sodium chicken broth

2 11-ounce cans mandarin oranges in light syrup

¼ cup chopped fresh cilantro

Salt and freshly ground black pepper

Five ingredients that taste like ten. Chicken sausage is flavorful on its own, but it's even better when simmered with toasted sesame oil, rice wine, and sweet mandarin oranges. The sauce is so good, make sure you serve this dish over rice, noodles, or mashed potatoes to sop it up.

1. Heat the oil in a large skillet over medium heat, and quickly add the sausage once the oil is hot in order to prevent the oil from smoking and burning. Cook the sausage for 5 minutes, or until golden brown on all sides. Add the rice wine and cook for 1 minute. Add the oranges with the liquid from the can and bring to a simmer. Simmer for 5 minutes, until the sausage is cooked through and the liquid reduces. Remove from the heat and stir in the cilantro. Season to taste with salt and pepper.

Serves 4

Quick Side Dish: Ginger-Soy Bok Choy

Heat 2 teaspoons toasted sesame oil and 2 teaspoons olive oil together in a large skillet over medium-high heat. To prevent the oil from smoking and burning, add 2 teaspoons minced peeled fresh ginger and 2 minced garlic cloves as soon as the oil is hot. Cook for 1 minute. Add 1 pound chopped bok choy, 2 tablespoons reduced-sodium soy sauce, and 1 tablespoon rice vinegar and cook for 3 to 5 minutes, until the bok choy is fork-tender. Season to taste with salt and freshly ground black pepper.

4-Ingredient Filo-Crusted Salmon with Olives and Goat Cheese

PREP TIME: 10 to 15 minutes • **COOK TIME: 15 to 20 minutes**

Cooking spray

4 sheets thawed filo dough

4 salmon fillets (about 5 ounces each)

Salt and freshly ground black pepper

½ cup soft fresh goat cheese

½ cup sliced pitted kalamata olives

This recipe idea comes from a dish I ate in a great little restaurant in Austin, Texas, that uses kataifi (also called knafa), very thin strands of partially cooked and dried wheat pastry, to make a crisp topping for fish. Because kataifi can be hard to find, I use shredded store-bought filo dough to make a dish that will dazzle guests.

1. Preheat the oven to 400°F. Coat a large baking sheet with cooking spray.

2. Using a sharp knife, cut the filo dough sheets lengthwise into quarters. Stack the filo quarters, and roll them together into a tight roll. Cut crosswise into very thin strips. Pull the strips apart, making a confetti-like pile.

3. Arrange the salmon on the prepared baking sheet and season with salt and pepper. Top each fillet with crumbled goat cheese and olives, making an even layer. Arrange filo strips in a pile to cover each piece of salmon and press down, making a crust. Spray the surface with cooking spray.

4. Bake for 15 to 20 minutes, until the salmon pulls apart when tested with a fork and the filo crust is golden brown.

Serves 4

Quick Side Dish: Broccoli Rabe with Sun-Dried Tomatoes and Cumin

Heat 1 tablespoon olive oil in a large skillet over medium-high heat. Add 1 pound chopped broccoli rabe, ½ cup diced drained oil-packed sun-dried tomatoes, and 1½ teaspoons ground cumin. Cover and cook for 3 to 5 minutes, until the broccoli rabe is tender. Season to taste with salt and freshly ground black pepper.

Seared Pork with Warm Sherry-Shallot Vinaigrette

PREP TIME: **10 minutes** • COOK TIME: **6 to 8 minutes**

3 tablespoons olive oil

4 boneless pork loin chops (about 5 ounces each)

Salt and freshly ground black pepper

½ cup reduced-sodium chicken broth or water

⅓ cup chopped shallots

⅓ cup fresh flat-leaf parsley leaves

2 tablespoons sherry vinegar

2 teaspoons Dijon mustard

It's amazing how simple it is to get tons of flavor from few ingredients. In this dish, shallots infuse their mild onion-garlic flavor into broth, and the sauce is livened up with fresh parsley, sweet sherry vinegar, and tangy Dijon mustard.

1. Heat 1 tablespoon of the oil in a large skillet over medium-high heat. Season both sides of the pork chops with salt and pepper and add to the hot pan. Cook for 2 to 3 minutes per side, until golden brown.

2. Meanwhile, to make the vinaigrette, in a blender combine the remaining 2 tablespoons oil, the broth, shallots, parsley, vinegar, and Dijon mustard. Puree until smooth.

3. Add the vinaigrette to the pork in the pan and cook for 2 minutes, until the pork is cooked through and still slightly pink in the center.

4. Serve the pork chops with the vinaigrette from the pan spooned over the top.

Serves 4

Morph to Another Meal ▶ ▶ ▶ Double the recipe for the pork portion, and use the extra pork in Pork Fried Rice with Cashews and Raisins (page 216), Black Bean–Mandarin Salad with Sliced Pork and Cilantro (page 109), or Alsatian Tart (page 44).

Quick Side Dish: Parmesan-Seared Polenta Rounds

Cut a prepared polenta log crosswise into ½-inch-thick rounds. Press each round into grated Parmesan cheese. Place the rounds in a hot pan or griddle that's been coated with cooking spray and cook for 2 minutes per side, until or golden brown.

Week 9

Roasted Chipotle–Honey Mustard Chicken
Quick Side Dish: Berry-Macadamia Salad with Raspberry Vinaigrette

Southwest Chicken Pot Pie
Quick Side Dish: Crisp Celery Salad

Pan-Seared Pork with Tomatoes, Capers, and Olives and Parmesan Pappardelle
Quick Dessert: Raspberry-Orange Sherbet

PREP LIST

* Cook extra chicken for the pot pie when you prepare the roasted chicken. (Refrigerate for up to 3 days or freeze for up to 3 months. Thaw overnight in the refrigerator or in the microwave on the defrost setting before using.)

* Chop the onion, bell pepper, and garlic for the pot pie. (Refrigerate for up to 3 days.)

* Assemble the pot pie. (Refrigerate for up to 3 days or freeze for up to 3 months; thaw overnight in the refrigerator before baking. I don't recommend thawing in the microwave.)

* Cook the pappardelle for the pork dish. (Refrigerate for up to 3 days. Reheat in the microwave before adding the oil and Parmesan cheese.)

Roasted Chipotle–Honey Mustard Chicken

PREP TIME: 10 minutes • COOK TIME: 25 to 30 minutes

Cooking spray

8 boneless skinless chicken breast halves (about 5 ounces each)

Salt and freshly ground black pepper

½ cup honey

1 tablespoon olive oil

1 tablespoon minced chipotle chiles in adobo sauce, plus 1 teaspoon sauce from the can or jar

2 teaspoons Dijon mustard

I love adding smoky heat by using chipotle chiles with all kinds of dishes, especially mild-flavored chicken. Sweet honey and tangy Dijon mustard add still more amazing layers of flavor. I like to serve this dish with quick-cooking rice or couscous on the side.

1. Preheat the oven to 400°F. Coat a large, rimmed baking sheet or roasting pan with cooking spray.

2. Arrange the chicken in the prepared pan and season with salt and pepper.

3. In a small bowl, whisk together the honey, oil, chipotle chiles with their sauce, and Dijon mustard. Brush the mixture all over the chicken.

4. Roast for 25 to 30 minutes, until the chicken is cooked through and no longer pink on the inside.

5. Serve 4 of the chicken breast halves with this meal. (Reserve the remaining 4 chicken breasts for the pot pie.)

Serves 4 (with leftover chicken for the pot pie)

Morph to Another Meal ▶ ▶ ▶ Instead of using the extra chicken in the pot pie, use it in one of the recipes listed in the box on page 23.

Quick Side Dish: Berry-Macadamia Salad with Raspberry Vinaigrette

Top mixed greens with fresh raspberries and blackberries and whole macadamia nuts. Whisk together ⅓ cup seedless raspberry preserves, 2 tablespoons olive oil, 2 tablespoons red wine vinegar, and 2 teaspoons Dijon mustard. Season the vinaigrette with salt and freshly ground black pepper and drizzle over the greens.

Southwest Chicken Pot Pie

PREP TIME: 10 minutes • COOK TIME: 25 to 35 minutes

1 tablespoon olive oil

½ cup diced onion

1 green bell pepper, seeded and chopped

3 garlic cloves, minced

2 teaspoons chili powder

1 teaspoon ground cumin

4 reserved cooked chicken breast halves, cubed (or 4 cups cubed cooked chicken)

1 cup fresh or frozen corn kernels

1 14-ounce can diced tomatoes

1½ cups reduced-sodium chicken broth

¼ cup chopped fresh cilantro

Salt and freshly ground black pepper

1 9-inch refrigerated pie crust

½ cup shredded cheddar cheese

As a resident of the Southwest, I couldn't let the traditional pot pie go untouched; in my opinion, it's screaming for a little more flavor! This one-dish winner comes alive with garlic, onion, chili powder, cumin, tomatoes, and cilantro—all nestled under a golden brown, cheesy crust.

1. Preheat the oven to 375°F.

2. Heat the oil in a large skillet over medium-high heat. Add the onion, bell pepper, and garlic and cook for 3 to 5 minutes, until the vegetables are soft. Add the chili powder and cumin and cook for 1 minute, until the spices are fragrant. Add the chicken, corn, tomatoes, and chicken broth and bring to a simmer. Simmer for 5 minutes. Remove from the heat and stir in the cilantro. Season to taste with salt and pepper.

3. Transfer the chicken mixture to a 9-inch pie plate. Unroll the pie crust and place over the chicken mixture. Using a fork or knife, make several holes or slits in the surface of the crust to allow steam to escape during baking. Top the crust with the cheddar cheese.

4. Bake for 15 to 20 minutes, until the crust is golden brown and the cheese is bubbly. Let cool slightly before serving.

Serves 4

Quick Side Dish: Crisp Celery Salad

In a large bowl, whisk together 2 tablespoons fresh lemon juice, 1 tablespoon olive oil, and 1 teaspoon honey mustard. Add 4 chopped celery stalks and 1 cup torn celery leaves. Season to taste with salt and freshly ground black pepper.

Pan-Seared Pork with Tomatoes, Capers, and Olives and Parmesan Pappardelle

PREP TIME: 10 minutes • COOK TIME: 15 to 20 minutes

12 ounces fresh or dried pappardelle pasta or fettuccine

2 tablespoons olive oil

2 to 3 tablespoons grated Parmesan cheese, to taste

Salt and freshly ground black pepper

4 boneless pork loin chops (about 5 ounces each)

½ cup vermouth, dry white wine, or reduced-sodium chicken broth

1 14-ounce can diced tomatoes

⅓ cup pitted kalamata olives, halved lengthwise

2 tablespoons drained capers

¼ cup chopped fresh basil

Since pork is mild in flavor, I love to spruce it up with salty ingredients like Greek olives, capers, and Parmesan cheese. Add tomatoes, basil, and wide pasta and the dish is completely awesome!

1. Cook the pasta according to the package directions. Drain and toss with 1 tablespoon of the olive oil and all of the Parmesan cheese. Season with salt and pepper.

2. Meanwhile, season both sides of the pork chops with salt and pepper. Heat the remaining tablespoon of olive oil in a large skillet over medium-high heat. Add the pork and cook for 1 to 2 minutes per side, until golden brown. Add the vermouth and cook for 1 minute. Add the tomatoes, olives, and capers and cook for 3 minutes, until the tomatoes start to break down and the pork is cooked through and still slightly pink in the center. Remove from the heat and stir in the basil.

3. Divide the pasta among 4 plates or shallow bowls and serve the pork and tomato mixture alongside.

Serves 4

Quick Dessert: Raspberry-Orange Sherbet

In a food processor, combine one 12-ounce package unsweetened frozen raspberries, ½ cup milk, ½ cup orange juice, ¼ cup sugar, and 1 teaspoon vanilla extract. Puree until smooth. Transfer to a container and freeze until firm, at least 30 minutes or up to 1 hour.

Week 10

Chicken with Maple-BBQ Cream Sauce and Edamame Succotash

Chicken Salad with Grilled Prosciutto and Creamy Balsamic Dressing

"Risotto" with Grilled Asparagus and Parmesan
Quick Side Dish: Arugula with Mango-Lime Dressing

PREP LIST

* Cook extra chicken for the salad when you prepare the chicken with maple-barbecue cream sauce. (Refrigerate for up to 3 days or freeze for up to 3 months. Thaw overnight in the refrigerator or in the microwave on the defrost setting before using.)

* Cook the rice for the chicken with maple-barbecue cream sauce and the "risotto." (Refrigerate for up to 3 days.)

* Chop the celery and onion for the chicken salad. (Refrigerate for up to 3 days.)

* Make the creamy balsamic dressing for the chicken salad. (Refrigerate for up to 2 days.)

* Grill the asparagus for the risotto. (Refrigerate for up to 3 days.)

Chicken with Maple-BBQ Cream Sauce and Edamame Succotash

PREP TIME: 15 minutes • COOK TIME: 25 to 30 minutes

Cooking spray

8 boneless skinless chicken breast halves (about 5 ounces each)

Salt and freshly ground black pepper

½ cup ketchup

¼ cup maple syrup, preferably 100% pure maple syrup

2 teaspoons Dijon mustard

2 teaspoons Worcestershire sauce

1 teaspoon ground cumin

½ cup heavy cream

2 cups fresh or frozen corn kernels

1 cup frozen shelled edamame

1 4-ounce jar diced pimientos, undrained

2 cups cooked white rice

Think of this as the perfect marriage: tangy barbecue sauce simmered with rich heavy cream. The cream cuts just enough of the tanginess to create a truly memorable sauce for chicken. And, using edamame instead of lima beans to make succotash is sure to become a new family favorite.

1. Preheat the oven to 400°F. Coat a shallow roasting pan with cooking spray.

2. Season both sides of the chicken breast halves with salt and pepper and arrange in the prepared pan. In a small bowl, whisk together the ketchup, maple syrup, Dijon mustard, Worcestershire sauce, and cumin. Brush a thin coating of the mixture all over the chicken and transfer the remaining mixture to a small saucepan.

3. Roast the chicken for 25 to 30 minutes, until cooked through and no longer pink on the inside.

4. Meanwhile, set the saucepan of reserved sauce over medium heat and bring to a simmer. Simmer for 5 minutes. Reduce the heat to low and add the heavy cream. Simmer for 5 more minutes.

5. In a separate saucepan, combine the corn, edamame, pimientos, and 2 tablespoons water. Set the pan over medium heat, partially cover, and cook for 5 minutes, or until the vegetables are tender. Season to taste with salt and pepper.

6. Serve 4 of the chicken breast halves with all of the cream sauce, all of the rice, and all of the succotash. (Reserve the remaining 4 chicken breast halves for the salad.)

Serves 4 (with leftovers for the chicken salad)

Chicken Salad with Grilled Prosciutto and Creamy Balsamic Dressing

PREP TIME: 15 minutes • COOK TIME: 2 to 4 minutes

Cooking spray

4 ounces thinly sliced prosciutto or ham

4 reserved cooked chicken breast halves, diced (or 4 cups diced cooked chicken)

1 cup diced mozzarella cheese

1 cup diced tomato

2 celery stalks, chopped

¼ cup diced red onion

¼ cup chopped fresh basil

½ cup sour cream

2 tablespoons balsamic vinegar

2 tablespoons honey

1 tablespoon grainy Dijon mustard

Salt and freshly ground black pepper

Grilling the prosciutto before adding it to the salad adds just enough smokiness, and another layer of flavor. Add that to mozzarella cheese, tomato, celery, onion, basil, and a creamy honey-vinegar dressing and you've got lots of layers!

1. Coat a stovetop grill pan or griddle with cooking spray and heat over medium-high heat. Put the prosciutto in the hot pan and grill for 1 to 2 minutes per side, until golden brown.

2. Remove from the heat and chop into 1-inch pieces. Transfer the prosciutto to a large bowl and add the chicken, mozzarella, tomatoes, celery, onion, and basil.

3. In a separate bowl, whisk together the sour cream, vinegar, honey, and mustard. Add the dressing to the chicken mixture and toss to combine. Season to taste with salt and pepper.

Serves 4

Morph from Another Meal ▶ ▶ ▶ Instead of using the extra chicken from the maple-barbecue chicken, make this dish with the reserved cooked chicken from one of the recipes listed in the box on page 169.

"Risotto" with Grilled Asparagus and Parmesan

PREP TIME: 10 minutes • **COOK TIME: 9 to 11 minutes**

Cooking spray

1 bunch fresh asparagus spears, woody ends trimmed

2 cups cooked white rice

¼ cup sherry

1 teaspoon dried thyme

1 cup reduced-sodium chicken broth

½ cup grated Parmesan cheese

1 tablespoon butter

Salt and freshly ground black pepper

Why the quotes? Because we're starting with pre-cooked white rice, not short-grain Arborio rice. When you start with cooked rice, you slash your risotto cooking time by more than half. But the trick to getting the same result is constant stirring, so make sure you keep moving the rice around the pan as it reheats. By releasing the starch from the rice, you'll create the creamy mixture you're looking for.

1. Coat a stovetop grill pan or griddle with cooking spray and heat to medium-high. Arrange the asparagus spears in the hot pan and grill for 2 to 3 minutes, until browned on all sides. Remove from the heat and chop into 1-inch pieces. Set aside.

2. In a medium saucepan, combine the rice, sherry, and thyme and set the pan over medium-high heat. Cook until the sherry is absorbed. Add the chicken broth and simmer, stirring constantly, for 5 minutes, or until the liquid is absorbed. Add the asparagus, cheese, and butter and cook, stirring constantly, for 2 minutes, or until the cheese melts. Season to taste with salt and pepper.

Serves 4

Quick Side Dish: Arugula with Mango-Lime Dressing

In a blender, combine 1 cup cubed fresh mango, ¼ cup fresh lime juice, 2 tablespoons olive oil, and 1 teaspoon Dijon mustard. Puree until smooth, adding a little water if necessary for a thinner dressing. Drizzle the dressing over 4 to 6 cups arugula leaves just before serving. Refrigerate the extra dressing for up to 3 days.

Week 11

Kyle's Cedar-Plank Tilapia with Tomato-Caper Relish and Roasted Asparagus

Manhattan Fish Chowder
Quick Side Dish: Artichoke Crostini with Romano Cheese

6-Ingredient Rigatoni with Asparagus and Wild Mushroom Cream Sauce
Quick Side Dish: Arugula Salad with Buttermilk-Chive Dressing

PREP LIST

* Cook extra fish for the chowder and extra asparagus for the rigatoni when you prepare the cedar-plank tilapia. (Refrigerate the fish for up to 2 days or freeze for up to 3 months. Thaw overnight in the refrigerator or in the microwave on the defrost setting before using. Refrigerate the asparagus for up to 3 days.)

* Chop the leeks, garlic, carrots, and bell pepper for the chowder. (Refrigerate for up to 3 days.)

* Cook the pasta for the rigatoni dish. (Refrigerate for up to 3 days.)

Kyle's Cedar-Plank Tilapia with Tomato-Caper Relish and Roasted Asparagus

PREP TIME: 10 minutes • COOK TIME: 15 minutes

Cooking spray

8 tilapia fillets (about 5 ounces each)

Salt and freshly ground black pepper

1 tablespoon chili powder

1 teaspoon ground cumin

1 teaspoon garlic powder

2 bunches asparagus, woody ends trimmed

1 cup finely diced beefsteak or plum tomato

2 tablespoons drained capers

2 tablespoons chopped fresh basil

My son Kyle is passionate about his tilapia. And, quite particular. The fish needs to be seasoned with chili powder, cumin, and garlic, and for the ultimate flavor, it should be cooked on a cedar plank. Once you try this, I'm sure you'll be passionate about it too!

1. Preheat the oven to 375°F. While the oven is heating, put an 11 x 17-inch untreated cedar plank in the oven to heat. (If not using a cedar plank, coat a large baking sheet with cooking spray.)

2. Season both sides of the fish fillets with salt and pepper.

3. In a small bowl, combine the chili powder, cumin, and garlic powder. Mix well. Sprinkle the mixture over one side of the fish fillets. Place the fish, spice side up, on the plank (or prepared baking sheet) and arrange the asparagus alongside. Spray the asparagus with cooking spray and season with salt and pepper.

4. Bake the fish and asparagus for 15 minutes, or until the fish pulls apart when tested with a fork and the asparagus is crisp-tender.

5. Meanwhile, to make the relish, in a medium bowl, combine the tomato, capers, and basil. Mix well and season to taste with salt and pepper.

6. Serve 4 of the fish fillets with half of the asparagus and all of the relish. (Reserve the remaining 4 fish fillets for the chowder and the remaining asparagus for the rigatoni.)

Serves 4 (with leftovers for the chowder and rigatoni)

Manhattan Fish Chowder

PREP TIME: 10 to 15 minutes • COOK TIME: 15 to 20 minutes

1 tablespoon olive oil

2 leeks, chopped and rinsed well

2 garlic cloves, minced

2 carrots, chopped

1 green bell pepper, seeded and chopped

1 teaspoon crushed red pepper flakes

1 teaspoon dried oregano

2 bay leaves

1 28-ounce can diced tomatoes

2 cups reduced-sodium chicken broth

2 cups bottled clam juice

2 medium Yukon Gold potatoes, diced

4 reserved cooked tilapia fillets, cut into 2-inch pieces (or 1 pound raw cod or halibut fillets, cut into 2-inch pieces)

¼ cup chopped fresh flat-leaf parsley

Salt and freshly ground black pepper

Manhattan-style chowder is tomato- and broth-based, and my version is crammed with vegetables (leeks, carrots, green bell pepper) and the bold flavors of crushed red pepper, oregano, and bay leaves. I also add Yukon Gold potatoes because they deliver the perfect combination of starch and sugar to the soup. Serve the chowder with crusty bread on the side (or the quick Artichoke Crostini, below).

1. Heat the oil in a large pot or Dutch oven over medium-high heat. Add the leeks and garlic and cook for 3 minutes, or until soft. Add the carrots and bell pepper and cook for 3 more minutes, or until soft. Add the red pepper flakes, oregano, and bay leaves and cook until the herbs are fragrant, about 1 minute.

2. Add the tomatoes, broth, and clam juice and bring to a boil. Add the potatoes and cook for 5 minutes. Add the fish and cook for 3 more minutes, or until the potatoes are fork tender (if using raw fish, cook until the fish pulls apart with a fork, 5 to 6 minutes). Remove from the heat, remove the bay leaves, and stir in the parsley. Season to taste with salt and pepper.

Serves 4

Quick Side Dish: Artichoke Crostini with Romano Cheese

In a food processor, combine one 6.5-ounce jar marinated artichoke hearts (undrained), 2 tablespoons grated Romano or Parmesan cheese, and 1 tablespoon fresh flat-leaf parsley leaves. Puree until smooth. Spread the mixture on toasted baguette slices.

6-Ingredient Rigatoni with Asparagus and Wild Mushroom Cream Sauce

PREP TIME: 15 to 20 minutes • COOK TIME: 10 minutes

1 ounce dried porcini, shiitake, or portobello mushrooms

12 ounces rigatoni or any tube-shaped pasta

2 cups heavy cream

2 tablespoons all-purpose flour

Reserved roasted asparagus, cut into 1-inch pieces (about 2 cups)

1 teaspoon dried thyme

Salt and freshly ground black pepper

You won't believe the amount of flavor just six ingredients can offer—as long as you pick the right six. Dried mushrooms lend incredible depth to a dish, and they have an added payoff: the soaking liquid used to rehydrate them is rich in wild mushroom flavor. I suggest topping the dish with shaved Romano or Pecorino cheese (use a vegetable peeler for perfect shavings).

1. In a small bowl, combine the dried mushrooms and ½ cup hot water. Let stand for 10 minutes. Drain the mushrooms through a fine sieve, reserving the soaking liquid, and then finely chop the mushrooms. Set aside.

2. Meanwhile, cook the pasta according to the package directions. Drain and set aside.

3. In a large saucepan, whisk together the cream and flour until the flour is blended. Set the pan over medium-high heat, add the reserved mushrooms, mushroom soaking liquid, asparagus, and thyme, and bring to a simmer. Simmer for about 5 minutes, stirring frequently, until the sauce thickens. Fold in the cooked pasta and season to taste with salt and pepper.

Serves 4

Quick Side Dish: Arugula Salad with Buttermilk-Chive Dressing

Whisk together ¼ cup buttermilk, 1 tablespoon cider vinegar, and 1 teaspoon each Dijon mustard and chopped fresh chives. Season to taste with salt and freshly ground black pepper. Drizzle the mixture over 6 cups arugula leaves just before serving.

Week 12

Cajun Pork Tenderloin
Quick Side Dish: Creamed Spinach

Pan-Seared Scallops with Orange-Tarragon Butter
Quick Side Dish: Pasta Salad with Olives, Broccoli, and Walnuts

Grilled Flank Steak with Malt Vinegar Aioli

PREP LIST

* Make the spice mixture for the pork. (Keep at room temperature for up to 3 months.)

* Rub the spice mixture all over the pork. (Refrigerate for up to 2 days.)

* Make the malt vinegar aioli. (Refrigerate for up to 24 hours.)

Cajun Pork Tenderloin

PREP TIME: 10 minutes • COOK TIME: 25 minutes

Cooking spray

1 pork tenderloin (about 1¼ pounds)

2 tablespoons sugar

2 teaspoons dried thyme

1 teaspoon ground cumin

1 teaspoon garlic powder

1 teaspoon onion powder

½ teaspoon ground ginger

½ teaspoon dry mustard powder

½ teaspoon salt

¼ teaspoon paprika, preferably smoked paprika

¼ teaspoon cayenne pepper

¼ teaspoon freshly ground black pepper

If this ingredient list seems long, don't worry! All the herbs and spices are pantry staples (or they should be). Double or triple the recipe for the spice blend and you can enjoy a future meal with half the prep work already done. In fact, make an extra batch of spice mixture and use it instead of the seasoning in Voodoo Chicken with Sweet-and-Sour Onions (page 28).

1. Preheat the oven to 400°F. Coat a shallow roasting pan with cooking spray. Put the pork in the pan.

2. In a small bowl, combine the sugar, thyme, cumin, garlic powder, onion powder, ginger, mustard powder, salt, paprika, cayenne, and black pepper. Mix well. Rub the mixture all over the top and sides of the pork tenderloin.

3. Roast for 25 minutes, or until a meat thermometer inserted into the center reads 160°F. Let stand for 5 minutes before slicing crosswise into ½-inch-thick slices.

Serves 4

Quick Side Dish: Creamed Spinach

Melt 2 tablespoons butter in a medium saucepan over medium heat. Whisk in 2 tablespoons all-purpose flour until blended and smooth, about 2 minutes. Whisk in ¾ cup milk and bring to a simmer. Add one 10-ounce package frozen chopped spinach (thawed and well drained), 2 teaspoons dried minced onion, ½ teaspoon salt, and ¼ teaspoon freshly ground black pepper. Cook for 1 minute to heat through.

Pan-Seared Scallops with Orange-Tarragon Butter

PREP TIME: 10 minutes • **COOK TIME: 5 to 7 minutes**

1 tablespoon olive oil

1½ to 2 pounds sea scallops, patted dry

2 tablespoons butter, preferably unsalted

Juice and grated zest of 2 oranges (or ½ cup orange juice and 1 teaspoon finely grated orange zest)

1 tablespoon chopped fresh tarragon

Salt and freshly ground black pepper

Scallops are uniquely sweet and they pair perfectly with this buttery orange sauce that's kicked up with anise-flavored tarragon. Few ingredients, major flavor.

1. Heat the oil in a large skillet over medium-high heat. Add the scallops and cook for 2 to 3 minutes per side, until opaque and cooked through. Remove the scallops from the pan, leaving the oil in the pan, cover with foil, and set them aside.

2. In the same pan, over medium-high heat, melt the butter. Add the orange juice, zest, and tarragon. Bring to a simmer. Return the scallops to the pan and simmer for 1 minute to heat through. Season to taste with salt and pepper.

3. Serve the scallops with the butter sauce spooned over the top.

Serves 4

Quick Side Dish: Pasta Salad with Olives, Broccoli, and Walnuts

Cook 8 ounces penne or spiral pasta according to the package directions, adding 2 cups broccoli florets for the last 30 seconds of cooking. Drain, transfer to a large bowl, and add 2 tablespoons olive oil, 1 tablespoon balsamic vinegar, and ⅓ cup each pitted and halved kalamata olives and toasted walnuts. Toss to combine and season to taste with salt and freshly ground black pepper.

Grilled Flank Steak with Malt Vinegar Aioli

PREP TIME: **5 to 10 minutes** • COOK TIME: **10 minutes**

Cooking spray

**1 flank steak
(1 to 1¼ pounds)**

Salt

**Coarsely ground black
pepper**

**2 teaspoons salt-free
garlic and herb
seasoning**

¼ cup mayonnaise

**1 tablespoon malt
vinegar or aged
balsamic vinegar**

**2 teaspoons chopped
fresh dill**

Flank steak is so easy to prepare, it's a weekly staple in my house. A simple "aioli" makes the perfect topping. Aioli is a mayonnaise-based sauce that usually contains garlic. In my version, I put the garlic on the steak and good vinegar in the mayonnaise—to get the maximum flavor combination. Malt vinegar is rich and sweet (I'm going for sweet and tangy here), a flavor you can also get from a good aged balsamic. I like to serve this steak with sautéed onions spooned over the top.

1. Coat a stovetop grill pan or griddle with cooking spray and heat over medium-high heat. Season both sides of the steak with salt, pepper, and the garlic and herb seasoning. Grill the steak for 5 minutes per side, for medium-rare. Remove the steak from the pan and let stand for 5 minutes.

2. Meanwhile, to make the aioli, in a small bowl, combine the mayonnaise, vinegar, and dill. Mix well and season to taste with salt and pepper.

3. Cut the steak crosswise, against the grain, into thin strips. Serve the steak with the aioli spooned over the top.

Serves 4

Morph to Another Meal ▶ ▶ ▶ Double the recipe for the steak portion of the meal, and use the steak in one of the recipes listed in the box on page 115.

Week 13

Roasted Chicken with Ginger-Peach Rémoulade
Quick Side Dish: Braised Kale with Pink Beans

Chicken Fra Diavolo

Roasted Asparagus Soup
Quick Side Dish: Parmesan-Crusted Pita Wedges

PREP LIST

* Cook extra chicken for the fra diavolo dish when you prepare the roasted chicken. (Refrigerate for up to 3 days or freeze for up to 3 months. Thaw overnight in the refrigerator or in the microwave on the defrost setting before using.)

* Cook the linguine for the fra diavolo dish. (Refrigerate for up to 3 days.)

* Roast the asparagus for the soup. (You can do this, if you'd like, when you roast the chicken. Refrigerate for up to 3 days.)

* Chop the leeks for the soup. (Refrigerate for up to 3 days.)

Roasted Chicken with Ginger-Peach Rémoulade

PREP TIME: 10 to 15 minutes • COOK TIME: 25 to 30 minutes

Cooking spray

8 boneless skinless chicken breast halves (about 5 ounces each)

Salt and freshly ground black pepper

1 tablespoon dried minced garlic

1 cup fresh peach slices (or frozen peaches, thawed, or drained canned peaches)

½ cup mayonnaise

2 teaspoons minced peeled fresh ginger

1 teaspoon chopped fresh tarragon or ½ teaspoon dried

1 teaspoon Dijon mustard

Rémoulade is pretty much just a fancy term for tartar sauce. Traditional recipes often include hard-boiled eggs, pickles, capers, and tarragon. In this recipe, I partner anise-flavored tarragon with sweet peaches and pungent ginger. It's a unique and flavorful blend.

1. Preheat the oven to 400°F. Coat a large, rimmed baking sheet with cooking spray.

2. Season both sides of the chicken breast halves with salt and pepper and place on the prepared baking sheet. Sprinkle with the minced garlic. Roast for 25 to 30 minutes, until the chicken is cooked through and no longer pink on the inside.

3. Meanwhile, to make the rémoulade, in a blender, combine the peaches, mayonnaise, ginger, tarragon, and Dijon mustard. Puree until smooth. Season to taste with salt and pepper.

4. Serve 4 of the chicken breast halves with all of the rémoulade spooned over the top. (Reserve the remaining 4 chicken breast halves for the fra diavolo dish.)

Serves 4 (with leftovers for the fra diavolo)

Morph to Another Meal ▶ ▶ ▶ Instead of using the extra chicken in the fra diavolo, use it in one of the recipes listed in the box on page 23.

Quick Side Dish: Braised Kale with Pink Beans

In a large skillet over medium-high heat, cook 2 to 3 diced bacon slices until crisp. Add 2 minced garlic cloves and cook for 1 minute. Add 1 pound chopped kale (tough stems removed), one 15-ounce can (rinsed and drained) pink beans, and ½ cup reduced-sodium chicken broth or water and bring to a simmer. Cover, reduce the heat to low, and cook for 10 minutes, or until the kale is tender. Season to taste with salt and freshly ground black pepper.

Chicken Fra Diavolo

PREP TIME: **15 minutes** • COOK TIME: **10 to 15 minutes**

12 ounces linguine

1 tablespoon olive oil

1 habanero or jalapeño chile pepper, seeded and minced

2 garlic cloves, minced

4 reserved cooked chicken breasts, cubed (or 4 cups cubed cooked or raw chicken)

1 teaspoon dried oregano

1 teaspoon crushed red pepper flakes

1 28-ounce can diced tomatoes

1 cup diced oil-packed sun-dried tomatoes

¼ cup chopped fresh basil

Fra diavolo is a spicy tomato sauce that's often served with shrimp. Since the flavors are strong, I like to serve the sauce over chicken. And, I kick up heat and depth of flavor in my sauce by adding a habanero chile and sun-dried tomatoes. You can also make this dish with cubed raw chicken (instead of leftover cooked chicken); just add a few minutes to the cooking time to make sure the chicken is cooked through and no longer pink on the inside. If you are out of linguine, serve this over any thin noodles, such as capellini (angel hair), or over rice.

1. Cook the linguine according to the package directions. Drain and set aside.

2. Meanwhile, heat the oil in a large, deep skillet over medium-high heat. Add the habanero and garlic and cook for 1 minute. Add the chicken and cook for 3 minutes, or until golden brown on all sides. Add the oregano and red pepper flakes and cook for 1 minute, or until the oregano is fragrant.

3. Add the diced tomatoes and sun-dried tomatoes and bring to a simmer. Simmer for 5 minutes.

4. Spoon the chicken and sauce over the linguine and top with the basil.

Serves 4

Morph from Another Meal ▶ ▶ ▶ Instead of using the extra chicken from the roasted chicken, make this dish with the reserved cooked chicken from one of the recipes listed in the box on page 169.

Roasted Asparagus Soup

PREP TIME: 10 to 15 minutes • **COOK TIME: 40 minutes**

Cooking spray

2 bunches (about
1½ pounds) fresh
asparagus, stem ends
trimmed

Salt and freshly ground
black pepper

1 tablespoon olive oil

2 leeks, chopped and
rinsed well

½ cup vermouth or
reduced-sodium chicken
broth

6 cups reduced-sodium
chicken broth

2 bay leaves

½ cup heavy cream

2 tablespoons chopped
fresh flat-leaf parsley

Soup crackers or oyster
crackers, for serving

Asparagus soup is awesome when made the traditional way (with steamed or blanched asparagus), so imagine how great the flavor is when you use grilled asparagus instead. The caramelized flavor truly shines through, adding to the soup's depth. As for presentation, make sure to reserve some of the asparagus tips for garnish. You can also top the soup with seasoned croutons instead of crackers.

1. Preheat the oven to 400°F. Coat a large, rimmed baking sheet with cooking spray.

2. Arrange the asparagus on the baking sheet and spray them with cooking spray. Season with salt and pepper. Roast for 25 minutes, or until golden brown and tender. When cool enough to handle, cut the asparagus into 3-inch pieces (set aside a few asparagus tips for garnish).

3. Heat the oil in a Dutch oven or large stockpot over medium-high heat. Add the leeks and cook for 5 minutes, or until soft. Add the vermouth and cook for 1 minute. Add the roasted asparagus pieces, chicken broth, and bay leaves and simmer for 5 minutes.

4. Discard the bay leaves. Remove the asparagus pieces with a slotted spoon and puree in a blender. Return the puree to the pot and add the heavy cream. Simmer for 2 minutes to heat through.

5. Stir in the parsley and season to taste with salt and pepper. Ladle the soup into bowls and top with the reserved asparagus tips and some crackers.

Serves 4

Quick Side Dish: Parmesan-Crusted Pita Wedges

Quarter 4 pita rounds and place on a baking sheet. Spray the pitas with cooking spray and sprinkle with grated Parmesan cheese. Bake at 400°F for 6 to 8 minutes, until golden brown.

Week 14

OPTIONAL HOLIDAY WEEK: This optional holiday week would be ideal for spring celebrations. Lamb not only is a holiday staple, but it also marries perfectly with spring mint. You can also create the recipe with pork chops instead—and serve it year-round!

Lamb Chops with Zucchini-Mint Pesto
Quick Side Dish: Baked Stuffed Onions

Grilled Portobello Burgers with Provolone
Quick Side Dish: Cavatappi Salad with White Beans, Shallots, and Cherry Tomatoes

Miso Mushroom Soup with Udon Noodles
Quick Side Dish: Steamed Asparagus with Caramelized Shallots

PREP LIST

* Make the pesto. (Refrigerate for up to 3 days.)

* Assemble the baked stuffed onion side dish, if desired. (Refrigerate for up to 3 days before baking.)

* Cook extra mushrooms for the soup when you prepare the portobello burgers. (Refrigerate for up to 2 days or freeze for up to 3 months. Thaw overnight in the refrigerator or in the microwave on the defrost setting before using.)

* Make the soup. (Refrigerate for up to 3 days or freeze for up to 3 months. Reheat—from frozen or thawed—in a saucepan or in the microwave, adding more broth if necessary.)

Lamb Chops with Zucchini-Mint Pesto

PREP TIME: 10 to 15 minutes • COOK TIME: **6 minutes**

1 tablespoon olive or vegetable oil

4 lamb chops (about 6 ounces each)

Salt and freshly ground black pepper

1/3 cup walnut pieces

1 medium zucchini, cut into 2-inch pieces

1/2 cup fresh mint leaves

2 garlic cloves

2 tablespoons olive oil

Simply seared lamb chops, served tender with a magnificent puree of toasted walnuts, zucchini, mint, and garlic, make a perfect springtime dish.

1. Heat the tablespoon of oil in a large skillet over medium-high heat. Season both sides of the lamb chops with salt and pepper. Add the lamb to the hot skillet and cook for about 3 minutes per side, until golden brown and cooked through but still slightly pink in the center.

2. Meanwhile, to make the pesto, put the walnuts in a small dry skillet over medium-high heat. Cook, shaking the pan frequently, for 3 to 5 minutes, until golden brown and fragrant. Transfer the walnuts to a blender and add the zucchini, mint, garlic, and 2 tablespoons of oil. Blend until smooth, adding a little water if necessary to create a thick paste. Season with salt and pepper.

3. Spoon the pesto over the lamb chops just before serving.

Serves 4

Quick Side Dish: Baked Stuffed Onions

Peel 4 medium yellow onions. Cut 1/2 inch off the top of each onion. Use a melon baller to hollow out the onions, leaving a 1/4-inch wall of 1 to 2 layers of onion on the sides and bottom; chop the inside of the onions and reserve for the stuffing. Cook 4 chopped slices bacon in a large skillet over medium-high heat until crisp. Add the chopped onion and cook for 2 minutes. Remove from the heat and add 2 diced slices sandwich bread, 1 cup shredded Gruyère or domestic Swiss cheese, 1 tablespoon chopped fresh flat-leaf parsley, 1/2 teaspoon salt, and 1/4 teaspoon freshly ground black pepper. Mix well and then spoon the mixture into the hollowed onions. Transfer the onions to a shallow baking dish and pour 1/2 cup reduced-sodium chicken broth into the bottom of the pan. Cover with foil and bake at 400°F for 20 minutes. Uncover and bake for 20 more minutes, or until the onions are tender and golden brown.

Grilled Portobello Burgers with Provolone

PREP TIME: **10 minutes** • COOK TIME: **7 minutes**

Cooking spray

6 large portobello mushroom caps

Salt and freshly ground black pepper

2 tablespoons balsamic vinegar

1 teaspoon dried thyme

4 teaspoons chopped fresh flat-leaf parsley

4 slices provolone cheese

4 hamburger buns, toasted if desired

Hearty enough to stand alone in a meat-free meal, these "burgers" truly satisfy. Fruity balsamic vinegar and thyme bring out the mushrooms' earthiness, and grilling adds a dose of caramelization. Serve the burgers with a mixed green salad topped with cucumbers, carrots, water chestnuts, canned whole baby corn, cherry tomatoes, and your favorite bottled dressing.

1. Coat a stovetop grill pan or griddle with cooking spray and heat over medium-high heat. Season both sides of the mushroom caps with salt and pepper and brush with balsamic vinegar. Rub the thyme into the stem side of 4 of the mushroom caps. Grill all 6 mushroom caps for 3 minutes per side, or until tender. Remove the 2 extra mushroom caps from the grill, and set aside.

2. Top the 4 thyme-rubbed mushrooms with the parsley and provolone cheese, tent with foil, and cook for 1 minute, until the cheese melts. Serve these mushrooms on the buns. (Reserve the remaining 2 mushrooms for the soup.)

Serves 4 (with leftovers for the soup)

Quick Side Dish: Cavatappi Salad with White Beans, Shallots, and Cherry Tomatoes

Cook 8 ounces cavatappi or small shell pasta according to the package directions. Drain and stir in one 15-ounce can (rinsed and drained) cannellini beans or small white beans, 1 cup halved cherry tomatoes, ¼ cup chopped fresh basil, 2 tablespoons each minced shallot, olive oil, and white wine vinegar, and 2 teaspoons Dijon mustard. Toss to combine and season to taste with salt and freshly ground black pepper.

Miso Mushroom Soup with Udon Noodles

PREP TIME: **10 minutes** • COOK TIME: **10 minutes**

7 cups reduced-sodium chicken broth

2 tablespoons reduced-sodium soy sauce

3 tablespoons miso paste

2 reserved grilled portobello mushrooms, cut into 2-inch strips (or 1 cup sliced mushrooms)

3 ounces udon noodles

¼ cup chopped scallions (white and green parts)

2 tablespoons chopped fresh cilantro

Here's a simple soup that boasts a rich, deep flavor from both grilled mushrooms and miso paste. If you're serving the soup as part of a meal for houseguests and want to make it more "substantial" or special, add eight ounces peeled and deveined fresh or frozen baby shrimp to the broth when you add the noodles.

1. In a large saucepan, whisk together the broth, soy sauce, and miso paste. Set the pan over high heat and bring to a boil. Add the mushrooms and noodles and cook for 3 to 5 minutes, until the noodles are tender. Remove from the heat and stir in the scallions and cilantro.

Serves 4

Quick Side Dish: Steamed Asparagus with Caramelized Shallots

Heat 1 tablespoon olive oil in a large skillet over medium-high heat. Add ⅓ cup thinly sliced shallots and 1 tablespoon sugar and cook for 5 minutes, or until the shallots are golden brown. Add 1 pound trimmed asparagus spears (preferably thin spears) and ¼ cup vermouth or water, cover, and steam for 5 minutes, or until the asparagus is crisp-tender. Uncover and cook until the liquid evaporates. Season to taste with salt and freshly ground black pepper.

17 Pantry Pastas

These sensational creations—made almost entirely from pantry and fridge staples—are for nights when you're craving a meal beyond spaghetti and meatballs. These winning recipes were inspired by the cuisines of the world, so you can enjoy a bounty of global flavors in the comfort of your own home in just minutes.

1. Spanish Pasta with Smoked Paprika: Combine cooked pasta, sliced stuffed Spanish olives, sliced anchovies, capers, diced tomatoes, extra-virgin olive oil, red wine vinegar, and smoked Spanish or Hungarian paprika. Toss to combine.

2. Thai Peanuty Noodles: Whisk together peanut butter, soy sauce, fresh lime juice, sesame oil, and a little hot sauce. Fold in cooked spaghetti or cooked somen or udon noodles and chopped fresh cilantro.

3. Tex-Mex Pasta Salad: Combine cooked orzo or small tube-shaped pasta, pre-pared salsa, diced cheddar cheese, diced ham, chopped red bell pepper, a small can of minced green chiles, and chopped fresh cilantro. Season to taste with salt and freshly ground black pepper.

4. Confetti Pasta: Combine cooked small shells, diced carrots, diced celery, diced yellow bell pepper, chopped scallions, shredded red cabbage, chopped fresh basil, red wine vinegar, and extra-virgin olive oil. Season to taste with salt and freshly ground black pepper.

5. Cheater's "Risotto": In a saucepan, combine cooked orzo pasta, heavy cream, grated Parmesan cheese, and garlic powder. Set the pan over medium-low heat and simmer until thick and creamy. Top with chopped fresh basil or flat-leaf parsley and season to taste with salt and freshly ground black pepper before serving.

6. Pasta Puglia: Combine cooked pasta, sliced sardines, steamed broccoli florets or broccoli rabe, chopped fresh garlic, minced shallots, chopped fresh flat-leaf parsley, extra-virgin olive oil, and fresh lemon juice. Season to taste with salt and freshly ground black pepper.

7. Artichoke Pasta Bake with Parmesan: In a buttered baking dish, combine cooked pasta, sour cream, chopped marinated artichoke hearts, chopped roasted red peppers, chopped fresh basil, grated Parmesan cheese, and freshly ground black pepper. Mix well and top with more grated Parmesan cheese. Bake at 375°F for 15 to 20 minutes, until the top is golden brown.

8. Creamy Caesar Pasta: Combine cooked pasta, mayonnaise, grated Parmesan cheese, garlic powder, lemon juice, minced anchovies, chopped fresh flat-leaf parsley, and freshly ground black pepper.

9. Pasta with Pears, Honey, Goat Cheese, and Walnuts: Combine cooked pasta, diced fresh pears, honey, white wine vinegar, crumbled goat cheese, toasted chopped walnuts, and chopped fresh mint. Season to taste with salt and freshly ground black pepper.

10. Yellow Curried Noodles: Whisk together sour cream, curry powder, salt, and freshly ground black pepper. Fold in cooked pasta, chopped hard-boiled egg, chopped scallions, and chopped fresh cilantro.

11. Fusilli in Parsley Broth: In a large, deep skillet, combine chicken or vegetable broth, chopped shallots, minced garlic, 2 bay leaves, and a good amount of chopped fresh flat-leaf parsley. Set the pan over medium heat and bring to a simmer. Stir in cooked fusilli, or any spiral pasta shape, and cook for 2 to 3 minutes to heat through. Remove the bay leaves. Season to taste with salt and freshly ground black pepper.

12. Penne with Caramelized Squash: Sauté sliced zucchini and/or yellow squash and minced garlic in olive oil until golden brown. Fold in cooked penne, minced red onion, fresh or dried thyme and oregano, and salt and freshly ground black pepper to taste.

13. Chili Cheese Rigatoni: In a large saucepan, combine milk, shredded cheddar cheese, prepared salsa, chili powder, and ground cumin. Set the pan over medium heat, and simmer until the cheese melts. Fold in cooked rigatoni or any tube-shaped pasta (and canned kidney beans if desired) and cook for 2 minutes to heat through. Stir in chopped fresh cilantro before serving.

14. Asian Stir-Fried Noodles with Mixed Veggies: Heat peanut oil and sesame oil together in a wok or large skillet. Add chopped scallions, minced peeled fresh ginger, minced garlic, sliced bell peppers, and snow or snap peas and cook until crisp-tender. Fold in cooked noodles (spaghetti, vermicelli, angel hair, or Asian noodles), soy sauce, and hot sauce, and cook for 1 minute to heat through (add more soy sauce or chicken broth to make a nice sauce).

15. Antipasto Pasta Salad: Combine cooked pasta, chopped roasted red peppers, diced salami and provolone cheese, pitted olives, chopped fresh basil, extra-virgin olive oil, and freshly ground black pepper.

16. Sesame Cellophane Noodles: Combine cooked cellophane (bean-thread) noodles, hoisin sauce, soy sauce, sesame oil, minced pickled ginger, and chopped scallions.

17. Udon Noodles in Miso Broth: In a saucepan, combine chicken broth, soy sauce, and miso paste. Bring to a simmer over medium heat. Add cooked udon noodles and simmer for 2 to 3 minutes to heat through. Add firm tofu chunks and scallions, if desired.

Week 15

Chicken Thighs with Bourbon Barbecue Sauce
Quick Side Dish: Parmesan Fries

Granddad's Maple-Soy Salmon
Quick Side Dish: Rice Vinegar Potatoes

Smoky Salmon Benedict
Quick Side Dish: Apple-Walnut Salad

PREP LIST

* Cook extra salmon for the Benedict when you prepare the maple-soy salmon. (Refrigerate the salmon for up to 2 days or freeze for up to 3 months. Thaw overnight in the refrigerator or in the microwave on the defrost setting before using.)

Chicken Thighs with Bourbon Barbecue Sauce

PREP TIME: 10 to 15 minutes • **COOK TIME: 35 to 40 minutes**

Cooking spray

2 pounds skinless chicken thighs

Salt and freshly ground black pepper

1 cup ketchup

¼ cup bourbon or ¼ cup apple juice mixed with ½ teaspoon vanilla extract

3 tablespoons light brown sugar

2 tablespoons red wine vinegar

2 teaspoons Worcestershire sauce

2 teaspoons reduced-sodium soy sauce

1 teaspoon garlic powder

½ teaspoon dry mustard powder

Adding bourbon to barbecue sauce is awesome. It adds a subtle sweetness and another layer of flavor. Here I add it to my ketchup-based barbecue sauce that's also spruced up with brown sugar, vinegar, Worcestershire sauce, soy sauce, garlic, and mustard powder. Instead of using chicken thighs, you can make this dish with skinless chicken breasts, which cook for just 25 to 35 minutes (25 minutes for boneless, 35 minutes for bone-in). I like to serve this chicken with a prepackaged rice pilaf mix (quick-cooking, of course!) or with the fries below.

1. Preheat the oven to 400°F. Coat a shallow roasting pan with cooking spray.

2. Arrange the chicken thighs in the prepared pan and season with salt and pepper.

3. In a medium bowl, whisk together the ketchup, bourbon, brown sugar, vinegar, Worcestershire sauce, soy sauce, garlic powder, and mustard powder. Brush the mixture all over the chicken thighs. Roast for 35 to 40 minutes, until the chicken is cooked through and no longer pink on the inside.

Serves 4

Quick Side Dish: Parmesan Fries

Peel and cut 2 large baking potatoes into ½-inch-thick strips and transfer to a large baking sheet that's been coated with cooking spray. Spread out in a single layer. Spray the potatoes with cooking spray, season with salt and pepper, and then sprinkle with Parmesan cheese. Bake at 400°F for 20 to 25 minutes, until tender and golden brown.

Granddad's Maple-Soy Salmon

PREP TIME: 10 minutes • **COOK TIME: 6 to 10 minutes**

Cooking spray

6 salmon fillets (about 5 ounces each)

Salt and freshly ground black pepper

⅓ cup maple syrup, preferably 100% pure maple syrup

2 tablespoons reduced-sodium soy sauce

2 teaspoons Dijon mustard

My father-in-law, Frank, is known for his incredibly tasty (and incredibly easy) salmon dish. A modest man, he gives all the credit to one of his best friends, Daljit, who gave him the recipe. Frank prefers to use wild salmon for this dish and likes to sprinkle it with chopped fresh chives or parsley just before serving.

1. Coat a stovetop grill pan, griddle, or large skillet with cooking spray and heat over medium-high heat.

2. Season both sides of the salmon fillets with salt and pepper.

3. In a small bowl, whisk together the maple syrup, soy sauce, and Dijon mustard. Brush the mixture all over the salmon. Grill the salmon for 3 to 5 minutes per side, until the fish pulls apart when tested with a fork.

4. Serve 4 of the salmon fillets with this meal. (Reserve the remaining 2 fillets for the salmon Benedict.)

Serves 4 (with leftovers for the Benedict dish)

Quick Side Dish: Rice Vinegar Potatoes

Place 2 pounds quartered small to medium red potatoes in a large saucepan. Add enough water to cover, set the pan over high heat, and bring to a boil. Boil for 8 to 10 minutes, until the potatoes are fork-tender. Drain and return the potatoes to the pan with ¼ cup chopped scallions (green and white parts), 2 tablespoons seasoned rice vinegar, 1 tablespoon olive oil, and 1 teaspoon dried thyme. Toss to coat. Season to taste with salt and freshly ground black pepper.

Smoky Salmon Benedict

PREP TIME: 10 minutes • **COOK TIME: 3 to 5 minutes**

1 teaspoon white vinegar

8 large eggs

4 English muffins, split and lightly toasted

2 reserved grilled salmon fillets, broken up into 2-inch pieces (or 2 cups cooked salmon pieces or smoked salmon)

8 slices smoked gouda or smoked mozzarella cheese

2 tablespoons chopped fresh chives

Why relegate eggs Benedict to breakfast? You've got almost all the food groups in one dish, so why not make it dinner? I consider it an excellent, protein-packed midweek surprise. You might notice there's no hollandaise on top. I like to use smoked cheese instead, for a more intense flavor and, quite frankly, because it's so much easier.

1. Preheat the broiler.

2. Fill a large pot with 3 inches of water. Bring the water to a gentle simmer over medium to medium-high heat. Add the vinegar. Carefully break the eggs into the simmering water. Cook for 2 to 3 minutes, until the whites are cooked and the yolks are slightly soft (or longer for fully-cooked yolks). Using a slotted spoon, remove the eggs from the water and dry on paper towels.

3. Put the English muffin halves on a foil-lined baking sheet. Top each English muffin half with salmon pieces and a poached egg. Arrange the cheese slices on top of the eggs. Broil for 1 to 2 minutes, until the cheese melts.

4. Top with the chives just before serving.

Serves 4

Morph from Another Meal ▶ ▶ ▶ Instead of using the extra salmon from the maple-soy salmon, use the 2 cups of reserved cooked salmon pieces from Roasted Salmon With Citrus Mustard Sauce (page 252).

Quick Side Dish: Apple-Walnut Salad

In a medium bowl, combine 2 diced McIntosh apples, ¼ cup toasted walnut pieces, 1 tablespoon cider vinegar, and 1 teaspoon olive oil. Season to taste with salt and freshly ground black pepper. Serve over 4 cups torn red lettuce leaves if desired.

Week 16

Grilled Shrimp with Curried Ginger Syrup
Quick Side Dish: Carrot-Coriander Puree

Mixed Greens with Shrimp, Crumbled Blue Cheese, and Peanut Brittle in Raspberry-Champagne Vinaigrette
Quick Side Dish: Rosemary–Olive Oil Pizzette

Maple-Glazed Chicken
Quick Side Dish: Baked Quesadillas with Brie and Chutney

PREP LIST

* Cook extra shrimp for the salad when you make the grilled shrimp. (Refrigerate for up to 2 days or freeze for up to 3 months. Thaw overnight in the refrigerator before using. I don't recommend thawing in the microwave.)

* Make the vinaigrette for the salad. (Refrigerate for up to 3 days.)

* Chop the onion for the chicken dish. (Refrigerate for up to 3 days.)

Grilled Shrimp with Curried Ginger Syrup

PREP TIME: **10 minutes** • COOK TIME: **10 minutes**

Cooking spray

4 pounds peeled and deveined fresh or thawed, frozen jumbo shrimp

Salt

Lemon pepper

1 cup reduced-sodium chicken broth

3 tablespoons honey

2 teaspoons minced peeled fresh ginger

1 teaspoon curry powder

This dish is great because it partners succulent shrimp with a sweet honey- and ginger-infused curry syrup. Since the curry syrup is drizzled over the shrimp after they're grilled, you can use a little or a lot—making these perfect for a family meal where some may want a lot of syrup and some little to none! I like to serve these shrimp over rice or cellophane noodles.

1. Coat a stovetop grill pan or griddle with cooking spray and heat over medium-high heat. Season the shrimp all over with salt and lemon pepper. Grill the shrimp for 2 to 3 minutes per side, until opaque and cooked through.

2. Meanwhile, to make the syrup, in a medium saucepan, whisk together the chicken broth, honey, ginger, and curry powder. Set the pan over medium-high heat and bring to a simmer. Simmer for 5 minutes, or until the liquid reduces to ½ cup.

3. Serve half of the shrimp with all of the syrup, spooning it over the top. (Reserve the remaining shrimp for the salad.)

Serves 4 (with leftovers for the salad)

Morph to Another Meal ▶ ▶ ▶ Use the extra shrimp in Panzanella and Shrimp Salad (page 293) instead of in the salad.

Quick Side Dish: Carrot-Coriander Puree

In a medium saucepan, combine 1 peeled and cubed Yukon Gold potato and 3 cups chopped peeled carrots. Add enough water to cover, set the pan over high heat, and bring to a boil. Boil for 8 minutes, or until the potato and carrots are tender. Drain and return the vegetables to the pan. Add ¼ cup milk, 1 tablespoon each butter and sugar, and 1 teaspoon ground coriander. Mash until almost smooth. Season to taste with salt and freshly ground black pepper.

Mixed Greens with Shrimp, Crumbled Blue Cheese, and Peanut Brittle in Raspberry-Champagne Vinaigrette

PREP TIME: 10 minutes

¼ cup olive oil

3 tablespoons champagne vinegar

1 tablespoon seedless raspberry preserves

2 teaspoons Dijon mustard

Salt and freshly ground black pepper

6 cups mixed greens

Reserved grilled shrimp (about 1½ pounds)

1 cup crumbled blue cheese

1 cup peanut brittle pieces

Peanut brittle in a salad? This idea came from my adventures in the South, where I've had some awesome peanut brittle. Seems a shame to limit its consumption to a sweet snack! The crunchy candy marries incredibly well with soft, salty blue cheese and grilled shrimp. The tangy raspberry vinaigrette ties everything together. Feel free to use any combination of greens—either pre-bagged or your favorites combined.

1. In a small bowl, whisk together the oil, vinegar, raspberry preserves, and Dijon mustard. Season to taste with salt and pepper.

2. Arrange the greens on individual plates. Top with the shrimp, blue cheese, and peanut brittle pieces. Drizzle the vinaigrette over the salad just before serving.

Serves 4

Quick Side Dish: Rosemary–Olive Oil Pizzette

Roll out one 13.8-ounce package refrigerated pizza dough to ¼ inch thick. Transfer the dough to a baking sheet and brush the top with olive oil. Sprinkle 2 tablespoons chopped fresh rosemary over the dough and then top with ¼ cup grated Parmesan cheese. Bake at 450°F for 12 minutes, or until golden brown.

Maple-Glazed Chicken

PREP TIME: 10 minutes • COOK TIME: 10 to 15 minutes

1 tablespoon olive oil

½ cup chopped red onion

1¼ pounds boneless skinless chicken breasts, cut into 2-inch pieces

1 teaspoon dried thyme

1 cup orange juice

⅓ cup maple syrup, preferably 100% pure maple syrup

1 tablespoon cornstarch

¼ cup chopped fresh mint or basil

Salt and freshly ground black pepper

Two of my favorite breakfast staples, orange juice and maple syrup, come together in a sauce for chicken. Because I always have these on hand, I can toss together this sweet, delicious meal any night of the week. I like to serve the chicken with angel hair pasta, quinoa, or couscous on the side.

1. Heat the oil in a large skillet over medium-high heat. Add the onion and cook for 3 minutes, or until soft. Add the chicken and cook for 3 to 5 minutes, until golden brown on all sides. Add the thyme and cook for 1 minute, or until the thyme is fragrant.

2. In a small bowl, whisk together the orange juice, maple syrup, and cornstarch. Add the mixture to the pan and bring to a simmer. Simmer for 2 to 3 minutes, until the sauce thickens and the chicken is cooked through and no longer pink on the inside.

3. Remove from the heat, stir in the mint, and season to taste with salt and pepper.

Serves 4

Quick Side Dish: Baked Quesadillas with Brie and Chutney

Spread one side of four 8- to 10-inch flour tortillas with mango (or any fruit) chutney. Top the chutney with thinly sliced Brie and some watercress leaves. Fold over the un-topped side and brush the half moons on both sides with olive oil. Transfer the quesadillas to a large baking sheet and bake at 400°F for 10 to 15 minutes, until the cheese melts and the quesadillas are golden brown.

Week 17

Seared Miso Pork with Udon Noodles
Quick Side Dish: Tamari Sugar Snap Peas

Black Bean–Mandarin Salad with Sliced Pork and Cilantro
Quick Side Dish: Broiled Ricotta Toast with Smoked Paprika

Chicken Penne with Artichokes, Tomatoes, and Pesto Cream
Quick Side Dish: Watercress Salad with Frisée and Pears

PREP LIST ·

* Cook extra pork for the salad when you prepare the pork and noodle dish. (Refrigerate for up to 3 days or freeze for up to 3 months. Thaw overnight in the refrigerator or in the microwave on the defrost setting before using.)

* Chop the onion for the salad. (Refrigerate for up to 3 days.)

* Cook the penne for the chicken dish. (Refrigerate for up to 3 days.)

Seared Miso Pork with Udon Noodles

PREP TIME: **10 minutes** • COOK TIME: **10 minutes**

12 ounces udon noodles

2 teaspoons toasted sesame oil

1 tablespoon peanut oil

6 boneless pork loin chops (about 5 ounces each)

Salt and freshly ground black pepper

Garlic powder

1½ cups reduced-sodium chicken broth

1 tablespoon miso paste

1 tablespoon minced lemongrass or 2 teaspoons finely grated lemon zest

½ cup chopped scallions (green and white parts)

Miso paste is a great one-stop-shop for flavor. It can range from mildly salty and savory to tangy, earthy, and fruity. Any variety will work in this dish. Look for it in the refrigerated section of well-stocked supermarkets. You'll find udon noodles, which cook up nice and chewy, in the Asian ingredients aisle.

1. Cook the udon noodles according to the package directions. Drain and toss with the sesame oil.

2. Meanwhile, heat the peanut oil in a large skillet over medium-high heat. Season both sides of the pork with salt, pepper, and garlic powder. Add the pork to the hot pan and cook for 1 to 2 minutes per side, until golden brown.

3. In a small bowl, whisk together the chicken broth and miso paste until the paste dissolves. Add the mixture to the pork with the lemongrass. Bring to a simmer and cook for 3 minutes, or until the pork is cooked through and still slightly pink in the center. Remove from the heat and add the scallions.

4. Arrange the udon noodles in 4 shallow bowls. Place 1 chop over each portion of noodles and pour the remaining broth on top, covering both the pork chops and noodles. (Reserve the remaining 2 pork chops for the salad.)

Serves 4 (with leftover pork for the salad)

Quick Side Dish: Tamari Sugar Snap Peas

Heat 2 teaspoons toasted sesame oil in a large skillet over medium heat. Add 2 teaspoons minced peeled fresh ginger and 2 minced garlic cloves and cook for 1 minute. Add 1 pound sugar snap peas and ¼ cup bottled tamari sauce and bring to a simmer. Cover and cook for 3 minutes or until the snap peas are crisp-tender.

Black Bean–Mandarin Salad with Sliced Pork and Cilantro

PREP TIME: 10 to 15 minutes

1 11-ounce can mandarin oranges in light syrup

1 15-ounce can black beans, rinsed and drained

¼ cup diced red onion

1 tablespoon olive oil

1 tablespoon fresh lime juice

1 teaspoon Dijon mustard

1 teaspoon ground cumin

¼ cup chopped fresh cilantro

Salt and freshly ground black pepper

6 cups torn or chopped lettuce leaves

2 reserved cooked pork chops, sliced into thin strips (or 2 cups sliced cooked pork or chicken)

Salty black beans pair nicely with sweet mandarin oranges, especially when the two are tossed together in a lime- and cumin-infused salad. This salad is also excellent with leftover chicken and shrimp.

1. Reserve 2 tablespoons syrup from the oranges, then drain the oranges, and put them in a medium bowl. Add the black beans and red onion.

2. In a small bowl, whisk together the reserved mandarin orange syrup, the olive oil, lime juice, Dijon mustard, and cumin. Pour the mixture over the black bean mixture and stir to combine (stir gently to prevent breaking up mandarin orange slices). Fold in the cilantro and season to taste with salt and pepper.

3. Arrange the lettuce on individual plates. Top with the bean mixture and pork slices. Serve chilled or at room temperature.

Serves 4

Quick Side Dish: Broiled Ricotta Toast with Smoked Paprika

Spread honey mustard over sliced whole-grain bread. Spread ricotta cheese on top of that and sprinkle with smoked paprika. Broil for 2 to 3 minutes, until the cheese is bubbly. Serve warm.

Chicken Penne with Artichokes, Tomatoes, and Pesto Cream

PREP TIME: **10 to 15 minutes** • COOK TIME: **10 minutes**

12 ounces penne pasta

1 tablespoon olive oil

2 boneless skinless chicken breast halves (6 oz. each), cubed

1 14-ounce can artichoke hearts, drained and halved

1 14-ounce can diced tomatoes, drained

1 cup heavy cream, or more as necessary

½ cup prepared basil pesto

¼ cup grated Parmesan cheese

Salt and freshly ground black pepper

A fancy name for a meal that's ready in just minutes! Thanks to flavorful canned artichokes, diced tomatoes, heavy cream, and prepared basil pesto, you can toss together an exotic-tasting meal with grocery-store staples.

1. Cook the pasta according to the package directions. Drain and set aside.

2. Meanwhile, heat the oil in a large, deep skillet over medium-high heat. Add the chicken and cook for 3 to 5 minutes, until golden brown on all sides. Add the artichoke hearts, tomatoes, cream, and pesto and bring to a simmer. Simmer, stirring frequently, for 3 minutes, or until the chicken is cooked through and no longer pink on the inside.

3. Fold in the cooked pasta and Parmesan cheese and cook for 1 minute to heat through, adding more cream or a little water if necessary to create a thinner sauce. Remove from the heat and season to taste with salt and pepper.

Serves 4

Morph from Another Meal ▶ ▶ ▶ Instead of using raw chicken, make this dish with 2 cups reserved, cubed cooked chicken (about 2 chicken breast halves), such as from one of the recipes listed on page 169, and add to the pan with the artichoke hearts, tomatoes, cream, and pesto.

Quick Side Dish: Watercress Salad with Frisée and Pears

In a large bowl, combine 4 cups fresh watercress leaves, 1 head torn frisée leaves, and 2 cored and sliced red or yellow Bartlett pears. In a small bowl, whisk together 3 tablespoons white wine vinegar, 3 tablespoons olive oil, and 1 teaspoon Dijon mustard. Pour the vinaigrette over the greens and pears and toss to coat. Season to taste with salt and freshly ground black pepper.

Week 18

Seared Teriyaki Beef Roll with
Gingered Vegetables
Quick Side Dish: Coconut-Almond Rice

Chimichangas Ranchero with Steak
and Pink Beans
Quick Side Dish: Hearts of Palm Salad with Mango and Lime

Tortilla-Crusted Salmon with
Tropical Fruit Salsa
Quick Side Dish: Ginger-Scallion Rice

PREP LIST

* Marinate the teriyaki beef. (Refrigerate for up to 24 hours.)

* Cook extra steak for the chimichangas when you prepare the teriyaki beef dish. (Refrigerate for up to 3 days or freeze for up to 3 months. Thaw overnight in the refrigerator or in the microwave on the defrost setting before using.)

* Chop the onion for the chimichangas. (Refrigerate for up to 3 days.)

* Assemble the chimichangas. (Refrigerate for up to 3 days or freeze for up to 3 months; thaw overnight in the refrigerator before baking. I don't recommend thawing in the microwave.)

* Make the salsa for the salmon dish. (Refrigerate for up to 3 days.)

* Crush the tortillas for the salmon. (Keep at room temperature.)

Seared Teriyaki Beef Roll with Gingered Vegetables

PREP TIME: 20 minutes • COOK TIME: 10 minutes

⅓ cup reduced-sodium soy sauce

2 tablespoons honey

1 sirloin steak (2 to 2½ pounds) or 2 steaks (1 to 1¼ pounds each), pounded to ½-inch thickness

4 teaspoons peanut or vegetable oil

1 red bell pepper, seeded and chopped

1 tablespoon minced peeled fresh ginger

2 garlic cloves, minced

2 scallions, chopped (green and white parts)

Salt and freshly ground black pepper

Sweet red peppers are sautéed with ginger and garlic before being tucked inside a steak "roll." As you slice the roll crosswise to serve, beautiful red pinwheels reveal themselves.

1. In a shallow dish, whisk together the soy sauce and honey. Add the steak, turn to coat, and set aside.

2. Heat 2 teaspoons of the oil in a large skillet over medium-high heat. Add the bell pepper, ginger, garlic, and scallions and cook, stirring frequently, for 3 to 5 minutes, until the vegetables are soft. Remove from the heat and season with salt and pepper.

3. Remove the steak from the marinade (reserve the marinade) and place on a flat surface. Top the steak with the vegetable mixture (wipe out and reserve the skillet). Starting from the smaller end, roll up the steak crosswise and secure with wooden picks.

4. Heat the remaining 2 teaspoons oil in the skillet over medium-high heat. Sear the steak for 30 seconds on each side. Add the marinade and simmer, turning the steak once, until the liquid evaporates and the steak is medium-rare, 5 minutes.

5. Transfer the steak to a cutting board and let stand for 5 minutes. Cut the steak crosswise into 1-inch-thick rounds. Serve most of the steak with this meal. (Reserve 2 to 3 rounds for the chimichangas.)

Serves 4 (with leftover beef for the chimichangas)

Quick Side Dish: Coconut-Almond Rice

Toast ¼ cup slivered almonds in a medium saucepan over medium heat for 3 minutes, or until golden brown. Add 2 cups quick-cooking white rice, one 14-ounce can unsweetened coconut milk, and ¼ cup water and bring to a boil. Cover, remove from the heat, and let stand for 5 minutes. Season with salt and freshly ground black pepper.

Chimichangas Ranchero with Steak and Pink Beans

PREP TIME: 10 minutes • **COOK TIME: 15 to 20 minutes**

Cooking spray

1 tablespoon vegetable oil

½ cup diced onion

2 to 3 reserved cooked steak rounds, diced (or 2 cups cubed cooked steak)

1 15-ounce can pink beans, rinsed and drained

1 4-ounce can diced green chiles

¼ cup red chili sauce

4 8-inch flour tortillas

1 14-ounce can diced tomatoes with onion and green pepper

1 teaspoon ground cumin

½ teaspoon garlic powder

1 cup shredded cheddar cheese

4 cups shredded or chopped lettuce

Guacamole (optional)

Sour cream (optional)

Salsa (optional)

Sliced black olives (optional)

A chimichanga is a meat-stuffed burrito that's deep-fried and served on a bed of lettuce with cheese and sauce. The chimichanga (or "chimi," to those who eat them regularly) has achieved cult status in Tucson, Arizona, where some say the dish was born. In fact, many restaurants boast large, overstuffed chimis that leave you waddling out the door. I add nutritious beans to my chimichangas, and I bake them instead of deep-frying. I also top my chimis with ranchero sauce, a tomato-based sauce with onions, garlic, and peppers. I know you'll love them, and I'm certain there won't be any waddling afterward!

1. Preheat the oven to 400°F. Coat a large, rimmed baking sheet or roasting pan with cooking spray.

2. Heat the oil in a large skillet over medium-high heat. Add the onion and steak and cook for 3 minutes, until the onion is golden brown. Add the beans, green chiles, and chili sauce and simmer until the liquid is absorbed, about 3 minutes.

3. Spoon the steak mixture onto the center of each tortilla. Roll up the tortillas halfway, fold in the sides, and finish rolling. Transfer the chimichangas to the prepared baking sheet.

4. In a small bowl, combine the tomatoes, cumin, and garlic powder. Mix well and spoon the mixture over the chimichangas. Top with the cheddar cheese. Bake for 10 to 15 minutes, until the tortillas are golden brown and the cheese melts.

5. Serve the chimichangas over the lettuce. Top with guacamole, sour cream, salsa, and black olives, if desired.

Serves 4

Morph from Another Meal ▶ ▶ ▶ Instead of using steak from the beef roll, use the reserved cooked steak from Skirt Steak with Cracked Black Pepper Butter (page 156), Grilled Steak with Shiitake Mushrooms, Wilted Arugula, and Shaved Parmesan (page 48), or Tandoori Steak Kebabs (page 53).

Quick Side Dish: Hearts of Palm Salad with Mango and Lime

In a large bowl, combine one 14.5-ounce can hearts of palm (drained and cut into 1-inch pieces), 1 diced mango, 2 tablespoons fresh lime juice, and 2 teaspoons honey mustard. Toss to combine and season to taste with salt and freshly ground black pepper. Serve over Boston or Bibb lettuce if desired.

Versatile Recipes for Leftover Steak

Leftover steak? Here are a few tempting ideas for "take two."

Steak Quesadillas with Spinach and Caramelized Onions and Chunky Ranch Guacamole (page 196)
BBQ Steak Kebabs over Avocado Puree (page 297)
Nacho Napoleons (page 157)
Beef Tart with Sun-Dried Tomatoes and Basil Vinaigrette (page 55)
Chimichangas Ranchero with Steak and Pink Beans (page 114)

Tortilla-Crusted Salmon with Tropical Fruit Salsa

PREP TIME: 10 to 15 minutes • COOK TIME: 12 to 15 minutes

Cooking spray

4 salmon fillets (about 5 ounces each)

Salt and freshly ground black pepper

1 tablespoon Dijon mustard

4 cups corn tortilla chips

1 mango, pitted and diced

1 papaya, peeled, seeded, and diced

½ cup diced fresh pineapple (or canned in juice, drained)

2 tablespoons minced red or white onion

2 tablespoons fresh lime juice

2 tablespoons chopped fresh cilantro

Ever wonder what to do with that big bag of tortilla chips before they go stale? Try crusting fish with them! Corn tortillas add a distinct salty corn flavor and crisp texture to salmon. The refreshing salsa combination of mango, papaya, and pineapple makes the perfect partner.

1. Preheat the oven to 400°F. Coat a large, rimmed baking sheet with cooking spray.

2. Season both sides of the salmon with salt and pepper. Brush the top side of the salmon with the mustard.

3. Put the chips in a plastic bag and, using a heavy rolling pin or the bottom of a heavy skillet, crush into fine crumbs. Transfer the crumbs to a shallow dish. Add the salmon to the chips, mustard side down, and press in the tortilla crumbs to coat.

4. Transfer the salmon to the prepared baking sheet, crumb side up, and bake for 12 to 15 minutes, until the fish pulls apart when tested with a fork.

5. Meanwhile, to make the salsa, in a small bowl, combine the mango, papaya, pineapple, onion, lime juice, and cilantro. Season to taste with salt and pepper.

6. Serve the salmon with the salsa spooned over the top.

Serves 4

Quick Side Dish: Ginger-Scallion Rice

In a medium saucepan, combine 2 cups reduced-sodium chicken broth, ¼ cup chopped scallions (green and white parts), and 2 teaspoons minced peeled fresh ginger. Bring to a boil over high heat. Add 2 cups quick-cooking white rice, cover, remove from the heat, and let stand for 5 minutes. Fluff with a fork and season with salt and freshly ground black pepper.

Week 19

Grilled Strip Steaks and Roasted
Vegetables with Two Cheeses

Sausage-Stuffed Mushrooms with
Spinach and Roasted Vegetables
Quick Side Dish: Mixed Baby Greens with Feta and Blueberries

Tuscan Pork Chops with White
Beans and Olives
Quick Side Dish: Broccoli Puree with Parmesan

PREP LIST

* Cook extra vegetables for the stuffed mushrooms when you prepare the strip steak dish. (Refrigerate for up to 3 days or freeze for up to 3 months. Thaw overnight in the refrigerator or in the microwave on the defrost setting before using.)

* Assemble the stuffed mushrooms. (Refrigerate for up to 2 days or freeze for up to 3 months. Thaw overnight in the refrigerator before baking. I don't recommend thawing in the microwave.)

Grilled Strip Steaks and Roasted Vegetables with Two Cheeses

PREP TIME: 10 to 15 minutes • COOK TIME: 40 to 45 minutes

2 medium zucchini, cut into 1-inch pieces

1 green bell pepper, seeded and cut into 1-inch pieces

1 red bell pepper, seeded and cut into 1-inch pieces

1 14-ounce can artichoke hearts, drained and quartered

1 small eggplant, peeled and cubed (1-inch pieces)

1 cup cherry tomatoes, halved

2 tablespoons olive oil

2 teaspoons chopped fresh rosemary

Salt and freshly ground black pepper

½ cup crumbled feta cheese

⅓ cup grated Parmesan cheese

Cooking spray

2 strip steaks (about 10 ounces each)

Strip steak is a large, tender cut that takes well to being cut up. It's often called porterhouse on restaurant menus. If you want, you can substitute skirt or flank steak for the strip. In this dish, the steak is simply grilled before serving with cheese-topped, caramelized roasted vegetables.

1. Preheat the oven to 400°F.

2. In a large bowl, combine the zucchini, both bell peppers, artichoke hearts, eggplant, and cherry tomatoes. Add the olive oil, rosemary, and ½ teaspoon each salt and pepper and toss to coat the vegetables. Transfer the vegetables to a large, rimmed baking sheet (or two to prevent crowding) and roast for 25 to 30 minutes, until tender and golden brown. Top the vegetables with both cheeses, return to the oven, and roast for 5 minutes, or until the cheese is golden and just begins to melt.

3. Meanwhile, coat a stovetop grill pan or griddle with cooking spray and heat over medium-high heat. Season both sides of the steaks with salt and pepper. Grill the steaks for 5 minutes per side, for medium-rare. Remove the steaks from the pan and let stand for 5 minutes.

3. Cut each steak in half, making 4 portions. Serve the steaks with all but 1 cup of the roasted vegetables. (Reserve the remaining vegetables for the stuffed mushrooms.)

Serves 4 (with leftovers for the stuffed mushrooms)

Morph to Another Meal ▶ ▶ ▶ Double the recipe for the steak, and use the extra steak in one of the recipes listed in the box on page 115.

Sausage-Stuffed Mushrooms with Spinach and Roasted Vegetables

PREP TIME: 10 to 15 minutes • COOK TIME: 15 minutes

2 teaspoons olive oil

1 pound sweet or hot turkey sausage, casing removed

1 cup reserved roasted vegetables, finely diced (or 1 cup sautéed mixed vegetables—any combination—finely diced)

2 cups baby spinach leaves, chopped

1/3 cup seasoned dry bread crumbs

1 teaspoon dried thyme

4 portobello mushroom caps

2 to 3 tablespoons grated Parmesan cheese, to taste

Portobello mushrooms make the perfect landing pad for savory fillings. In this dish, I mound up a sausage-vegetable filling on the caps before topping with cheese and baking. As the mushrooms soften in the oven, the flavors of the filling soak into the flesh. You're gonna love this one.

1. Preheat the oven to 375°F.

2. Heat the oil in a large skillet over medium-high heat. Add the sausage and cook, breaking up the meat as it cooks, for 3 to 5 minutes, until cooked through. Add the vegetables, spinach, bread crumbs, and thyme and cook for 2 minutes, or until the spinach wilts and the thyme is fragrant.

3. Spoon the mixture into the mushroom caps and, using your hands, shape the filling into a mound. Transfer the mushrooms to a large, rimmed baking sheet and sprinkle the tops with the Parmesan cheese. Bake for 15 minutes, or until the mushrooms soften and the cheese is golden brown. Serve warm.

Serves 4 to 6

Quick Side Dish: Mixed Baby Greens with Feta and Blueberries

Top 6 cups baby salad greens with 1/2 cup crumbled feta cheese and 1 cup fresh blueberries. In a small bowl, whisk together 3 tablespoons olive oil, 2 tablespoons sherry vinegar, and 2 teaspoons honey mustard. Season to taste with salt and freshly ground black pepper. Drizzle the dressing over the salad just before serving.

Tuscan Pork Chops with White Beans and Olives

PREP TIME: 10 to 15 minutes • COOK TIME: 6 to 8 minutes

1 tablespoon olive oil

4 boneless pork loin chops (about 5 ounces each)

Salt and freshly ground black pepper

2 garlic cloves, minced

1 14-ounce can diced tomatoes, with juice

1 cup reduced-sodium chicken broth

½ cup sliced drained, oil-packed sun-dried tomatoes

1 15-ounce can cannellini or white beans, rinsed and drained

1 12-ounce jar marinated artichoke hearts, drained

½ cup pitted kalamata olives

¼ cup chopped fresh flat-leaf parsley

Go to Tuscany, if just for one night—and in your own kitchen. What makes these pork chops Tuscan in my mind is the rustic addition of sun-dried tomatoes, white beans, artichoke hearts, and olives. This is a super-flavorful and incredibly easy dish.

1. Heat the oil in a large skillet over medium-high heat. Season both sides of the pork chops with salt and pepper and add to the hot pan. Cook for 1 to 2 minutes per side, until golden brown. Remove the pork from the pan and set aside.

2. To the same pan over medium-high heat, add the garlic and cook for 1 minute. Add the canned tomatoes, broth, sun-dried tomatoes, beans, artichokes, and olives. Bring to a simmer. Return the pork chops to the pan and cook for 3 to 5 minutes, until the pork is cooked through and still slightly pink in the center and the sauce reduces.

3. Spoon the sauce over the pork chops, sprinkle with the parsley, and serve.

Serves 4

Quick Side Dish: Broccoli Puree with Parmesan

Spread out 1 peeled and cubed large baking potato in a large saucepan. Add enough water to cover by 3 inches, set the pan over high heat, and bring to a boil. Boil for 6 minutes. Add 4 cups fresh or frozen, thawed broccoli florets, partially cover, and boil for 2 to 4 more minutes, until the potato and broccoli are tender. Drain and return the vegetables to the pan. Add ⅓ cup grated Parmesan cheese, ⅓ cup sour cream or plain yogurt, and ½ teaspoon garlic powder. Mash until almost smooth. Season to taste with salt and freshly ground black pepper.

Week 20

Clams with Fennel-Lemon Broth over Rice
Quick Side Dish: Chili-Spiked Carrots

Spaghetti with Clams and Chorizo
Quick Side Dish: Mixed Greens with Hazelnuts and Oranges

Hearty Minestrone Soup
Quick Side Dish: Garlic-Parmesan Bread Sticks

PREP LIST

* Cook extra clams for the spaghetti when you prepare the clam dish. (Refrigerate for up to 2 days or freeze for up to 3 months. Thaw overnight in the refrigerator before using. I don't recommend thawing in the microwave.)

* Cook the spaghetti. (Refrigerate for up to 3 days).

* Chop the onion, carrots, celery, cabbage, and garlic for the soup. (Refrigerate for up to 3 days.)

* Cook the rice for the soup. (Refrigerate for up to 3 days.)

* Make the soup. (Refrigerate for up to 3 days or freeze for up to 3 months. Reheat—from frozen or thawed—in a large saucepan or in the microwave.)

Clams with Fennel-Lemon Broth over Rice

PREP TIME: 10 minutes • **COOK TIME: 10 to 15 minutes**

2 tablespoons butter, preferably unsalted

1 fennel bulb, cored and sliced into thin strips

2 to 3 garlic cloves, to taste, minced

5 pounds littleneck clams (60 to 72), washed and drained

1 cup vermouth, dry white wine, or reduced-sodium chicken broth

1 cup reduced-sodium chicken or vegetable broth

1 tablespoon fresh lemon juice

2 cups cooked white rice (regular or quick-cooking)

¼ cup chopped fresh flat-leaf parsley

Anise-flavored fennel is a unique and fabulous addition to this dish that also boasts tart lemon and sweet butter. I serve everything over rice so you won't miss an ounce of the sauce.

1. Melt the butter in a large, deep skillet over medium heat. Add the fennel and garlic and cook for 3 minutes, or until both are soft.

2. Add the clams and increase the heat to high. Cook for 1 minute, stirring constantly. Add the vermouth, broth, and lemon juice, cover, and cook for 5 to 8 minutes, until the clam shells open (discard any that do not eventually open).

3. Remove from the heat. Arrange half to three quarters of the clams (in their shells) over all of the rice in bowls. Pour the broth on top and garnish with the parsley. (Reserve the remaining clams—2 cups, without their shells—for the spaghetti.)

Serves 4 (with leftovers for the spaghetti)

Quick Side Dish: Chili-Spiked Carrots

Heat 1 tablespoon olive oil in a large skillet over medium-high heat. Add one 8-ounce bag of baby carrots and 1 teaspoon chili powder. Cook for 3 minutes, or until the carrots are crisp-tender. Season to taste with salt and freshly ground black pepper.

Spaghetti with Clams and Chorizo

PREP TIME: 15 minutes • **COOK TIME: 6 to 10 minutes**

12 ounces spaghetti

1 tablespoon olive oil

1 cup diced cooked chorizo or andouille sausage

**2 cups reserved shelled, cooked clams or
2 11-ounce cans whole baby clams, drained**

1 cup reduced-sodium chicken broth

¼ cup grated Parmesan cheese

¼ cup chopped fresh basil

Salt and freshly ground black pepper

Garlicky and mildly spicy, chorizo really sends this dish sky-high. Just a few ingredients combine for a stellar weeknight meal. No leftover clams? Substitute canned and you'll be fine.

1. Cook the spaghetti according to the package directions. Drain and set aside.

2. Meanwhile, heat the oil in a large, deep skillet over medium-high heat. Add the chorizo and cook for 3 minutes, or until golden brown. Add the clams and cook, stirring frequently, for 2 minutes. Add the chicken broth and bring to a simmer. Add the spaghetti and Parmesan cheese and cook for 1 minute to heat through.

3. Remove from the heat and stir in the basil. Season to taste with salt and pepper.

Serves 4

Quick Side Dish: Mixed Greens with Hazelnuts and Oranges

Top 6 cups torn Bibb lettuce with one 11-ounce can mandarin oranges in light syrup (drained) and ½ cup toasted, chopped hazelnuts. In a small bowl, whisk together 2 tablespoons each orange juice, orange marmalade, and sherry vinegar; 1 tablespoon olive oil; and 1 teaspoon Dijon mustard. Season to taste with salt and freshly ground black pepper. Drizzle the dressing over the salad just before serving.

Hearty Minestrone Soup

PREP TIME: 10 to 15 minutes • **COOK TIME: 10 to 20 minutes**

1 tablespoon olive oil

½ cup diced onion

2 carrots, diced

2 celery stalks, diced

½ small head green cabbage, chopped

2 garlic cloves, minced

1 teaspoon dried oregano

1 28-ounce can petite diced tomatoes

4 cups reduced-sodium chicken or vegetable broth

1 15-ounce can pink beans, rinsed and drained

1 15-ounce can black beans, rinsed and drained

½ cup quick-cooking brown or white rice

¼ cup chopped fresh basil

Salt and freshly ground black pepper

Think of this soup on your next visit to the salad bar. Load up on onions, carrots, celery, and cabbage (and any other vegetables you like, such as broccoli, cauliflower, and bell peppers) and you won't have any prep work at all! I like to top this soup with shaved or grated Parmesan cheese for extra depth of flavor.

1. Heat the oil in a large Dutch oven or stockpot over medium-high heat. Add the onion, carrots, celery, cabbage, and garlic and cook for 5 to 7 minutes, until the vegetables are tender. Add the oregano and cook for 1 minute, or until the oregano is fragrant.

2. Add the tomatoes, chicken broth, both types of beans, and rice and bring to a simmer. Reduce the heat to low, cover, and simmer for 5 to 10 minutes, until the rice is tender (5 minutes for white rice, 10 minutes for brown). Remove from the heat, stir in the basil, and season to taste with salt and pepper.

Serves 4 to 6

Quick Side Dish: Garlic-Parmesan Bread Sticks

Unroll refrigerated bread stick dough on a flat surface. Separate bread sticks (as directed) and roll them in a mixture of ½ cup grated Parmesan cheese and 2 teaspoons salt-free garlic and herb seasoning. Transfer to a baking sheet and bake as directed.

Week 21

Veracruz Chicken
Quick Dessert: Strawberry-Spiked Mango Sorbet in Mini Sponge Cakes

Pan-Fried Chicken Enchiladas with Spinach and Cheese
Quick Side Dish: Tomato-Mango Salsa Salad In Lettuce Cups

Shrimp Pomodoro over Angel Hair
Quick Dessert: Peach Tiramisù Parfaits

PREP LIST

* Cook extra chicken for the enchiladas when you make the Veracruz chicken. (Refrigerate for up to 3 days or freeze for up to 3 months. Thaw overnight in the refrigerator or in the microwave on the defrost setting before using.)

* Make the quick salsa side dish, if desired. (Refrigerate for up to 2 days.)

* Assemble the enchiladas. (Refrigerate for up to 3 days or freeze for up to 3 months before cooking. Thaw overnight in the refrigerator before baking. I don't recommend thawing in the microwave.)

* Cook the pasta for the shrimp dish. (Refrigerate for up to 3 days.)

Veracruz Chicken

PREP TIME: 10 to 15 minutes • COOK TIME: 25 to 30 minutes

Cooking spray

8 boneless skinless chicken breast halves (about 5 ounces each)

Salt and freshly ground black pepper

1 14-ounce can diced tomatoes, drained

½ cup halved Spanish olives

2 tablespoons drained capers

3 garlic cloves, minced

1 jalapeño chile pepper, seeded and minced

1 teaspoon dried Mexican oregano or regular oregano

This recipe idea comes from one of my favorite New York City restaurants, Dos Caminos. Not just a great bar, they have fabulous food, like this incredible combination of chicken, tomatoes, olives, capers, garlic, and jalapeño. I like to serve this dish over rice or couscous so I don't miss a drop of the sauce.

1. Preheat the oven to 400°F.

2. Coat a shallow roasting pan with cooking spray. Season both sides of the chicken breast halves with salt and pepper and arrange in the pan.

3. In a medium bowl, combine the tomatoes, olives, capers, garlic, jalapeño, and oregano. Mix well and spoon the mixture over 4 of the chicken breasts halves. Bake for 25 to 30 minutes, until the chicken is cooked through and no longer pink on the inside.

4. Serve the 4 topped chicken breast halves with this meal. (Reserve the remaining 4 chicken breast halves for the enchiladas.)

Serves 4 (with leftovers for the enchiladas)

Morph to Another Meal ▶ ▶ ▶ Instead of using the extra chicken in the enchiladas, use it in one of the recipes listed in the box on page 23.

Quick Dessert: Strawberry-Spiked Mango Sorbet in Mini Sponge Cakes

Slightly thaw 2 cups prepared mango sorbet. Stir in 1 cup chopped strawberries and return the sorbet to the freezer. Freeze for about 30 minutes, until firm. Spread 4 teaspoons seedless strawberry preserves into the bottom of 4 mini sponge cakes. Spoon the sorbet into the cakes and garnish with fresh strawberry slices if desired.

Pan-Fried Chicken Enchiladas with Spinach and Cheese

PREP TIME: **10 to 15 minutes** • COOK TIME: **10 minutes**

4 reserved cooked chicken breasts halves, cubed or shredded (or 4 cups cubed or shredded cooked chicken)

1 cup sour cream

1 cup shredded Mexican cheese blend or cheddar cheese

1 10-ounce package frozen chopped spinach, thawed and well drained

1 teaspoon chili powder

1 teaspoon garlic powder

½ teaspoon ground cumin

4 8-inch flour tortillas

1 tablespoon olive or vegetable oil

1 cup prepared salsa

Enchiladas are my go-to for "morphing" because you can transform leftovers (chicken, steak, fish, shellfish, vegetables) into something completely different. These enchiladas are stuffed with a savory blend of chicken, sour cream, cheese, spinach, and spices before they're pan-fried (instead of deep-fried or baked) and topped with salsa.

1. In a large bowl, combine the chicken, sour cream, cheese, spinach, chili powder, garlic powder, and cumin. Mix well. Spoon the chicken mixture onto the center of each tortilla. Roll up the tortillas halfway, fold in the sides, and finish rolling up.

2. Heat the oil in a large skillet over medium-high heat. Add the enchiladas and cook for 2 minutes per side, until golden brown. Reduce the heat to medium-low, tent with foil, and cook for 5 more minutes, or until the cheese melts.

3. Serve the enchiladas with salsa spooned over the top.

Serves 4

Quick Side Dish: Tomato-Mango Salsa Salad in Lettuce Cups

In a medium bowl, combine 2 cups diced mango, 1 cup diced tomato, ¼ cup minced red onion, and 2 tablespoons each chopped cilantro and fresh lime juice. Season to taste with salt and freshly ground black pepper. Spoon the mixture into 4 butter lettuce leaves.

Shrimp Pomodoro over Angel Hair

PREP TIME: 10 to 15 minutes • COOK TIME: 10 to 15 minutes

12 ounces angel hair or capellini pasta

1 tablespoon olive oil

¼ cup minced shallot

2 to 3 garlic cloves, minced, to taste

1 teaspoon dried oregano

1½ pounds peeled and deveined fresh shrimp or thawed frozen jumbo shrimp

½ cup vermouth or dry white wine

1 28-ounce can diced tomatoes

1 tablespoon sugar

Salt and freshly ground black pepper

¼ cup chopped fresh basil

Because shrimp cooks fast, it's the ultimate midweek fast meal. My pomodoro sauce is a flavorful blend of tomatoes, shallot, garlic, oregano, and fresh basil. The addition of vermouth and sugar creates a slightly sweet sauce that's awesome with the shrimp and pasta.

1. Cook the pasta according to the package directions. Drain and set aside.

2. Meanwhile, heat the oil in a large, deep skillet over medium-high heat. Add the shallot and garlic and cook for 3 minutes, or until soft. Add the oregano and cook for 1 minute, or until the oregano is fragrant. Add the shrimp and cook for 1 to 2 minutes, until golden brown.

3. Add the vermouth and cook for 1 minute. Add the tomatoes and sugar and bring to a simmer. Cook for 3 to 4 minutes, until the shrimp are opaque and cooked through. Season to taste with salt and pepper.

4. Transfer the pasta to a serving platter, pour the shrimp mixture on top, and sprinkle with the basil.

Serves 4

Quick Dessert: Peach Tiramisù Parfaits

In a mixing bowl or food processor, combine 8 ounces mascarpone cheese or cream cheese, ¼ cup milk, 2 tablespoons sugar, and 1½ teaspoons vanilla extract. Mix or puree until smooth. Layer in 4 tall glasses: crumbled ladyfingers, the mascarpone mixture, and sliced fresh or thawed frozen peaches. Repeat the layers, ending with peaches. Top with whipped cream and shaved chocolate (or sifted cocoa powder), if desired.

13 Pantry Grain Meals (Beyond Pasta)

Don't relegate grains to boring side dishes. Use hearty, filling grains as the star attraction in a variety of fun and flavorful main courses. Super-satisfying and chock-full of nutrients and fiber, grains are now available in quick-cooking varieties. You can also cook up extra rice on the weekend to have available during the week.

1. Moroccan Couscous: Combine cooked couscous, canned chickpeas (drained), sour cream, curry powder, ground cumin, and chopped fresh cilantro. Season to taste with salt and freshly ground black pepper.

2. Red Beans and Rice: Combine cooked white or brown rice, canned kidney beans (drained), chopped scallions, prepared salsa, chili powder, garlic powder, and fresh lime juice. Season to taste with salt and freshly ground black pepper.

3. Nutty Quinoa: Combine cooked quinoa, toasted slivered almonds, minced shallots, chopped fresh flat-leaf parsley, and dried oregano. Season to taste with salt and freshly ground black pepper. For added protein and a more substantial meal, add 2 cups diced cooked pork or chicken.

4. Wild Rice Pilaf: Combine cooked brown or white rice, cooked wild rice, toasted pine nuts, golden raisins, ground cumin, and chopped fresh flat-leaf parsley. Season to taste with salt and freshly ground black pepper. For more protein and a more substantial meal, add 2 cups cooked and cleaned small to medium shrimp.

5. Rice Salad with Papaya, Peanuts, and Lime: Combine cooked white or brown rice, diced fresh papaya, fresh lime juice, and dry-roasted peanuts. Season to taste with salt and freshly ground black pepper.

6. Chicken and Rice Soup with Egg and Lemon: In a large saucepan, combine chicken broth, shredded or cubed cooked chicken, uncooked white rice, chopped yellow onion, 2 bay leaves, dried thyme, and salt-free lemon and herb seasoning. Set the pan over high heat and bring to a boil. Reduce the heat to low and simmer until the rice is cooked. Remove the bay leaves, stir in chopped hard-boiled egg, and season to taste with salt and freshly ground black pepper before serving.

7. Pineapple Fried Rice with Macadamia Nuts and Coconut: In a large skillet or wok, combine cooked white or brown rice, soy sauce, chopped pineapple (fresh or canned), minced red onion, chopped macadamia nuts, and shredded coconut. Set the pan over medium-high heat and cook for 3 to 5 minutes, until the rice is golden brown.

8. Greek Barley Salad: Combine cooked barley, diced seedless cucumber, pitted kalamata olives, crumbled feta cheese, chopped fresh basil, dried oregano, and fresh lemon juice.

9. Quinoa Waldorf Salad with Apples, Walnuts, and Blue Cheese:

Combine cooked quinoa, diced Granny Smith apples, toasted walnuts, crumbled blue cheese, chopped fresh flat-leaf parsley, a little honey, and salt and freshly ground black pepper to taste.

10. Rice and Goat Cheese Cakes:

Combine cooked white or brown rice, crumbled fresh goat cheese, dried oregano, and enough sour cream or yogurt so that the mixture comes together enough to shape into cakes. Season to taste with salt and freshly ground black pepper. With your hands, shape the mixture into cakes, each about 1 inch thick. Sear both sides of the cakes in olive oil in a large skillet over medium heat. Top with chopped fresh flat-leaf parsley before serving.

11. Mexican Couscous:

Combine cooked couscous, minced pickled jalapeños, chopped tomato, diced avocado, chopped fresh cilantro, fresh lime juice, and ground cumin. Season to taste with salt and freshly ground black pepper. For added protein and a more substantial meal, add 2 cups diced cooked chicken or steak.

12. Jasmine Rice with Apricots and Almonds:

Combine cooked jasmine rice, minced dried apricots, toasted almonds, chopped fresh or dried thyme, sherry vinegar, and extra-virgin olive oil. Season to taste with salt and freshly ground black pepper. For added protein and a more substantial meal, add 2 cups diced cooked pork or chicken.

13. Cilantro Rice Patties with Sesame-Soy Drizzle:

Combine cooked white or brown rice, chopped fresh cilantro, minced garlic, and enough mayonnaise so that the mixture comes together enough to shape into patties. Season to taste with salt and freshly ground black pepper. With your hands, shape the mixture into patties, each about 1 inch thick. Sear both sides of the patties in olive oil in a large skillet over medium heat. Serve with a mixture of soy sauce and sesame oil drizzled over the top.

Week 22

Pan-Seared Tilapia with Roasted
Red Pepper Broth
Quick Side Dish: Curried Couscous with Chickpeas

Fish Soft Tacos with Black Beans
Quick Side Dish: Salsa Rice

Spanish Sausage and Vegetable
Kebabs
Quick Side Dish: Orzo Salad with Olives and Capers

PREP LIST

* Cook extra fish for the tacos when you prepare the pan-seared tilapia. (Refrigerate the remaining fish for up to 2 days or freeze for up to 3 months. Thaw overnight in the refrigerator or in the microwave on the defrost setting before using.)

* Slice the bell pepper and onion for the tacos. (Refrigerate for up to 3 days.)

* Make the kebab marinade. (Refrigerate for up to 3 days.)

* Chop the scallions for the kebabs. (Refrigerate for up to 3 days.)

* Make the quick orzo side dish for the kebabs, if desired. (Refrigerate for up to 3 days.)

Pan-Seared Tilapia with Roasted Red Pepper Broth

PREP TIME: 10 to 15 minutes • **COOK TIME: 4 to 6 minutes**

1½ cups reduced-sodium chicken broth

½ cup chopped roasted red bell peppers

1 garlic clove, chopped

1 to 2 tablespoons olive oil

8 tilapia fillets (about 5 ounces each)

Salt and freshly ground black pepper

¼ cup chopped fresh basil

Tilapia is a mildly sweet white fish that partners well with most ingredients. Add a few amazing flavors—like the roasted red peppers, garlic, and basil used here—and you have a simple and elegant dish in just minutes.

1. In a blender, combine the chicken broth, roasted red peppers, and garlic. Puree until smooth. Set aside.

2. Heat the oil in one or two large skillets over medium-high heat (use two skillets if necessary to prevent crowding the fish; you want the fish to sear, not steam). Season both sides of the tilapia fillets with salt and pepper and add the fish to the hot pan. Sear for 1 to 2 minutes per side, until golden brown.

3. Add the red pepper mixture to the pan and bring to a simmer. Simmer for 2 minutes, or until the fish pulls apart when tested with a fork. Serve 4 of the fish fillets with all of the broth and basil sprinkled over top. (Reserve the remaining 4 fish fillets for the soft tacos.)

Serves 4 (with leftovers for the tacos)

Morph to Another Meal ▶ ▶ ▶ Instead of using the extra fish in the tacos, use it in Manhattan Fish Chowder (page 77).

Quick Side Dish: Curried Couscous with Chickpeas

Bring 1¼ cups reduced-sodium chicken broth or water to a boil in a medium saucepan over high heat. Add 1 teaspoon curry powder, 1 cup couscous, and one 15-ounce can (rinsed and drained) chickpeas and mix well. Remove from the heat, cover, and let stand for 5 minutes. Stir in 2 tablespoons chopped cilantro and fluff with a fork. Season to taste with salt and freshly ground black pepper.

Fish Soft Tacos with Black Beans

PREP TIME: 10 to 15 minutes • COOK TIME: 6 to 8 minutes

1 tablespoon vegetable oil

1 green bell pepper, seeded and sliced into thin strips

1 cup sliced onion

1 15-ounce can black beans, rinsed and drained

½ cup sour cream

½ teaspoon ground cumin

4 reserved cooked tilapia fillets, broken up into bite-size pieces (or 4 cups cooked seafood pieces, such as cod, flounder, halibut, and shrimp)

8 6-inch flour tortillas, warmed in the microwave if desired

Shredded cheddar cheese, for serving

Diced tomato, for serving

Shredded lettuce, for serving

Who says you need chicken or steak? Fish makes an excellent addition to soft tacos, especially when partnered with sautéed onion, bell pepper, and black beans.

1. Heat the oil in a large skillet over medium-high heat. Add the bell pepper and onion and cook for 3 to 5 minutes, until soft. Remove from the heat and set aside.

2. In a small saucepan, combine the black beans, sour cream, and cumin. Set the pan over medium-low heat and cook for 3 minutes, just until hot. Remove from the heat.

3. If desired, reheat the fish in the microwave for 30 seconds on high.

4. Spoon the black bean mixture onto the flour tortillas. Top with the bell pepper and onion and the fish pieces. Serve cheese, tomato, and lettuce on the side for stuffing into the tacos.

Serves 4

Quick Side Dish: Salsa Rice

In a medium saucepan, combine 2 cups quick-cooking white rice, 2 cups reduced-sodium chicken or vegetable broth or water, and ⅓ cup prepared salsa. Set the pan over high heat and bring to a boil. Remove from the heat, cover, and let stand for 5 minutes. Fluff with a fork and season to taste with salt and freshly ground black pepper.

Spanish Sausage and Vegetable Kebabs

PREP TIME: 10 to 15 minutes • **COOK TIME: 6 minutes**

Cooking spray

2 tablespoons olive oil

1 tablespoon sherry vinegar

1 teaspoon paprika, preferably smoked paprika

½ teaspoon ground cumin

¼ teaspoon ground sage

1 pound cooked chorizo sausage, cut into 2-inch pieces

16 to 20 button or cremini mushrooms

8 thick scallions, cut into 2-inch pieces

2 cups cherry or grape tomatoes

Salt and freshly ground black pepper

Chorizo is a fabulous pork sausage that's cured with paprika and garlic. It's a superstar on its own, but it also makes a great addition to all types of skewers. Here, I pair the sausage with mushrooms, scallions, and cherry tomatoes for a feast on a stick. If desired, you can also cook the kebabs under the broiler (cooking time remains the same). I like to serve the kebabs with yellow rice or the orzo dish below.

> **Note:** When using wooden skewers, soak them in water for at least 20 minutes prior to using to prevent burning.

1. Coat a stovetop grill pan or griddle with cooking spray and heat over medium-high heat.

2. In a shallow bowl, whisk together the oil, vinegar, paprika, cumin, and sage. Add the sausage and toss to coat. Skewer alternating pieces of sausage, mushrooms, scallions, and tomatoes on metal or wooden skewers. Season with salt and black pepper.

3. Grill the skewers, turning and basting with any remaining marinade, until the vegetables are tender and slightly charred, about 6 minutes.

Serves 4

Quick Side Dish: Orzo Salad with Olives and Capers

Cook 8 ounces orzo pasta according to the package directions. Drain and transfer to a large bowl. Add ½ cup sliced Spanish olives, 2 tablespoons drained capers, 1 tablespoon each red wine vinegar and olive oil, and 1 tablespoon chopped fresh basil. Toss to combine and season to taste with salt and freshly ground black pepper.

Week 23

Chicken with Sweet Tomato–Pine Nut Sauce

Corn Tortilla Soup with Chicken and Lime
Quick Dessert: Virgin Piña Colada Pudding

Grilled Moroccan Steak with Charred Zucchini–Mint Salsa

PREP LIST

* Cook extra chicken for the soup when you prepare the chicken dish. (Refrigerate for up to 3 days or freeze for up to 3 months. Thaw overnight in the refrigerator or in the microwave on the defrost setting before using.)

* Chop the scallions, celery, and garlic for the soup. (Refrigerate for up to 3 days.)

* Make the soup. (Refrigerate for up to 3 days or freeze for up to 3 months. Reheat—from frozen or thawed—in a large saucepan or in the microwave.)

* Make the spice mixture for the steak. (Refrigerate for up to 2 days.)

* Make the salsa for the steak. (Refrigerate for up to 2 days.)

Chicken with Sweet Tomato–Pine Nut Sauce

PREP TIME: 15 minutes • COOK TIME: 25 to 30 minutes

Cooking spray

8 boneless skinless chicken breast halves (about 5 ounces each)

Salt and freshly ground black pepper

1 tablespoon salt-free garlic and herb seasoning

¼ cup pine nuts

1 8-ounce can tomato sauce

1 cup drained oil-packed sun-dried tomatoes

2 garlic cloves, chopped

2 tablespoons grated Parmesan cheese

¼ cup chopped fresh basil

I call the sauce for the chicken "sweet" because it's made with sun-dried tomatoes. It's also nutty from toasted pine nuts and cheesy from Parmesan cheese. In fact, it's perfect! I like to use oil-packed sun-dried tomatoes for most dishes because not only do they come already tender and ready to eat, I use the leftover oil from the jar to sauté other ingredients in other dishes (one ingredient, many uses!).

1. Preheat the oven to 400°F. Coat a large, rimmed baking sheet with cooking spray.

2. Season both sides of the chicken breast halves with salt and pepper and place on the prepared baking sheet. Season the top of the chicken with the garlic and herb seasoning. Set aside.

3. Put the pine nuts in a small dry skillet and set the pan over medium heat. Cook, shaking the pan frequently, for 3 minutes, or until golden brown. Transfer the nuts to a blender and add the tomato sauce, sun-dried tomatoes, garlic, and Parmesan cheese. Process until smooth. Season to taste with salt and pepper.

4. Spoon the tomato mixture over 4 of the chicken breast halves. Bake the chicken for 25 to 30 minutes, until cooked through and no longer pink on the inside.

5. Sprinkle the tomato-topped chicken with basil just before serving. (Reserve the remaining 4 chicken breast halves for the soup.)

Serves 4 (with leftovers for the soup)

Corn Tortilla Soup with Chicken and Lime

PREP TIME: 10 to 15 minutes • **COOK TIME: 15 to 20 minutes**

1 tablespoon olive oil

½ cup chopped scallions (green and white parts)

2 celery stalks, chopped

2 garlic cloves, minced

4 reserved cooked chicken breast halves, cubed (or 4 cups cubed cooked chicken)

1 teaspoon dried oregano

1 28-ounce can crushed tomatoes

3 cups reduced-sodium chicken broth

1½ cups fresh or frozen corn

1 4-ounce can minced green chiles, drained

2 bay leaves

2 to 3 tablespoons fresh lime juice, to taste

¼ cup chopped fresh cilantro

Salt and freshly ground black pepper

2 cups crumbled tortilla chips

You see similar recipes on restaurant menus all the time, but when you make those dishes yourself, you can make them better because *you* control the ingredients. In my rendition of tortilla soup, I add chicken, scallions, celery, tomatoes, corn, green chiles, lime, and cilantro to simmering broth and let the flavors get acquainted. Once the soup is ladled into bowls, it's topped with crunchy corn tortilla chips. Fun and delicious!

1. Heat the oil in a large Dutch oven or stockpot over medium-high heat. Add the scallions, celery, and garlic and cook for 3 minutes, or until soft. Add the chicken and oregano and cook for about 1 minute, until the oregano is fragrant. Add the tomatoes, broth, corn, chiles, and bay leaves and bring to a simmer. Simmer for 10 minutes.

2. Remove the bay leaves and add the lime juice and cilantro. Season to taste with salt and pepper. Ladle the soup into bowls and top with crumbled chips.

Serves 4

Quick Dessert: Virgin Piña Colada Pudding

In a large bowl, whisk together 2 cups prepared vanilla pudding, ¼ cup sweetened coconut milk, and ½ teaspoon vanilla extract. Fold in 1 cup cubed fresh pineapple (or canned in juice, drained). Garnish with shredded coconut if desired.

Grilled Moroccan Steak with Charred Zucchini–Mint Salsa

PREP TIME: **10 to 15 minutes** • COOK TIME: **10 minutes**

Cooking spray

2 tablespoons olive oil

1 teaspoon ground cumin

1 teaspoon dried marjoram

½ teaspoon ground cinnamon

½ teaspoon ground cardamom

Salt and freshly ground black pepper

¼ teaspoon ground nutmeg

1 flank or skirt steak (1 to 1¼ pounds)

2 medium zucchini, cut into ½-inch-thick rounds

½ cup diced tomato

2 tablespoons chopped fresh flat-leaf parsley

2 tablespoons chopped fresh mint

2 tablespoons chopped red onion

1 tablespoon fresh lemon juice

Yeah, I know, it seems like a long spice list, but read on: most of the spices are pantry staples. While you're making this dish, double or triple the spice mixture and leave out the olive oil. Now you have a great spice rub ready for a future meal! (It will keep in an airtight jar at room temperature for up to 3 months.) It's all about the planning . . .

1. Coat a stovetop grill pan or griddle with cooking spray and heat over medium-high heat.

2. In a small bowl, whisk together the oil, cumin, marjoram, cinnamon, cardamom, ½ teaspoon salt, ½ teaspoon pepper, and nutmeg. Mix well and brush the mixture all over both sides of the steak. Grill the steak for 5 minutes per side for medium-rare. Remove the steak from the pan and let stand for 5 minutes.

3. Meanwhile, to make the salsa, arrange the zucchini slices around the steak on the grill pan. Grill for 2 minutes per side, until charred and tender. Remove from the pan and dice the zucchini. Transfer to a medium bowl and add the tomato, parsley, mint, onion, and lemon juice. Season to taste with salt and pepper.

4. Cut the steak crosswise, against the grain, into thin strips. Top the steak with the salsa just before serving.

Serves 4

Morph to Another Meal ▶ ▶ ▶ Double the recipe for the steak, and use the extra steak in one of the recipes listed in the box on page 115.

Week 24

Grilled Chicken with Sherried
Caramelized Wild Mushrooms

Baja Chicken Soft Tacos
Quick Side Dish: Olive- and Tomato-Spiked Rice

Seared Tuna with Miso Broth and
Sesame Soba Noodles
Quick Side Dish: Chunky Tomato Salad

PREP LIST

* Cook extra chicken for the tacos when you make the grilled chicken. (Refrigerate for up to 3 days or freeze for up to 3 months. Thaw overnight in the refrigerator or in the microwave on the defrost setting before using.)

* Cook the soba noodles for the tuna dish; toss with oil as directed. (Refrigerate for up to 2 days.)

Grilled Chicken with Sherried Caramelized Wild Mushrooms

PREP TIME: 10 to 15 minutes • COOK TIME: 10 minutes

Cooking spray

8 boneless skinless chicken breast halves (about 5 ounces each)

Salt and freshly ground black pepper

1 tablespoon olive oil

¼ cup diced white onion

2 garlic cloves, minced

4 cups sliced mixed wild mushrooms (cremini, portobello, shiitake, oyster)

1 tablespoon chopped fresh thyme or 1 teaspoon dried

½ cup dry sherry or ½ cup reduced-sodium chicken broth with ¼ teaspoon vanilla extract

¼ cup chopped fresh flat-leaf parsley

Sherry is a great cooking wine because it adds just enough sweetness without overpowering a dish. I also love sherry's sweetness partnered with earthy wild mushrooms.

1. Coat a stovetop grill pan or griddle with cooking spray and preheat to medium-high. Season both sides of the chicken with salt and pepper and add to the hot pan. Grill the chicken for 3 to 5 minutes per side, until cooked through and no longer pink on the inside.

2. Meanwhile, heat the oil in a large skillet over medium-high heat. Add the onion and garlic and cook for 2 minutes. Add the mushrooms and cook for 5 minutes, or until the mushrooms soften and release their juice. Add the thyme and cook for about 1 minute, until the thyme is fragrant. Add the sherry and cook for 1 minute. Remove from the heat, stir in the parsley, and season to taste with salt and pepper.

3. Serve 4 of the chicken breast halves with all of the mushrooms spooned over top. (Reserve the remaining 4 chicken breast halves for the tacos.)

Serves 4 (with leftovers for the tacos)

Morph to Another Meal ▶ ▶ ▶ Instead of using the extra chicken in the tacos, use it in one of the recipes listed in the box on page 23.

Baja Chicken Soft Tacos

PREP TIME: 10 to 15 minutes • COOK TIME: 6 minutes

1 tablespoon vegetable oil

½ cup chopped scallions (green and white parts)

4 reserved cooked chicken breast halves, shredded (or 4 cups shredded cooked chicken)

1½ teaspoons chili powder

1 teaspoon ground cumin

2 tablespoons fresh lime juice

1 teaspoon minced chipotle chiles in adobo sauce

1 cup prepared refried beans

8 6-inch flour tortillas, warmed in the microwave if desired

Sour cream, for serving

Prepared salsa, for serving

Shredded lettuce, for serving

When in doubt, pull the tacos out! That's my motto because tacos are a hectic cook's best friend at the end of a crazy day. These winners are simple to prepare because they use precooked chicken and a few potent ingredients—chipotle chiles, lime juice, refried beans—that send flavors soaring.

1. Heat the oil in a large skillet over medium-high heat. Add the scallions and cook for 1 minute. Add the chicken and cook for 2 minutes, until golden brown on all sides. Add the chili powder and cumin and stir to coat the chicken and scallions. Cook for 1 minute, or until the spices are fragrant. Add the lime juice and chipotle chiles and cook for 2 minutes to heat through.

2. Spread refried beans on the flour tortillas and top with the chicken mixture. Serve with sour cream, salsa, and shredded lettuce on the side.

Serves 4

Quick Side Dish: Olive- and Tomato-Spiked Rice

In a medium saucepan, combine 2 cups reduced-sodium chicken broth, 2 cups quick-cooking white or brown rice, and 1 teaspoon dried oregano. Set the pan over high heat and bring to a boil. Cover, remove from the heat, and let stand for 5 minutes. Stir in ½ cup sliced pitted black olives and ⅓ cup chopped drained, oil-packed sun-dried tomatoes and toss to combine. Season to taste with salt and freshly ground black pepper.

Seared Tuna with Miso Broth and Sesame Soba Noodles

PREP TIME: **10 to 15 minutes** • COOK TIME: **10 minutes**

8 ounces soba noodles

2 teaspoons toasted sesame oil

1 tablespoon sesame seeds

1 tablespoon olive oil

4 tuna steaks (about 5 ounces each)

Salt and freshly ground black pepper

1 cup reduced-sodium chicken broth

2 tablespoons miso paste

1 tablespoon tamari, teriyaki sauce, or reduced-sodium soy sauce

¼ cup chopped fresh cilantro

When was the last time you made miso broth on a Tuesday? It should be more often, because making miso broth is a quick and easy way to create an interesting and completely different weeknight meal. Now's your chance. Miso's unique flavor is a terrific addition to hearty tuna and sesame noodles.

1. Cook the noodles according to the package directions. Drain, transfer to a large bowl, and toss with the sesame oil.

2. Meanwhile, put the sesame seeds in a small dry skillet and set the pan over medium heat. Cook the seeds, shaking the pan frequently to prevent burning, for 2 to 3 minutes, until golden brown. Add the seeds to the soba noodles and toss to combine.

3. Heat the olive oil in a large skillet over medium-high heat. Season both sides of the tuna with salt and pepper and add to the hot pan. Sear for 1 to 2 minutes per side, until golden brown on the outside and pink in the center.

4. In a small bowl, whisk together the chicken broth, miso paste, and tamari sauce until the miso dissolves. Add the mixture to the tuna and bring to a simmer. Simmer for 1 to 2 minutes for the tuna to reach medium-rare (or longer for medium-well).

5. Serve the tuna over the noodles and top with the cilantro.

Serves 4

Quick Side Dish: Chunky Tomato Salad

In a large bowl, combine 3 cups quartered cherry tomatoes (a combination of yellow and red tomatoes makes a nice presentation), 2 tablespoons each chopped fresh basil and minced red onion, and 1 tablespoon each olive oil, red wine vinegar, and balsamic vinegar. Toss to combine and season to taste with salt and freshly ground black pepper.

Week 25

Chicken Burgers with Guacamole, Cheddar, and Charred Tomatoes

Thai Chicken in Puff Pastry
Quick Side Dish: Navy Bean Salad with Roasted Red Peppers

Corn and Zucchini Quesadillas with Charred Tomato–Basil Salsa

PREP LIST

* Form the burgers. (Refrigerate for up to 3 days or freeze for up to 3 months. Thaw overnight in the refrigerator or in the microwave on the defrost setting before cooking.)

* Make the guacamole. (Refrigerate for up to 2 days.)

* Cook extra chicken burgers for the Thai chicken dish and extra tomatoes for the salsa to serve with the quesadillas when you make the chicken burgers. (Refrigerate for up to 3 days or freeze for up to 3 months. Thaw overnight in the refrigerator or in the microwave on the defrost setting.)

* Assemble the Thai chicken dish. (Refrigerate for up to 3 days or freeze for up to 3 months. Thaw overnight in the refrigerator before baking. I don't recommend thawing in the microwave.)

* Assemble the quesadillas. (Refrigerate for up to 3 days or freeze for up to 3 months. Thaw overnight in the refrigerator before cooking. I don't recommend thawing in the microwave.)

Chicken Burgers with Guacamole, Cheddar, and Charred Tomatoes

PREP TIME: 10 to 15 minutes • **COOK TIME: 7 minutes**

Cooking spray

2 pounds ground chicken or turkey

3 tablespoons chopped fresh cilantro

3 tablespoons seasoned dry bread crumbs

Salt and freshly ground black pepper

4 ripe beefsteak tomatoes, halved

1 ripe avocado, pitted and coarsely chopped

2 tablespoons minced white onion

1 tablespoon fresh lime juice

1 teaspoon garlic powder

1 cup shredded cheddar cheese

4 hamburger buns, toasted if desired

This is not your average burger, and it's about to become your favorite! Lean ground chicken is first blended with cilantro and seasoned bread crumbs, and then crowned with southwestern toppings of seared tomatoes and garlicky guacamole.

1. Coat a stovetop grill pan, griddle, or large skillet with cooking spray and heat over medium-high heat.

2. In a large bowl, combine the chicken, cilantro, bread crumbs, 1 teaspoon salt, and ½ teaspoon pepper. Mix well and shape into 8 patties, each about 1 inch thick. Place the burgers on the hot pan and arrange the tomato halves, flesh side down, alongside. Cook for 3 minutes per side, or until the burgers are cooked through and the tomatoes are charred.

3. Meanwhile, to make the guacamole, in a small bowl, combine the avocado, onion, lime juice, and garlic powder. Mix well with a fork, slightly smashing the avocado into small pieces. Season to taste with salt and pepper.

4. Transfer the tomatoes to a cutting board. Top the burgers with cheddar cheese, tent with foil, and cook for about 1 minute, until the cheese melts. Chop all of the charred tomatoes into small pieces.

5. Serve 4 burgers on the hamburger buns with half of the charred tomatoes and all of the guacamole. (Reserve the remaining 4 burgers for the Thai chicken dish and the remaining tomatoes for the salsa.)

Serves 4 (with leftovers for the Thai chicken and for the quesadillas)

Thai Chicken in Puff Pastry

PREP TIME: 10 to 15 minutes • **COOK TIME: 30 to 35 minutes**

⅓ cup sour cream

2 tablespoons creamy or crunchy peanut butter

2 tablespoons reduced-sodium soy sauce

2 teaspoons toasted sesame oil

4 reserved cooked chicken burgers, broken up into ¼-inch pieces (or 2 cups shredded or diced cooked chicken)

1 cup diced fresh pineapple or drained canned pineapple

⅓ cup chopped scallions (green and white parts)

1 sheet frozen puff pastry, thawed according to package directions

1 egg

1 tablespoon sesame seeds

If you think working with puff pastry is too hard or time-consuming, think again. This dish simply requires that you roll out store-bought pastry, fill it, and roll it back up. The oven does the rest!

1. Preheat the oven to 375°F.

2. In a large bowl, whisk together the sour cream, peanut butter, soy sauce, and sesame oil. Mix in the chicken burger pieces, pineapple, and scallions.

3. Unfold the pastry on a flat surface. Roll into a 16 x 12-inch rectangle. Spread the chicken mixture onto the pastry to within 1½ inches of the edges. Starting at the shorter side, roll up like a jelly roll. Place seam side down on a large, rimmed baking sheet. Tuck the ends under to seal.

4. In a small bowl, whisk together the egg and 1 tablespoon water. Brush the egg mixture all over the puff pastry and sprinkle the surface with the sesame seeds.

5. Bake for 30 to 35 minutes, until the pastry is golden brown. Let cool for 10 minutes before slicing crosswise into 2-inch-thick slices and serving.

Serves 4

Quick Side Dish: Navy Bean Salad with Roasted Red Peppers

In a bowl, combine two 15-ounce cans (rinsed and drained) navy beans, 1 cup diced roasted red bell peppers, and 2 tablespoons chopped fresh basil. Season to taste with salt and freshly ground black pepper.

Corn and Zucchini Quesadillas with Charred Tomato–Basil Salsa

PREP TIME: **10 minutes** • COOK TIME: **10 to 15 minutes**

2 cups fresh or frozen corn, thawed

2 reserved charred tomatoes, diced (or 1 14-ounce can fire-roasted diced tomatoes)

2 tablespoons minced red onion

2 tablespoons chopped fresh basil

1 tablespoon fresh lime juice

1 teaspoon ground cumin

Salt and freshly ground black pepper

Cooking spray

4 8- to 10-inch flour tortillas

1 cup shredded cheddar cheese

1 cup shredded Monterey Jack or pepper Jack cheese

2 small zucchini, thinly sliced

1 4-ounce can minced green chiles, drained

This is a great dish for the vegetarians in the crowd. Sautéing corn brings out its natural sweetness and the golden corn pairs beautifully with cheddar and Jack cheeses, zucchini, and chiles. Plus, the salsa has a delightfully deep tomato flavor thanks to the reserved charred tomatoes.

1. Put the corn in a large nonstick skillet and set the pan over medium-high heat. Cook for 6 minutes, or until the corn is golden brown on all sides, shaking the pan frequently to prevent burning. Set aside.

2. Meanwhile, to make the salsa, in a medium bowl, combine the charred tomatoes, onion, basil, lime juice, and cumin. Mix well and season to taste with salt and pepper. Set aside.

3. Coat a stovetop griddle or large skillet with cooking spray and heat over medium-high heat.

4. Arrange the tortillas on a flat surface. Top half of each tortilla with both kinds of shredded cheese, the zucchini, reserved corn, and green chiles. Fold over the un-topped side, making a half moon. Place the quesadillas on the hot pan and cook for 2 to 3 minutes per side, until the tortillas are golden brown and the cheese melts.

5. Serve the quesadillas with the salsa on the side.

Serves 4

Week 26

Skirt Steak with Cracked Black Pepper Butter
Quick Side Dish: Pasta with Zucchini and Oregano

Nacho Napoleons
Quick Side Dish: Corn and Pinto Bean Salad

Prosciutto-Wrapped Halibut with Macadamia Couscous
Quick Side Dish: Asian Cabbage Salad

PREP LIST

* Cook extra steak for the napoleons when you prepare the skirt steak dish. (Refrigerate for up to 3 days or freeze for up to 3 months. Thaw overnight in the refrigerator or in the microwave on the defrost setting before using.)

* Make the couscous for the halibut dish. (Refrigerate for up to 2 days.)

Skirt Steak with Cracked Black Pepper Butter

PREP TIME: 5 minutes • COOK TIME: 10 minutes

Cooking spray

1 skirt or flank steak (1¾ to 2 pounds), or 2 steaks (12 ounces to 1 pound each)

Salt and freshly ground black pepper

4 tablespoons (½ stick) butter

1 teaspoon cracked black pepper

Just salt and pepper? Really? Cooked to perfection, that's all a tasty steak needs. Drizzle butter that's been steeped with cracked black pepper over the top just before serving for extra flavor and richness. So divine and easy—this recipe is perfect for entertaining.

1. Coat a stovetop grill pan or griddle with cooking spray and heat over medium-high heat. Season both sides of the steak with salt and ground pepper. Grill for 5 minutes per side, for medium-rare. Remove the steak from the pan and let stand for 5 minutes.

2. Meanwhile, melt the butter and cracked black pepper together in a medium saucepan over low heat.

3. Slice the steak crosswise, against the grain, into thin strips. Serve all but 1 cup of steak slices with all of the butter drizzled over the top (serve any remaining butter alongside). (Reserve the remaining steak slices for the napoleons.)

Serves 4 (with leftovers for the napoleons)

Morph to Another Meal ▶ ▶ ▶ Instead of using the extra steak in the napoleons, use it in one of the recipes listed in the box on page 115.

Quick Side Dish: Pasta with Zucchini and Oregano

Cook 8 ounces orecchiette (ear-shaped) pasta according to the package directions, adding 2 cups chopped zucchini for the last 30 seconds of cooking. Drain and transfer to a large bowl. Add 2 tablespoons olive oil and 2 teaspoons each dried oregano and dried minced garlic and toss to combine. Season to taste with salt and freshly ground black pepper.

Nacho Napoleons

PREP TIME: 10 to 15 minutes • COOK TIME: 15 to 20 minutes

Cooking spray

12 6-inch corn tortillas

1 cup reserved sliced cooked skirt steak, diced (or 1 cup diced cooked steak or ground beef)

1 cup shredded cheddar cheese

½ cup sour cream

⅓ cup prepared salsa

1 teaspoon chili powder

Salt

½ cup prepared guacamole

¼ cup sliced black olives

I love layering ingredients—not just to combine flavors, but also to make a dazzling presentation. Check out this fun dish that boasts layers of steak (mixed with sour cream, cheese, and salsa) and crunchy corn tortillas. Guacamole and sliced olives are the (savory) icing on top!

1. Preheat the oven to 375°F. Coat a large baking sheet with cooking spray.

2. Trim the round edges from the tortillas, making twelve 4-inch squares. Arrange 4 squares on the prepared baking sheet.

3. In a medium bowl, combine the steak, cheese, sour cream, salsa, and chili powder. Mix well. Spoon half of the steak mixture onto the tortillas on the baking sheet. Top each stack with a second tortilla square. Spoon the remaining steak mixture on top and cover with the last tortilla squares. Spray the top layer with cooking spray and season with salt.

4. Bake for 15 to 20 minutes, until the tortillas are golden brown and the cheese melts. Top the napoleons with a dollop of guacamole and sprinkle with black olives just before serving.

Serves 4

Quick Side Dish: Corn and Pinto Bean Salad

In a large bowl, combine one 10-ounce bag thawed, frozen corn, one 15-ounce can (rinsed and drained) pinto beans, one 14-ounce can drained, diced tomatoes, one 4-ounce can minced green chiles, 2 tablespoons chopped fresh cilantro, and 1 tablespoon fresh lime juice. Toss to combine and season to taste with salt and freshly ground black pepper.

Prosciutto-Wrapped Halibut with Macadamia Couscous

PREP TIME: **10 to 15 minutes** • COOK TIME: **12 to 15 minutes**

Cooking spray

4 halibut fillets (about 5 ounces each)

Salt and freshly ground black pepper

½ pound thinly sliced prosciutto

½ cup unsalted roasted macadamia nuts, chopped

1 cup couscous

1 teaspoon ground cumin

1¼ cups reduced-sodium chicken broth or water

Because halibut is a mild-tasting fish, I often pair it with stronger flavors. Prosciutto is the ideal partner here because it adds a distinct saltiness without overpowering the dish. If desired, you can substitute flounder, tilapia, cod, bass, snapper, or grouper for the halibut.

1. Preheat the oven to 400°F. Coat a large baking sheet with cooking spray.

2. Season both sides of the fish fillets with salt and pepper. Wrap prosciutto slices around the pieces of fish, making a thin, even layer. Transfer the fish to the prepared baking sheet and bake for 12 to 15 minutes, until the fish pulls apart when tested with a fork.

3. Meanwhile, to make the couscous, put the macadamia nuts in a medium saucepan and place the pan over medium heat. Cook, shaking the pan frequently, for 2 minutes, or until the nuts are toasted and golden brown. Add the couscous and cumin and cook for about 30 seconds, until the cumin is fragrant. Add the chicken broth and bring to a boil. Remove from the heat, cover, and let stand for 5 minutes. Fluff with a fork and season with salt and pepper.

4. Serve the halibut with the couscous on the side.

Serves 4

Quick Side Dish: Asian Cabbage Salad

In a large bowl, combine 6 cups shredded red cabbage (about 1 small head), 1 cup shredded carrots, and ½ cup chopped scallions (green and white parts). In a medium bowl, whisk together ¼ cup cider vinegar, ¼ cup mayonnaise, 2 teaspoons finely grated peeled fresh ginger, and 2 teaspoons toasted sesame oil. Add the dressing to the cabbage mixture and toss to coat. Season to taste with salt and freshly ground black pepper.

Week 27

Kung Pow Turkey Tenderloin
Quick Side Dish: Cilantro-Lime Broccoli

Turkey Reubens with Ham and Swiss
Quick Side Dish: Red Potato Salad

Halibut with Red Pepper Pesto
Quick Side Dish: Brown Ale Rice

* Cook extra turkey for the Reubens when you make the kung pow turkey dish. (Refrigerate for up to 3 days or freeze for up to 3 months. Thaw overnight in the refrigerator or in the microwave on the defrost setting before using.)

* Make the mayonnaise mixture for the Reubens. (Refrigerate for up to 2 days.)

* Make the pesto for the halibut. (Refrigerate for up to 3 days or freeze for up to 3 months. Thaw overnight in the refrigerator before serving.)

Kung Pow Turkey Tenderloin

PREP TIME: 10 to 15 minutes • **COOK TIME: 7 to 9 minutes**

1 tablespoon peanut oil

1 turkey tenderloin
(2 to 2½ pounds),
cut crosswise into ½-
inch-thick slices

Salt and freshly ground
black pepper

1 cup reduced-sodium
chicken broth

2 tablespoons reduced-
sodium soy sauce

1 tablespoon dry sherry

2 teaspoons cornstarch

1 teaspoon rice wine
vinegar

1 teaspoon toasted
sesame oil

1 teaspoon Chinese
chile sauce with garlic

½ cup chopped dry-
roasted peanuts

¼ cup chopped scallions
(green and white parts)

No need to order in Chinese tonight! You can make your favorite restaurant dish in your own kitchen by using pantry staples (chile sauce happens to be a pantry staple in my house; if it's not in yours, it should be). And you can feel guilt-free after this meal because it's much lower in calories and fat than the restaurant version. It also works with chicken breasts and pork tenderloin.

1. Heat the peanut oil in a large skillet over medium-high heat. Season both sides of the turkey slices with salt and pepper. Add the turkey to the hot pan and cook for 2 minutes per side, or until golden brown.

2. In a small bowl, whisk together the chicken broth, soy sauce, sherry, cornstarch, vinegar, sesame oil, and chile sauce. Add the mixture to the turkey and bring to a simmer. Simmer for 3 to 5 minutes, until the sauce thickens and the turkey is cooked through and no longer pink on the inside.

3. Serve half of the turkey topped with all of the peanuts and scallions. (Reserve the remaining turkey for the Reubens.)

Serves 4 (with leftovers for the Reubens)

Quick Side Dish: Cilantro-Lime Broccoli

Heat 2 teaspoons toasted sesame oil in a large skillet over medium heat. To prevent the oil from smoking and burning, quickly add 2 minced garlic cloves and 6 cups broccoli florets to the pan once the oil is hot. Cook for 1 minute. Add ¼ cup reduced-sodium chicken broth or water, and bring to a simmer. Cover and simmer for 3 minutes, or until the broccoli is crisp-tender. Uncover and simmer until the liquid evaporates. Remove from the heat, add ¼ cup chopped fresh cilantro and 1 tablespoon each fresh lime juice and ponzu sauce (or soy sauce), and toss to coat. Season to taste with salt and freshly ground black pepper.

10 Fast Meals from Leftover Steak

Instead of searching to find uses for leftovers, PLAN them! Cook extra steak (or chicken and pork) so you can enjoy two or more meals with little extra effort. Leftover steak from one meal can quickly evolve into a fabulous new meal on a busy weeknight. You can also pick up delicious cooked steak from the supermarket in a pinch. See page 115 for more recipes using leftover steak.

1. Seared Steak with Sherry Garlic Butter: Thinly slice cooked steak and quickly sear the slices in a little olive oil. Add butter, salt-free garlic and herb seasoning, sherry, and freshly ground black pepper, and simmer until the sauce thickens slightly.

2. Steak and Mozzarella Bruschetta with Balsamic-Marinated Tomatoes and Red Onions: In a bowl, combine thinly sliced tomatoes, thinly sliced red onions, balsamic vinegar, and a little olive oil (this mixture may be refrigerated for up to 2 days before using). Top thinly sliced bread (preferably a baguette-style loaf cut on the diagonal) with sliced cooked steak, the tomato-onion mixture, and shredded mozzarella cheese. Place the open-faced sandwiches under the broiler and broil for 2 to 3 minutes, until the cheese melts.

3. Spicy Asian Steak Pizza with Miso: In a bowl, combine hoisin sauce, soy sauce, miso paste, and hot sauce. Spread the mixture over a refrigerated or prepared pizza crust. Top with thinly sliced cooked steak, chopped scallions, and shredded Fontina cheese. Bake at 400°F for 12 to 15 minutes, until the cheese melts.

4. Margarita Steak with Chiles and Lime: In a large skillet, combine thinly sliced cooked steak, canned diced tomatoes (undrained), canned minced green chiles (undrained), fresh lime juice, tequila (optional), ground cumin, and dried oregano. Set the pan over medium heat and bring to a simmer. Simmer for 5 minutes. Stir in chopped fresh cilantro before serving.

5. Cuban Steak Sandwiches: In a bowl, combine thinly sliced cooked steak, minced garlic, chopped fresh mint, fresh lime juice, and freshly ground black pepper. Place the mixture on long sandwich rolls and top with shredded cheddar cheese. Wrap the sandwiches in foil and place in a 350°F oven for 10 to 15 minutes, until the cheese melts.

6. Cheese Steak Empanadas: Roll a 9-inch refrigerated pie crust into a 1/4-inch-thick circle. Cut the circle into quarters. In a bowl, combine chopped cooked steak, chopped onions, and shredded provolone cheese. Place a mound of the steak mixture on the center of each pie crust piece. Fold the dough over the mixture into triangles, and seal the edges. Transfer the empanadas to a baking sheet, cut slits in the tops (to allow steam to escape), and bake at 375°F for 12 minutes, or until golden brown. Serve with ketchup on the side.

7. Steak Kebabs with Horseradish Marmalade: Skewer alternating pieces of cooked steak, cremini mushrooms, cherry tomatoes, and sliced zucchini onto skewers.

Cook on a hot grill pan or griddle for 3 to 5 minutes, until the steak and vegetables are seared. In a bowl, combine orange marmalade, mayonnaise, and horseradish. Serve the marmalade mixture alongside the steak kebabs for dunking.

8. Steak with Wild Mushroom Gravy and Blue Cheese Mashed Potatoes:
Sauté a combination of sliced wild mushrooms (shiitake, cremini, portobello, oyster, chanterelle) in a little olive oil until the mushrooms are tender and release their liquid. Whisk a little flour into beef broth and add to the mushrooms. Add some dried thyme and freshly ground black pepper. Bring to a simmer, add thinly sliced cooked steak, and cook for 1 minute to heat the steak through. To make the mashed potatoes, boil cubed Yukon Gold potatoes in water or broth for 8 minutes, until fork-tender. Drain, and return the potatoes to the pan with crumbled blue cheese and sour cream. Mash the potatoes until smooth or almost smooth. Serve the steak and mushroom gravy alongside or on top of the mashed potatoes.

9. Steak and Artichoke Strudel with Herbed Goat Cheese:
Unfold a sheet of thawed frozen puff pastry on a flat surface, and roll it into a 12 x 16-inch rectangle. Spread herbed goat cheese (such as Boursin or Alouette) all over the pastry, to within 1 inch of the edges. Top the cheese with chopped cooked steak and chopped marinated artichoke hearts. Starting at the shorter side, roll up the pastry like a jelly roll. Place the strudel seam side down on a large, rimmed baking sheet, and tuck the ends under to seal. Bake at 375°F for 20 to 30 minutes, until the pastry is golden brown. Cool for 10 minutes before slicing crosswise into 2-inch-thick slices.

10. Panzanella-Caprese Salad with Steak, Mozzarella, and Tomato:
In a bowl, combine thinly sliced cooked steak, toasted cubed country-style bread or unseasoned croutons, chopped tomatoes, chopped mozzarella cheese, chopped fresh basil, red wine or balsamic vinegar, and extra-virgin olive oil. Season with salt and freshly ground black pepper to taste, and serve over romaine lettuce if desired.

Turkey Reubens with Ham and Swiss

PREP TIME: 10 to 15 minutes • COOK TIME: 4 to 6 minutes

Cooking spray

¼ cup mayonnaise

1 tablespoon ketchup

1 tablespoon pickle rel-
ish

8 thick slices rye bread
(each ½ inch thick)

Reserved cooked turkey,
thinly sliced (or 3 to
4 cups sliced cooked
turkey or chicken)

½ pound thinly sliced
baked ham

1 cup prepared sauer-
kraut

8 slices Swiss cheese or
1 cup shredded Swiss
cheese

Now here's a sandwich worthy of a complete meal (especially when coupled with the potato salad below). I use ham in my Reuben sandwiches because it's leaner than the more traditional corned beef or pastrami.

1. Coat a stovetop grill pan or griddle with cooking spray and heat over medium-high heat.

2. In a small bowl, combine the mayonnaise, ketchup, and relish. Mix well and spread onto 4 of the bread slices. Top the mayonnaise mixture with the turkey slices, ham, sauerkraut, Swiss cheese, and the second slice of bread.

3. Place the sandwiches on the hot pan and cook for 2 to 3 minutes per side, until the sandwiches are golden brown and the cheese melts.

Serves 4

Morph from Another Meal ► ► ► Instead of using the extra turkey, make this dish with the reserved cooked chicken from one of the recipes listed in the box on page 169.

Quick Side Dish: Red Potato Salad

Place 2 pounds quartered small to medium red potatoes in a large saucepan. Add enough water to cover, set the pan over high heat, and bring to a boil. Boil for 8 minutes, or until the potatoes are fork-tender. Drain and transfer to a large bowl. While still warm, add one 14-ounce can diced tomatoes (drained), ½ cup each chopped celery and red onion, ¼ cup chopped fresh flat-leaf parsley, and 2 tablespoons each olive oil and red wine vinegar. Toss to combine and season to taste with salt and freshly ground black pepper.

Halibut with Red Pepper Pesto

PREP TIME: 10 to 15 minutes • COOK TIME: 4 to 7 minutes

1 cup roasted red bell peppers, drained

½ cup reduced-sodium chicken broth

2 tablespoons grated Parmesan cheese

2 garlic cloves, chopped

1 tablespoon olive oil

4 halibut fillets (about 5 ounces each)

Salt and freshly ground black pepper

¼ cup chopped fresh chives

This pesto is so deeply delicious, you'll want to stock several batches in the freezer for future meals. Although I don't use pine nuts (or any nuts) in this pesto, you still get a nutty flavor from the Parmesan cheese. This sweet and smoky pesto is perfect with halibut or other mild-flavored fish, such as tilapia, flounder, bass, snapper, cod, and grouper.

1. In a blender, combine the roasted red peppers, broth, Parmesan cheese, and garlic. Puree until smooth. Set aside.

2. Heat the oil in a large skillet over medium-high heat. Season both sides of the halibut fillets with salt and pepper and add to the hot pan. Cook for 1 to 2 minutes per side, until golden brown.

3. Add the red pepper pesto and bring to a simmer. Simmer for 2 to 3 minutes, until the fish pulls apart when tested with a fork.

4. Top the halibut with the chives just before serving.

Serves 4

Quick Side Dish: Brown Ale Rice

In a medium saucepan, combine 1 cup brown ale (or reduced-sodium beef broth), 1 cup reduced-sodium beef broth, 2 cups quick-cooking white or brown rice, and 1 teaspoon dried thyme. Set the pan over high heat and bring to a boil. Cover, remove from the heat, and let stand for 5 minutes. Fluff with a fork and season to taste with salt and freshly ground black pepper.

Week 28

5-Ingredient Spicy Apricot Chicken
Quick Side Dish: Thai Bok Choy "Slaw"

Curried Cashew Chicken Salad with Toasted Raisin Bread

Popcorn Shrimp with Cajun Mayo

PREP LIST

* Make the optional slaw side dish for the apricot chicken, if desired. (Refrigerate for up to 2 days before serving.)

* Cook extra chicken for the salad when you prepare the apricot chicken. (Refrigerate for up to 3 days or freeze for up to 3 months. Thaw overnight in the refrigerator or in the microwave on the defrost setting before using.)

* Assemble the chicken salad. (Refrigerate for up to 2 days before serving.)

* Combine the bread-crumb mixture for the popcorn shrimp. (Store at room temperature for up to 5 days.)

* Make the Cajun mayo for the shrimp. (Refrigerate for up to 3 days.)

5-Ingredient Spicy Apricot Chicken

PREP TIME: **10 minutes** • COOK TIME: **25 to 30 minutes**

Cooking spray

8 boneless skinless chicken breasts (about 5 ounces each)

Salt and freshly ground black pepper

¾ cup apricot nectar

⅓ cup apricot preserves

2 tablespoons reduced-sodium soy sauce

1 teaspoon prepared Chinese hot mustard, or ½ teaspoon mustard powder

My pantry is never without a jar of apricot preserves. The sweet jam is great in sugary desserts and it's an excellent base for savory dishes. In this recipe, I kick up the apricot flavor with apricot nectar and then add salty soy sauce and spicy hot mustard. It's the perfect balance of flavors, all for just 5 ingredients.

1. Preheat the oven to 400°F. Coat a shallow roasting pan with cooking spray.

2. Season both sides of the chicken breast halves with salt and pepper and arrange in the prepared pan. In a small bowl, whisk together the apricot nectar, apricot preserves, soy sauce, and mustard. Pour the mixture all over the chicken.

3. Roast for 25 to 30 minutes, until the chicken is cooked through and no longer pink on the inside. Serve 4 of the chicken breast halves with this meal. (Reserve the remaining 4 chicken breast halves for the curried chicken salad.)

Serves 4 (with leftovers for the salad)

Quick Side Dish: Thai Bok Choy "Slaw"

In a large bowl, combine 3 cups shredded red cabbage, 1 cup shredded bok choy, and ½ cup shredded carrots. In a small bowl, whisk together ½ cup mayonnaise, 1 tablespoon peanut butter, and 1 tablespoon each fresh lime juice and reduced-sodium soy sauce. Add the dressing to the cabbage mixture and toss to combine. Season to taste with salt and black pepper. Garnish with chopped peanuts if desired.

Curried Cashew Chicken Salad with Toasted Raisin Bread

PREP TIME: **15 minutes**

½ cup mayonnaise or sour cream

1 teaspoon white wine vinegar

1 teaspoon curry powder

4 reserved cooked chicken breast halves, cubed (or 4 cups cubed cooked chicken)

½ cup roasted, salted whole cashews or cashew pieces

1 Granny Smith apple, cored and diced

1 celery stalk, chopped

2 tablespoons chopped fresh chives

2 tablespoons chopped fresh flat-leaf parsley

Salt and freshly ground black pepper

4 cups torn red lettuce leaves

4 slices raisin bread, toasted

Take your chicken salad over the top by adding sweet, salty cashews, tart Granny Smith apples, and lots of fresh herbs. Served with raisin bread, it makes an amazing meal for the whole family. This is also a great dish for luncheons.

1. In a large bowl, whisk together the mayonnaise, vinegar, and curry powder. Add the chicken, cashews, apple, celery, chives, and parsley and mix to combine. Season to taste with salt and pepper.

2. Serve the chicken salad over the lettuce with the raisin bread on the side.

Serves 4

Plan Ahead

These recipes all make plenty of leftover chicken to use for a second meal. Make these when you have time on your hands, and your next meal will be only minutes away.

Chicken with Sweet Tomato–Pine Nut Sauce (page 141)

Chicken with Roasted Mushrooms and Pearl Onions (page 210)

Grilled Chicken with Sherried Caramelized Wild Mushrooms (page 146)

Roasted Chicken with Ginger-Peach Rémoulade (page 86)

5-Ingredient Spicy Apricot Chicken (page 168)

Roasted Chipotle–Honey Mustard Chicken (page 66)

Popcorn Shrimp with Cajun Mayo

PREP TIME: 15 minutes • COOK TIME: 4 minutes

2 large eggs

2 tablespoons milk

1 cup seasoned dry bread crumbs

1 teaspoon garlic powder

1 teaspoon onion powder

½ teaspoon paprika, preferably smoked paprika

½ teaspoon salt

¼ teaspoon freshly ground black pepper

1¼ pounds peeled and deveined fresh medium shrimp or thawed frozen medium shrimp

2 to 3 tablespoons vegetable oil, as needed

⅓ cup mayonnaise

1 teaspoon Cajun or Creole seasoning

Lemon wedges, for serving (optional)

I can't remember the last time I deep-fried anything. It's just not my style. But I still enjoy foods that are typically deep-fried. So in this recipe, I batter shrimp with a highly seasoned coating of bread crumbs before searing them in oil. Golden brown and tender, they're awesome when dunked in a Cajun-spiked mayo. I like to serve the shrimp with lemon wedges on the side and with couscous or rice that's been tossed with a little prepared salsa or pesto.

1. In a shallow dish, whisk together the eggs and milk. In a separate shallow dish, combine the bread crumbs, garlic powder, onion powder, paprika, salt, and pepper. Mix well to combine. Working in batches, add the shrimp to the egg mixture and turn to coat. Transfer the shrimp to the bread-crumb mixture and turn to coat. Shake off any excess bread crumbs.

2. Heat the oil in a large, deep skillet over medium-high heat. Add the shrimp to the hot oil and cook for 2 minutes per side, or until the shrimp are opaque and cooked through and the crumb coating is golden brown.

3. Meanwhile, to make the Cajun mayonnaise, in a small bowl, whisk together the mayonnaise and Cajun seasoning.

4. Serve the shrimp with the Cajun mayonnaise on the side for dipping and pass the lemon wedges (the lemon can be squeezed over the shrimp or into the mayonnaise).

Serves 4

Week 29

Cornmeal Seared Scallops
Quick Side Dish: Spicy Eggplant Ratatouille

Roast Beef Empanadas with Cilantro Sour Cream
Quick Side Dish: Sautéed Corn with Roasted Red Peppers

Chicken with Citrus-Soy BBQ Sauce over Pickled Ginger Noodles

PREP LIST

* Make the ratatouille optional side dish for the scallops. (Refrigerate for up to 3 days. Reheat in a saucepan or in the microwave.)

* Sauté the vegetables for the empanadas. (Refrigerate for up to 3 days.)

* Assemble the empanadas. (Refrigerate for up to 2 days or freeze for up to 3 months before baking. No need to thaw before baking; just add 5 to 10 minutes to the cooking time.)

* Make the cilantro sour cream for the empanadas. (Refrigerate for up to 2 days).

* Make the barbecue sauce and marinate the chicken. (Refrigerate the sauce for up to 3 days; marinate the chicken for up to 24 hours in the refrigerator).

* Make the soba noodles for the chicken. (Refrigerate for up to 2 days. Reheat in the microwave if desired.)

Cornmeal Seared Scallops

PREP TIME: 10 to 15 minutes • **COOK TIME: 6 minutes**

½ cup yellow cornmeal

2 tablespoons grated
Parmesan cheese

1 teaspoon dried thyme

2 pounds sea scallops,
patted dry

Salt and freshly ground
black pepper

1 tablespoon olive oil

Cornmeal adds a distinct crunch and subtle sweetness to already sweet scallops. As the scallops sear, the crust becomes golden brown and crisp. This dish is simple yet incredibly flavorful. I sometimes serve the scallops on top of my favorite bottled tomato sauce.

1. In a shallow dish, combine the cornmeal, Parmesan cheese, and thyme. Season both sides of the scallops with salt and pepper and then add them to the cornmeal mixture. Turn to coat both sides.

2. Heat the oil in a large skillet over medium-high heat. Add the scallops to the hot pan and cook for 3 minutes per side, or until opaque and cooked through.

Serves 4

Quick Side Dish: Spicy Eggplant Ratatouille

Heat 1 tablespoon olive oil in a large saucepan over medium-high heat. Add ½ cup chopped onion and 2 minced garlic cloves and cook for 2 minutes. Add 2 peeled and chopped medium eggplants (about 1 pound total) and cook for 5 minutes, or until the eggplant is golden brown on all sides. Add one 14-ounce can diced tomatoes (undrained), ½ cup chopped roasted red pepper, 3 tablespoons balsamic vinegar, 4 minced anchovy fillets, 1 teaspoon smoked paprika, and ½ teaspoon crushed red pepper flakes. Bring to a simmer. Partially cover and simmer for 5 to 7 minutes, until the eggplant breaks down and the sauce thickens. Season to taste with salt and freshly ground black pepper.

Roast Beef Empanadas with Cilantro Sour Cream

PREP TIME: 15 to 20 minutes • **COOK TIME: 15 minutes**

Cooking spray

2 cups shredded roast beef

1 cup prepared salsa

½ cup chopped roasted red bell peppers

½ cup shredded Monterey Jack cheese

½ cup shredded cheddar cheese

1 teaspoon ground cumin

2 9-inch refrigerated pie crusts

½ cup sour cream

1 tablespoon fresh lime juice

2 tablespoons chopped fresh cilantro

Salt and freshly ground black pepper

These half-moon–shaped pastries are stuffed with an amazing mixture of roast beef, salsa, red peppers, and cheese and served with cilantro sour cream.

1. Preheat the oven to 425°F. Coat a large baking sheet with cooking spray.

2. In a large bowl, combine the roast beef, salsa, roasted red peppers, both types of cheese, and cumin. Mix well to combine.

3. Roll each pie crust into a 12-inch circle. Divide the beef mixture into four equal portions on top of one crust, placing one mound on each of four "quadrants." Top with the second crust. Using a pizza slicer or pastry wheel, cut the circle into four equal wedges. Pinch the edges together to seal and transfer the empanadas to the prepared baking sheet. Using a fork, press into the edges of each empanada to ensure the seal. Using a sharp knife, make small slits in the top of each empanada to allow steam to escape during baking.

4. Bake for 15 minutes, until the crust is golden brown.

5. Meanwhile, to make the cilantro sour cream, in a small bowl, whisk together the sour cream, lime juice, and cilantro. Season to taste with salt and pepper.

6. Serve the empanadas with the cilantro sour cream on the side for dipping.

Serves 4

Quick Side Dish: Sautéed Corn with Roasted Red Peppers

Heat 1 tablespoon olive oil in a large skillet over medium-high heat. Add 3 cups fresh or frozen corn and ½ cup chopped scallions (green and white parts) and cook for 3 to 5 minutes, until the corn is golden brown. Add ½ cup diced roasted red bell peppers and cook for 2 minutes, to heat through. Season to taste with salt and freshly ground black pepper.

Chicken with Citrus-Soy BBQ Sauce over Pickled Ginger Noodles

PREP TIME: 10 to 15 minutes • COOK TIME: 25 to 30 minutes

Cooking spray

4 boneless skinless chicken breast halves (about 5 ounces each)

Salt and freshly ground black pepper

½ cup orange juice

¼ cup ketchup

1 tablespoon reduced-sodium soy sauce

1 tablespoon light brown sugar

1 teaspoon chili powder

½ teaspoon liquid smoke

8 ounces soba noodles

2 cups thinly sliced baby spinach leaves

1 tablespoon rice wine vinegar

1 tablespoon minced pickled ginger

2 teaspoons toasted sesame oil

This barbecue sauce is tangy, sweet, and smoky at the same time. Tangy from the orange juice and ketchup, sweet from the brown sugar, and smoky from the chili powder and liquid smoke. The noodles get their pickle flavor and subtle heat from pickled ginger, added color from shredded spinach, and nutty flavor from toasted sesame oil.

1. Preheat the oven to 400°F. Coat a shallow roasting pan with cooking spray.

2. Season both sides of the chicken with salt and pepper and arrange in the prepared pan. In a small bowl, whisk together the orange juice, ketchup, soy sauce, brown sugar, chili powder, and liquid smoke. Spoon the mixture all over the chicken. Roast for 25 to 30 minutes, until the chicken is cooked through and no longer pink on the inside.

3. Meanwhile, to make the noodles, cook the soba noodles according to the package directions. Drain and transfer to a large bowl. While the noodles are still hot, fold in the spinach. Add the vinegar, ginger, and sesame oil and toss to combine. Season to taste with salt and pepper.

4. Serve the chicken over the noodles.

Serves 4

Morph to Another Meal ▶ ▶ ▶ Double the recipe for the chicken portion, and use the extra chicken in one of the recipes listed in the box on page 23.

Week 30

Sweet Ginger Shrimp with
Coconut–Red Curry Dip

Corn Chowder with Grilled Tomatoes
Quick Side Dish: Bruschetta with Artichoke-Fennel Caponata

Mushroom-Watercress Rolls with
Herbed Goat Cheese
Quick Side Dish: Thousand Island Shells
Quick Dessert: Blueberry-Cran Sorbet

PREP LIST

* Grill the tomatoes for the soup when you prepare the shrimp dish. (Refrigerate for up to 3 days.)

* Make the coconut–red curry dip for the shrimp. (Refrigerate for up to 3 days. Reheat in a small saucepan over medium heat or in the microwave before serving.)

* Chop the leeks and celery for the soup. (Refrigerate for up to 3 days.)

* Make the caponata for the optional bruschetta side dish for the soup, if desired. (Refrigerate for up to 3 days. If desired, reheat in the microwave before serving.)

* Cook the mushroom filling for the rolls. (Refrigerate for up to 3 days. Reheat in the microwave before making the rolls.)

* Assemble the rolls. (Refrigerate for up to 24 hours before serving.)

Sweet Ginger Shrimp with Coconut–Red Curry Dip

PREP TIME: 15 minutes • COOK TIME: 6 minutes

Cooking spray

½ cup seedless straw-berry preserves

1 tablespoon balsamic vinegar

2 teaspoons minced peeled fresh ginger

2 teaspoons Dijon mus-tard

1½ to 2 pounds peeled and deveined fresh or thawed, frozen large or jumbo shrimp

1 green bell pepper, seeded and cut into 2-inch pieces

1 medium red onion, cut into 2-inch pieces

16 cherry tomatoes

Salt and freshly ground black pepper

1 cup canned unsweet-ened coconut milk

1 tablespoon red curry paste

2 teaspoons fresh lime juice

2 teaspoons sugar

Strawberry preserves are superbly sweet, so to add strawberry flavor to a savory dish, I add opposing ingredients to balance the flavor. In this dish, tangy balsamic vinegar, Dijon mustard, and pungent ginger help make the intense glaze. Once the shrimp grill to perfection (alongside fresh vegetables), I dunk them in a sweet and slightly tangy coconut sauce.

> **Note:** When using wooden skewers, soak them in water for at least 20 minutes prior to using to prevent burning. Red curry paste is sold with the other Asian ingredients in the grocery store.

1. Coat a stovetop grill pan or griddle with cooking spray and heat over medium-high heat.

2. In a large bowl, whisk together the strawberry preserves, vinegar, ginger, and Dijon mustard. Add the shrimp and toss to coat. Skewer alternating pieces of shrimp, bell pepper, and onion on metal or wooden skewers. Skewer cherry tomatoes on differ-ent skewers. Season all of the skewers with salt and pepper.

3. Grill the skewers, turning and basting with any remaining strawberry mixture, for 6 minutes, or until the shrimp are opaque and cooked through and the vegetables are tender and slightly charred.

4. Meanwhile, to make the sauce, in a small saucepan, com-bine the coconut milk, curry paste, lime juice, and sugar. Set the pan over medium heat and bring to a simmer. Simmer for 5 minutes, or until the mixture thickens and reduces.

5. Serve the shrimp skewers with sauce on the side. (Reserve the tomato skewers for the soup.)

Serves 4 (with leftovers for the soup)

Corn Chowder with Grilled Tomatoes

PREP TIME: 10 to 15 minutes • COOK TIME: **15 to 20 minutes**

1 tablespoon butter

2 leeks, rinsed well and chopped

1 celery stalk, chopped

1 teaspoon dried thyme

1 11-ounce can creamed corn

1 15-ounce can whole kernel corn, drained

2 cups diced red potatoes

1 12-ounce can evaporated milk

1½ cups reduced-sodium chicken or vegetable broth

½ cup sour cream

Salt and freshly ground black pepper

16 reserved grilled cherry tomatoes, coarsely chopped

Corn chowder is the ultimate comfort food. In this dish, leeks sweeten the pot, as does the combination of creamed corn and whole kernel corn. I also add potatoes for a more substantial meal. The addition of grilled tomatoes at the end adds incredible color and flavor to an already great soup.

1. Melt the butter in a large saucepan over medium-high heat. Add the leeks and celery and cook for 3 minutes, or until soft. Add the thyme and cook for about 1 minute, until the thyme is fragrant. Add the creamed corn, whole kernel corn, potatoes, evaporated milk, and broth and bring to a simmer. Partially cover and simmer for 8 to 10 minutes, until the potatoes are fork-tender.

2. Reduce the heat to low, add the sour cream, and simmer for 1 to 2 minutes, to heat through. Season to taste with salt and pepper.

3. Ladle the soup into bowls and top with the chopped tomatoes.

Serves 4

Quick Side Dish: Bruschetta with Artichoke-Fennel Caponata

In a medium saucepan, combine one 14-ounce can artichoke hearts (drained and chopped); ½ cup each chopped onion, chopped fennel bulb, and raisins; ¼ cup red wine vinegar; 3 tablespoons sugar; and 1 teaspoon ground cumin. Set the pan over medium heat and bring to a simmer. Simmer for 5 minutes, or until the vegetables are soft and the liquid evaporates. Season to taste with salt and freshly ground black pepper. Spoon the mixture (warm or chilled) over toasted baguette slices.

Mushroom-Watercress Rolls with Herbed Goat Cheese

PREP TIME: **10 to 15 minutes** • COOK TIME: **5 to 7 minutes**

1 tablespoon olive oil

2 cups sliced portobello mushroom caps

1 cup sliced roasted red bell peppers

½ cup sliced, drained oil-packed sun-dried tomatoes

1 tablespoon balsamic vinegar

4 ounces herbed goat cheese

1 cup fresh watercress leaves

4 6-inch flour tortillas (spinach or regular)

Tortillas are one of my best friends in the kitchen because they're great for holding all types of ingredients, like this tasty blend of wild mushrooms, sweet roasted red peppers, sun-dried tomatoes, peppery watercress, and tangy goat cheese. Roll 'em up and serve to happy faces.

1. Heat the oil in a large skillet over medium-high heat. Add the mushrooms and cook for 3 to 5 minutes, until the mushrooms soften and release their juice. Add the red peppers, sun-dried tomatoes, and vinegar and cook for 2 minutes, until the liquid evaporates. Remove from the heat.

2. Spread the goat cheese on the tortillas. Top with watercress leaves and then the mushroom mixture. Roll up and serve.

Serves 4

Quick Side Dish: Thousand Island Shells

Cook 8 ounces small shell pasta (or elbow macaroni) according to the package directions. Drain and transfer to a large bowl. In a small bowl, whisk together ½ cup mayonnaise, 2 tablespoons each pickle relish and ketchup, 1 tablespoon olive oil, and 1 teaspoon Dijon mustard. Add the mixture to the shells and toss to coat. Season to taste with salt and freshly ground black pepper. Serve warm or cold.

Quick Dessert: Blueberry-Cran Sorbet

In a blender, combine 2 cups cranberry juice, one 10-ounce bag frozen blueberries, 2 tablespoons sugar, and ½ teaspoon vanilla extract. Puree until smooth. Serve immediately or freeze until ready to serve.

Week 31

Strawberry-Citrus Chicken with Roasted Vegetables
Quick Side Dish: Cellophane Noodles with Soy and Sesame

Creole Shrimp and Chicken
Quick Side Dish: Creamy Cucumber Salad

Garden Vegetable Alfredo in Parmesan Cream Sauce
Quick Side Dish: Mixed Greens with Lemon-Rosemary Dressing

PREP LIST

* Cook extra chicken for the Creole dish and extra vegetables for the pasta dish when you prepare the strawberry-citrus chicken. (Refrigerate for up to 3 days or freeze for up to 3 months. Thaw overnight in the refrigerator or in the microwave on the defrost setting before using.)

* Cook the rice for the Creole dish. (Refrigerate for up to 3 days.)

* Chop the onion, celery, bell pepper, and garlic for the Creole dish. (Refrigerate for up to 3 days.)

* Cook the fettuccine for the Alfredo dish. (Refrigerate for up to 3 days.)

Strawberry-Citrus Chicken with Roasted Vegetables

PREP TIME: **10 to 15 minutes** • COOK TIME: **25 to 30 minutes**

Cooking spray

6 boneless skinless chicken breast halves (about 5 ounces each)

Salt and freshly ground black pepper

¾ cup seedless strawberry preserves

2 tablespoons finely grated lemon zest

2 teaspoons garlic powder

2 medium zucchini, chopped

1 red bell pepper, seeded and chopped

2 cups broccoli florets

1½ cups baby carrots

1 cup sliced red onion

Many of my recipe ideas come from raiding my own pantry. I discovered this awesome combination when I paired a generous amount of pepper with sweet strawberry preserves. It's a keeper.

1. Preheat the oven to 400°F. Coat a shallow roasting pan with cooking spray.

2. Arrange the chicken in the prepared pan and season with salt and a generous amount of black pepper. In a small bowl, whisk together the strawberry preserves, lemon zest, and garlic powder. Brush the mixture all over the chicken.

3. Arrange the vegetables all around the chicken in the pan. Spray the vegetables with cooking spray and season with salt and pepper. Roast for 25 to 30 minutes, until the chicken is cooked through and no longer pink on the inside and the vegetables are tender.

4. Serve 4 of the chicken breast halves with half of the vegetables. (Reserve the remaining 2 chicken breast halves for the Creole dish and the remaining vegetables for the pasta dish.)

Serves 4 (with leftovers for the Creole dish)

Quick Side Dish: Cellophane Noodles with Soy and Sesame

Soak 8 ounces cellophane (bean thread) noodles in enough hot water to cover until soft, about 10 minutes. Drain and transfer to a large bowl. Add ¼ cup chopped fresh cilantro, 2 tablespoons reduced-sodium soy sauce, and 2 teaspoons toasted sesame oil and toss to combine. Season to taste with salt and freshly ground black pepper.

Creole Shrimp and Chicken

PREP TIME: **15 minutes** · COOK TIME: **10 to 15 minutes**

1 tablespoon olive oil

½ cup chopped onion

½ cup chopped celery

1 green bell pepper, seeded and chopped

2 garlic cloves, minced

4 ounces cooked andouille or other smoked sausage, diced

2 reserved cooked chicken breast halves, cubed (or 2 cups cubed cooked chicken)

2 teaspoons Creole or Cajun seasoning

1 teaspoon dried thyme

1 14-ounce can diced tomatoes

1 cup reduced-sodium chicken broth

1 pound peeled and deveined fresh large shrimp or thawed frozen large shrimp

1 cup frozen cut okra

1 cup cooked white rice

Salt and freshly ground black pepper

No need to take a trip to the Bayou to enjoy those classic flavors (although it would be nice). Thanks to prepared Creole and Cajun seasonings and spice blends, you can get the same wonderful aromas and flavors in your own kitchen. This hearty, stew-like dish boasts a bounty of textures and taste sensations, and it comes together very quickly thanks to the precooked chicken.

1. Heat the oil in a large saucepan over medium-high heat. Add the onion, celery, bell pepper, and garlic and cook for 2 minutes, or until soft. Add the andouille, chicken, Creole seasoning, and thyme and cook for 1 minute, or until the seasonings are fragrant.

2. Add the tomatoes and chicken broth and bring to a simmer. Add the shrimp and okra and cook for 5 minutes, or until the shrimp are opaque and cooked through and the okra is tender.

3. Stir in the rice and cook for 1 minute to heat through. Season to taste with salt and pepper.

Serves 4

Quick Side Dish: Creamy Cucumber Salad

In a medium bowl, combine 4 cups thinly sliced cucumber (preferably seedless, unwaxed cucumber), ½ cup thinly sliced red onion, ½ cup plain yogurt, 1 tablespoon chopped fresh dill, and ½ teaspoon garlic powder. Toss to combine and season to taste with salt and freshly ground black pepper.

Garden Vegetable Alfredo in Parmesan Cream Sauce

PREP TIME: 15 to 20 minutes • COOK TIME: 10 to 12 minutes

1 pound spinach fettuccine

2 tablespoons butter

1 cup sliced cremini or button mushrooms

2 tablespoons all-purpose flour

2 cups milk

½ cup grated Parmesan cheese

Pinch of ground nutmeg

2 cups reserved roasted vegetables

Salt and freshly ground black pepper

If you don't have leftover vegetables from the Strawberry-Citrus Chicken, simply hit up the salad bar or the freezer aisle at your favorite grocery store for already chopped veggies. (You'll need about 2 cups.) Give the veggies a quick sauté in a little oil before starting this dish and you can whip up the rest with ease!

1. Cook the fettuccine according to the package directions. Drain and set aside.

2. Melt the butter in a large saucepan over medium-high heat. Add the mushrooms and cook for 3 minutes, or until they soften and release their juice. Add the flour and stir to coat. Whisk in the milk and bring to a simmer. Simmer for 2 minutes, or until the sauce thickens.

3. Add the Parmesan cheese and nutmeg and simmer, stirring frequently, for 1 to 2 minutes, until the cheese melts. Add the vegetables and simmer for 1 minute to heat through. Season to taste with salt and pepper.

4. Transfer the fettuccine to a serving platter or individual bowls and top with the vegetable-cheese mixture.

Serves 4

Quick Side Dish: Mixed Greens with Lemon-Rosemary Dressing

In a blender, combine ½ cup reduced-sodium chicken or vegetable broth, 2 tablespoons olive oil, 2 tablespoons fresh lemon juice, 1 tablespoon fresh rosemary leaves, and 1 teaspoon each grated fresh lemon zest and honey-Dijon mustard. Puree until smooth and season to taste with salt and freshly ground black pepper. Drizzle the dressing over 6 cups mixed greens or baby spinach leaves just before serving.

Week 32

Moroccan Turkey Burgers with Goat Cheese and Figs
Quick Side Dish: Butternut Squash Puree

Black Pepper Shrimp
Quick Side Dish: Capellini with Diced Tomatoes, Basil, and Smoked Mozzarella

Roast Beef Sandwiches with Horseradish Cream and Ale Jus
Quick Side Dish: Cajun Sweet Potato Fries

PREP LIST

* Form the burgers. (Refrigerate for up to 3 days or freeze for up to 3 months. Thaw overnight in the refrigerator or in the microwave on the defrost setting before cooking.)

* Make the horseradish cream for the sandwiches. (Refrigerate for up to 24 hours.)

Moroccan Turkey Burgers with Goat Cheese and Figs

PREP TIME: **10 to 15 minutes** • COOK TIME: **7 minutes**

Cooking spray

1¼ pounds ground turkey

½ cup diced figs

½ cup seasoned dry bread crumbs

2 teaspoons ground cumin

½ teaspoon salt

¼ teaspoon freshly ground black pepper

⅛ teaspoon ground cinnamon

1 cup crumbled fresh goat cheese

4 hamburger buns or English muffins, toasted if desired

Sliced beefsteak tomato, for serving

¼ cup fresh cilantro leaves

The flavors of Morocco (figs, cumin, goat cheese, cinnamon, cilantro) come alive in this dish, transforming regular old turkey burgers into something spectacular.

1. Coat a stovetop grill pan, griddle, or large skillet with cooking spray and heat over medium-high heat.

2. In a large bowl, combine the ground turkey, figs, bread crumbs, cumin, salt, pepper, and cinnamon. Mix well and shape the mixture into 4 patties, each about 1 inch thick. Cook the burgers in the hot pan for 3 minutes per side, or until cooked through. Top the burgers with the goat cheese, tent with foil, and cook for 1 minute, or until the cheese melts.

3. Serve on hamburger buns with tomato slices and fresh cilantro leaves.

Serves 4

Quick Side Dish: Butternut Squash Puree

Peel and cut 1 medium butternut squash (about 2 pounds) into 2-inch cubes. Put the cubes in a large saucepan and add enough water to cover. Set the pan over high heat and bring to a boil. Boil for 8 minutes, or until the squash is fork-tender. Drain and return the squash to the pan. Add 2 tablespoons butter, 1 tablespoon sugar, and 1 teaspoon ground coriander and mash until smooth. Season to taste with salt and freshly ground black pepper.

Black Pepper Shrimp

PREP TIME: **5 to 10 minutes** • COOK TIME: **8 minutes**

2 tablespoons butter

1 tablespoon olive oil

3 garlic cloves, minced

2 pounds peeled and deveined fresh jumbo shrimp or thawed frozen jumbo shrimp

2 tablespoons fresh lemon juice

2 teaspoons freshly ground black pepper

¼ cup chopped fresh flat-leaf parsley

Salt

Succulent, sweet shrimp need little else to taste divine. So, in this dish, they get a dousing of black pepper, a little garlic, and a squirt of fresh lemon juice. The result is fantastic. I like to serve these shrimp over rice or with the quick-cooking capellini dish below.

1. Heat the butter and oil together in a large, deep skillet over medium-high heat. Add the garlic and cook for 3 minutes, or until soft. Add the shrimp, lemon juice, and black pepper. Cook, stirring frequently, for 5 minutes, or until the shrimp are opaque and cooked through. Remove from the heat and stir in the parsley. Season with salt.

Serves 4

Morph to Another Meal ▶ ▶ ▶ Cook double the shrimp you need for this recipe, and use the extra shrimp in Panzanella and Shrimp Salad (page 293).

Quick Side Dish: Capellini with Diced Tomatoes, Basil, and Smoked Mozzarella

Cook 8 ounces capellini or angel hair pasta according to the package directions. Drain and transfer to a large bowl. Add one 14-ounce can petite diced tomatoes (drained), 1 cup diced smoked mozzarella cheese, ¼ cup chopped fresh basil, and 1 tablespoon olive oil and toss to combine. Season to taste with salt and freshly ground black pepper.

10 Fast Meals from Leftover Seafood

Chicken, beef, and pork aren't the only ingredients that take well to reinvention. Leftover fish and shellfish can be woven into additional meals with a few simple ingredients and easy preparation methods. Precooked seafood is available at most supermarkets, too, and it's an easy beginning for any weeknight meal.

1. Salmon Burgers: In a bowl, combine cooked and flaked salmon, seasoned dry bread crumbs, minced white onion, egg, and enough mayonnaise to make the mixture come together. Season to taste with salt and freshly ground black pepper. With your hands, shape the mixture into burgers, each about 1 inch thick. Press the burgers into seasoned bread crumbs to coat both sides. Sear the burgers in olive oil in a large skillet. Transfer the burgers to a large baking sheet and bake at 375°F for 10 minutes, or until cooked through.

2. Mixed Seafood Stew: In a stockpot, combine chicken or vegetable broth, diced red potatoes, canned diced tomatoes (undrained), chopped celery, 2 bay leaves, dried thyme and dried oregano, and salt and freshly ground black pepper to taste. Set the pot over high heat and bring to a boil; boil for 5 minutes, then add leftover seafood and/or shellfish. Continue boiling for 8 minutes, or until the potatoes are fork-tender. Remove the bay leaves and stir in chopped fresh flat-leaf parsley before serving.

3. Seafood Enchiladas: In a bowl, combine flaked cooked seafood and/or shellfish, prepared salsa, and sour cream (and leftover cooked rice if desired). Spoon the mixture onto the center of flour or whole-wheat tortillas, and roll up. Place the enchiladas side by side in a shallow baking dish and top with shredded Monterey Jack cheese, cheddar cheese, or a shredded Mexican cheese blend. Cover with foil and bake at 375°F for 12 to 15 minutes, until the cheese melts.

4. Greek Pasta Salad with Seafood: In a bowl, combine cooked pasta (such as orzo), flaked cooked seafood and/or shellfish, canned tomatoes (drained), capers, crumbled feta cheese, chopped fresh basil, dried oregano, red wine vinegar, and extra-virgin olive oil. Season with freshly ground black pepper.

5. Quick Fish Quiche: Press a refrigerated pie crust into a pie plate or tart pan. In a bowl, combine flaked cooked seafood, lightly beaten eggs, milk, chopped scallions, chopped thawed (if frozen) broccoli florets, crumbled fresh goat cheese, and dried oregano and dried thyme. Season with salt and freshly ground black pepper to taste. Mix well, and pour the mixture into the pie shell. Bake at 375°F for 30 to 40 minutes, until the center is set.

6. Spicy Gazpacho with Seafood: In a bowl, combine canned pureed tomatoes or tomato juice, flaked cooked seafood and/or shellfish, diced celery, diced cucumber, diced green bell pepper, diced white onion, diced jalapeño, fresh lemon juice, hot sauce, chopped fresh flat-leaf parsley, and salt and freshly ground black pepper to taste. Refrigerate until ready to serve.

7. Seafood Salad in Melon Bowls:
In a bowl, combine flaked cooked seafood and/or shellfish, mayonnaise, Dijon mustard, diced celery, chopped roasted red bell peppers, diced gherkins, and chopped fresh flat-leaf parsley. Spoon the mixture into hollowed cantaloupe or honeydew melon halves.

8. Mixed Seafood Stromboli: Roll out refrigerated or thawed frozen pizza dough into a large rectangle (about 12 x 15 inches). In a bowl, combine flaked cooked seafood and/or shellfish, ricotta cheese, shredded mozzarella cheese, grated Parmesan cheese, chopped fresh basil, and salt and freshly ground black pepper to taste. Spoon the mixture onto the center of the dough. Starting from the longer side, fold over the dough, covering the filling, and pinch the edges together to seal. Transfer the stromboli to a large oiled baking sheet, and bake at 400°F for 12 to 15 minutes, until golden brown.

9. Salmon Beggar's Purses: In a bowl, combine flaked cooked salmon, shredded cabbage and carrots (coleslaw mix), soy sauce, and sesame oil. Spoon the mixture onto the center of wonton wrappers. Fold up the corners and pinch them together to seal. Sear the bottom of the purses in a little peanut oil in a large skillet over medium heat. Add a little chicken broth or water to the skillet, cover, and cook for 2 more minutes, or until the wontons are translucent. Serve with soy or tamari sauce on the side for dunking.

10. Fish with Jamaican Rum Butter over Rice: Melt butter and spiced rum together in a large skillet over medium heat. Add flaked cooked fish and/or shellfish and simmer for 2 minutes to heat through. Stir in chopped fresh mint and serve over cooked white or brown rice.

Roast Beef Sandwiches with Horseradish Cream and Ale Jus

PREP TIME: 5 to 10 minutes • **COOK TIME: 10 minutes**

1 12-ounce bottle ale or amber beer

1 cup reduced-sodium beef broth

½ teaspoon garlic powder

12 ounces thinly sliced roast beef

3 tablespoons mayonnaise

1 tablespoon prepared horseradish

8 slices sourdough or rye bread (about ½ inch thick)

Sometimes the middle of a hectic week just cries out for a comforting sandwich. I loved soup-and-sandwich night when I was a little girl, and I still do. What's more comforting than warm roast beef, simmered in a garlicky beer broth, nestled on tangy bread with horseradish-spiked mayonnaise?

1. In a medium saucepan, combine the ale, broth, and garlic powder. Set the pan over medium-high heat and bring to a simmer. Simmer for 5 minutes, or until the liquid reduces to 1½ cups. Add the roast beef and simmer for 5 minutes to heat through.

2. Meanwhile, in a small bowl, combine the mayonnaise and horseradish. Mix well and spread on 4 of the bread slices. Using tongs, remove the roast beef from the ale mixture and place on the horseradish-topped bread. Top each sandwich with a second slice of bread. Serve the remaining ale sauce on the side for dipping.

Serves 4

Quick Side Dish: Cajun Sweet Potato Fries

Peel and cut 2 pounds sweet potatoes (2 to 3 medium) into thin strips (fries). Transfer to a baking sheet that's been coated with cooking spray and spread out in a single layer. Spray with cooking spray and season with Cajun or Creole seasoning and freshly ground black pepper. Roast at 400°F for 25 to 30 minutes, until golden brown and tender.

Chicken Burgers with Guacamole, Cheddar, and Charred Tomatoes, page 151.

Spanish Sausage and Vegetable Kebabs, page 138.

Below: **Lasagna Rolls with Herbed Cheese,** page 35.
Right: **5-Ingredient Spicy Apricot Chicken,** page 168.
Opposite: **Kung Pow Turkey Tenderloin,** page 161.

Above: **Peanut-Crusted Chicken with Apple-Gorgonzola Relish,** page 220.
Opposite: **Creamy Peanut Chicken Fettuccine with Broccoli,** page 221.

Above: **Mixed Greens with Shrimp, Crumbled Blue Cheese, and Peanut Brittle in Raspberry-Champagne Vinaigrette, page 104. Opposite: Grilled Steak with Shiitake Mushrooms, Wilted Arugula, and Shaved Parmesan,** page 48.

Above: **Corn Tortilla Soup with Chicken and Lime,** page 142.
Opposite: **Grilled Moroccan Steak with Charred Zucchini–Mint Salsa,** page 143.

Above: **Pan-Seared Scallops with Spinach-Mushroom Sauté**, page 257.
Opposite: **Pasta Paella with Saffron Broth**, page 258.

Above: **Seared Teriyaki Beef Roll with Gingered Vegetables,** page 113. Opposite: **Tortilla-Crusted Salmon with Tropical Fruit Salsa,** page 116.

Seared Tuna with Miso Broth and Sesame Soba Noodles, page 148.

Week 33

Grilled Flank Steak with Blue Cheese–Crumb Topping
Quick Side Dish: Maple-Glazed Sweet Potatoes

Steak Quesadillas with Spinach and Caramelized Onions and Chunky Ranch Guacamole

Lemongrass Poached Salmon with Wasabi-Soy Mayo
Quick Side Dish: Chunky Buttermilk Mashed Potatoes

PREP LIST

* Cook extra steak for the quesadillas when you prepare the flank steak. (Refrigerate for up to 3 days or freeze for up to 3 months. Thaw overnight in the refrigerator or in the microwave on the defrost setting before using.)

* Assemble the quesadillas. (Refrigerate for up to 3 days or freeze for up to 3 months. Thaw overnight in the refrigerator before cooking. I don't recommend thawing in the microwave.)

* Make the guacamole for the quesadillas. (Refrigerate for up to 2 days; I don't recommend freezing.)

* Poach the salmon. (Refrigerate for up to 2 days. Serve chilled or reheat in the microwave for 30 seconds to 1 minute on high.)

* Make the wasabi-soy mayo for the salmon. (Refrigerate for up to 2 days.)

Grilled Flank Steak with Blue Cheese–Crumb Topping

PREP TIME: 10 minutes • COOK TIME: 10 minutes

Cooking spray

1 flank steak (2 to 2½ pounds), or 2 flank steaks (1 to 1¼ pounds each)

Salt and freshly ground black pepper

2 teaspoons olive oil

2 garlic cloves, minced

½ cup seasoned dry bread crumbs

½ cup crumbled blue cheese

This is a simple way to take an everyday steak over the top. Since it takes just a few minutes (and practically zero effort) to make the creamy-crunchy topping, think of this for your next dinner party.

1. Coat a stovetop grill pan or griddle with cooking spray and heat over medium-high heat. Season both sides of the steak with salt and pepper and add to the hot pan. Cook for 5 minutes per side for medium-rare. Remove the steak from the pan and let stand for 5 minutes.

2. Meanwhile, to make the crumb topping, heat the oil in a large skillet over medium heat. Add the garlic and cook for 2 to 3 minutes, until soft. Add the bread crumbs and cook for 2 minutes, or until golden brown. Add the blue cheese and cook for 1 to 2 minutes, until the cheese starts to melt and the mixture is crumbly.

3. Cut the steak crosswise, against the grain, into thin strips. Serve half of the steak with all of the blue cheese mixture sprinkled over the top. (Reserve the remaining steak for the quesadillas.)

Serves 4 (with leftovers for the quesadillas)

Quick Side Dish: Maple-Glazed Sweet Potatoes

Peel and cube 2 pounds sweet potatoes (2 to 3 medium) and toss with 1 tablespoon olive oil, ½ teaspoon salt, and ¼ teaspoon freshly ground black pepper. Transfer the potatoes to a large, rimmed baking sheet, in a single layer, and roast at 400°F for 25 to 30 minutes, until tender. While still hot, toss the sweet potatoes with a mixture of ¼ cup 100% pure maple syrup and 2 teaspoons Dijon mustard.

Steak Quesadillas with Spinach and Caramelized Onions and Chunky Ranch Guacamole

PREP TIME: 15 minutes • **COOK TIME: 15 minutes**

1 tablespoon olive oil

1 cup sliced yellow or red onion

1 tablespoon sugar

2 ripe avocados, pitted, peeled, and coarsely chopped

¼ cup prepared ranch dressing

2 teaspoons fresh lime juice

½ cup diced ripe beefsteak or plum tomato

1 to 2 tablespoons chopped fresh cilantro, to taste

Salt and freshly ground black pepper

Cooking spray

4 8- to 10-inch flour tortillas

2 cups shredded Monterey Jack cheese

2 cups baby spinach leaves

Reserved cooked steak slices (or 3 to 4 cups sliced cooked steak or chicken)

We love quesadillas in our house, so I'm always creating a new version. This simple combination contains tortillas stuffed with steak, cheese, spinach, and caramelized onions. What takes them over the top is the guacamole on the side—an awesome (and ridiculously simple) blend of avocados, ranch dressing, lime juice, tomato, and cilantro.

1. Heat the oil in a large skillet over medium heat. Add the onion and sugar and cook for 7 to 8 minutes, until soft and golden brown.

2. Meanwhile, to make the guacamole, in a medium bowl, combine the avocado, ranch dressing, and lime juice. Mash with a fork until blended. Stir in the tomato and cilantro. Season to taste with salt and pepper. Set aside.

3. Coat a stovetop griddle or large skillet with cooking spray and heat over medium-high heat.

4. Arrange the tortillas on a flat surface. Top half of each tortilla with shredded cheese, spinach, reserved steak, and caramelized onions. Fold over the un-topped side, making a half moon. Place the quesadillas on the hot pan and cook for 2 to 3 minutes per side, until the tortillas are golden brown and the cheese melts.

5. Serve the quesadillas with the guacamole on the side.

Serves 4

Lemongrass Poached Salmon with Wasabi-Soy Mayo

PREP TIME: **10 minutes** • COOK TIME: **10 to 15 minutes**

1 stalk lemongrass, cut into 2-inch pieces (or 3 to 4 thin strips of fresh lemon zest)

3 teaspoons chopped peeled fresh ginger

2 garlic cloves, chopped

4 salmon fillets or steaks (about 5 ounces each)

¼ cup mayonnaise

2 teaspoons wasabi paste

2 teaspoons reduced-sodium soy sauce

2 teaspoons toasted sesame oil

Salt and freshly ground black pepper

The stalk of lemongrass is too hard and fibrous to eat (except for the soft inner portion), but it lends a wonderful citrus flavor to poached dishes. You'll love the balance of flavors here: lemon-infused salmon topped with a creamy blend of mayonnaise, wasabi, soy sauce, and sesame oil.

1. Combine 4 cups water, the lemongrass, ginger, and garlic in a large saucepan and set the pan over high heat. Bring to a boil. Reduce the heat to medium and bring to a simmer. Add the salmon to the simmering liquid and cook for 10 minutes, or until the fish pulls apart when tested with a fork.

2. Meanwhile, to make the wasabi-soy mayo, in a small bowl, whisk together the mayonnaise, wasabi paste, soy sauce, and sesame oil.

3. Transfer the salmon to a serving platter, arranging bits of ginger and garlic over the top (discard the lemongrass). Season the top of the salmon with salt and pepper and serve with the mayonnaise mixture spooned over the top.

Serves 4

Quick Side Dish: Chunky Buttermilk Mashed Potatoes

Put 2 pounds quartered small red potatoes in a large saucepan. Add enough water to cover, set the pan over high heat, and bring to a boil. Boil for 8 to 10 minutes, until the potatoes are fork-tender. Drain and return the potatoes to the pan. Add ½ cup buttermilk, 1 teaspoon garlic powder, and 1 teaspoon celery salt and mash until chunky. Season to taste with salt and freshly ground black pepper.

Week 34

Grilled Tuna with Parsley-Parmesan Vinaigrette
Quick Side Dish: Parmesan-Roasted Cauliflower and Artichokes

Tuna Salad with Pimiento-Spiked Mayo
Quick Dessert: Dessert Crostini with Fresh Berries and Apricot Sauce

Nanny's Pasta Pepperoni Cake
Quick Side Dish: Mixed Greens with Creamy Honey-Mint Dressing

PREP LIST

* Cook extra tuna for the salad when you prepare the grilled tuna dish. (Refrigerate for up to 2 days or freeze for up to 3 months. Thaw overnight in the refrigerator or in the microwave on the defrost setting before using.)

* Make the vinaigrette for the tuna. (Refrigerate for up to 2 days.)

* Chop the celery, onion, and pickles for the salad. (Refrigerate for up to 3 days.)

* Assemble the pasta pepperoni cake. (Refrigerate for up to 2 days or freeze for up to 3 months before baking. Thaw overnight in the refrigerator before baking. I don't recommend thawing in the microwave.)

Grilled Tuna with Parsley-Parmesan Vinaigrette

PREP TIME: 10 to 15 minutes • COOK TIME: 6 minutes

Cooking spray

6 tuna steaks (about 5 ounces each)

Salt

Lemon pepper

½ cup chopped fresh flat-leaf parsley

¼ cup reduced-sodium chicken broth or water, plus more as needed

2 tablespoons grated Parmesan cheese

2 tablespoons olive oil

2 tablespoons red wine vinegar

2 to 3 garlic cloves, to taste, chopped

This tuna is drizzled with a refreshing blend of fresh parsley, garlic, and Parmesan cheese. The vinaigrette is also excellent with shellfish (particularly shrimp and scallops) and mixed greens.

1. Coat a stovetop grill pan or griddle with cooking spray and heat over medium-high heat. Season both sides of the tuna steaks with salt and lemon pepper and add to the hot pan. Grill for 3 minutes per side for medium-rare. Remove from the pan and let stand for 5 minutes.

2. Meanwhile, to make the vinaigrette, in a blender, combine the parsley, chicken broth, Parmesan cheese, oil, vinegar, and garlic. Process until smooth and thin, adding more broth or water as necessary.

3. Serve 4 of the tuna steaks with all of the vinaigrette spooned over the top. (Reserve the remaining 2 tuna steaks for the salad.)

Serves 4 (with leftovers for the salad)

Morph to Another Meal ▶ ▶ ▶ Instead of using the extra tuna in the salad, use it in Fish Soft Tacos with Black Beans (page 137) or instead of shrimp in Mixed Greens with Shrimp, Crumbled Blue Cheese, and Peanut Brittle in Raspberry-Champagne Vinaigrette (page 104).

Quick Side Dish: Parmesan-Roasted Cauliflower and Artichokes

In a large bowl, combine 4 cups cauliflower florets, two 14-ounce cans artichoke hearts (drained and halved), ¼ cup grated Parmesan cheese, and 2 tablespoons each chopped fresh flat-leaf parsley and olive oil. Toss to coat. Transfer the vegetables to a large, rimmed baking sheet, in a single layer, and season with salt and freshly ground black pepper. Roast at 450°F for 20 minutes, or until golden brown.

Tuna Salad with Pimiento-Spiked Mayo

PREP TIME: **10 to 15 minutes**

⅓ cup mayonnaise

¼ cup diced pimientos

2 teaspoons Dijon mustard

2 reserved cooked tuna steaks (or two 6-ounce cans white tuna in water, drained), pulled apart with two forks into 1-inch chunks

2 celery stalks, chopped

¼ cup minced red onion

2 tablespoons chopped fresh flat-leaf parsley

1 tablespoon minced gherkin pickles

Salt and freshly ground black pepper

6 cups torn red lettuce leaves

Using grilled tuna instead of canned really turns a tuna salad into a stellar tuna salad. I love the addition of pimientos in this recipe for their color and for their smoky-sweet flavor.

1. In a large bowl, whisk together the mayonnaise, pimientos, and Dijon mustard. Fold in the tuna, celery, onion, parsley, and pickles. Mix well and season to taste with salt and pepper.

2. Arrange the lettuce on individual plates and top with the tuna mixture.

Serves 4

Morph from Another Meal ▶ ▶ ▶ Instead of using tuna, make this dish with the reserved cooked chicken from one of the recipes listed in the box on page 169.

Quick Dessert: Dessert Crostini with Fresh Berries and Apricot Sauce

In a small bowl, whisk together 1 cup softened cream cheese and 2 to 3 tablespoons confectioners' sugar, to taste. Spread the mixture on toasted cinnamon-swirl bread and top with fresh berries (strawberries, raspberries, blueberries, blackberries). Warm ½ cup apricot preserves in the microwave until thin (about 30 seconds). Drizzle the preserves over the crostini just before serving (or drizzle with honey instead of preserves).

Nanny's Pasta Pepperoni Cake

PREP TIME: 15 minutes • **COOK TIME: 40 to 50 minutes**

Cooking spray

1 pound acini di pepe pasta or orzo pasta

8 ounces pepperoni, diced

12 large eggs, lightly beaten

8 ounces shredded mozzarella cheese

1 teaspoon freshly ground black pepper

¼ cup chopped fresh basil

My grandmother used to make this dish for family get-togethers. It's amazingly easy to prepare and can serve lots of people depending on how large the servings are (and what you serve alongside). The pasta used is called "acini di pepe," which is Italian for peppercorns, because the pasta looks like tiny beads. I like to serve this dish with warmed tomato sauce on the side, in case anyone wants "gravy."

1. Preheat the oven to 350°F. Coat a 12-cup Bundt or tube pan with cooking spray.

2. Cook the pasta according to the package directions. Drain and transfer to a large bowl. Add the pepperoni, eggs, cheese, and pepper. Mix well, then transfer the mixture to the prepared pan and press down slightly to make a smooth top.

3. Bake for 40 to 50 minutes, until set. Let stand for 5 to 10 minutes before inverting onto a platter and slicing. Garnish with the basil.

Serves 6 to 8

Quick Side Dish: Mixed Greens with Creamy Honey-Mint Dressing

In a food processor, combine 1 cup plain yogurt, ½ cup cottage cheese, 2 tablespoons honey, and 1 tablespoon chopped fresh mint. Puree until smooth and season to taste with salt and freshly ground black pepper. Drizzle the mixture over 6 cups mixed greens or chopped lettuce just before serving.

Week 35

Roasted Chicken Florentine with Artichokes and Pimiento
Quick Side Dish: Parsnip Fries

Miso-Marinated Chicken Paninis with Ginger Mayo
Quick Side Dish: Buttermilk Onion Rings

Vegetable Lasagna with Pesto Cream Sauce

PREP LIST

* Make the spinach mixture for the chicken florentine. (Refrigerate for up to 3 days.)

* Cook extra chicken for the paninis when you prepare the chicken florentine. (Refrigerate for up to 3 days or freeze for up to 3 months. Thaw overnight in the refrigerator or in the microwave on the defrost setting before using.)

* Assemble the paninis. (Refrigerate for up to 2 days before cooking.)

* Assemble the lasagna. (Refrigerate for up to 3 days or freeze for up to 3 months. Thaw overnight in the refrigerator before baking. I don't recommend thawing in the microwave.)

Roasted Chicken Florentine with Artichokes and Pimiento

PREP TIME: 10 to 15 minutes • COOK TIME: 25 to 30 minutes

Cooking spray

8 boneless skinless chicken breast halves (about 5 ounces each)

Salt and freshly ground black pepper

1 14-ounce can artichoke hearts, drained

1 10-ounce package frozen chopped spinach, thawed and well drained

½ cup sour cream

2 tablespoons grated Parmesan cheese

1 teaspoon dried minced garlic

½ cup diced pimientos

This isn't your average Florentine sauce. I spruce up the spinach-based cream sauce with artichoke hearts, sour cream, Parmesan cheese, and garlic and garnish it with pimiento. And check out the parsnip fries below: they cook at the same time and temperature as the chicken—the way a side dish should!

1. Preheat the oven to 400°F. Coat a large, rimmed baking sheet with cooking spray.

2. Arrange the chicken in a single layer on the prepared baking sheet and season with salt and pepper.

3. In a food processor, combine the artichoke hearts, spinach, sour cream, Parmesan cheese, and minced garlic. Spoon the mixture over 4 of the chicken breast halves. Roast for 25 to 30 minutes, until the chicken is cooked through and no longer pink on the inside.

4. Serve the 4 coated chicken breast halves with the pimientos spooned over the top. (Reserve the remaining 4 chicken breast halves for the paninis.)

Serves 4 (with leftover chicken for the paninis)

Quick Side Dish: Parsnip Fries

Peel and cut 2 pounds of parsnips into thin strips (fries). Transfer to a rimmed baking sheet that's been coated with cooking spray and spread out in a single layer. Spray the parsnips with cooking spray and season with salt and freshly ground black pepper. Roast at 400°F for 25 to 30 minutes, until golden brown and tender.

Miso-Marinated Chicken Paninis with Ginger Mayo

PREP TIME: **10 minutes** • COOK TIME: **2 to 4 minutes**

Cooking spray

1 tablespoon miso paste

2 teaspoons reduced-sodium soy sauce

4 reserved cooked chicken breast halves, sliced into thin strips (or 4 cups sliced cooked chicken or turkey)

½ cup mayonnaise

1 teaspoon ground ginger

8 slices sourdough bread (about ½ inch thick), or any bread variety

8 slices Fontina cheese

1 cup thinly sliced roasted red bell peppers

1 cup baby spinach leaves

I like to marinate chicken in a miso-soy mixture and then make chicken sandwiches that also boast a gingery mayonnaise, roasted red peppers, and baby spinach. Just make sure you put the Fontina on each slice of bread because the melted cheese holds these fat sandwiches together!

1. Coat a stovetop grill pan, griddle, or panini press with cooking spray and heat over medium-high heat.

2. In a small bowl, whisk together until smooth 1 tablespoon water with the miso paste and soy sauce. Pour the mixture into a shallow dish, add the chicken, and turn to coat.

3. In a small bowl, whisk together the mayonnaise and ginger. Spread on the bread slices and top with the cheese. Top 4 of the bread slices with miso-marinated chicken, roasted red peppers, and spinach. Place a second cheese-topped bread slice over the top, making a sandwich.

4. Place the sandwiches in the hot pan and cover with a baking sheet with a few heavy cans in it to weight down the sandwiches (or press down in a panini press). Cook for 1 to 2 minutes. Flip, return the baking sheet with the weights, and cook for 1 to 2 more minutes, until the cheese melts.

Serves 4

Quick Side Dish: Buttermilk Onion Rings

In a large bowl, toss together 2 sliced medium white onions and ¾ cup buttermilk. Drain the onions and dredge in a mixture of 1 cup all-purpose flour, ½ teaspoon smoked paprika, ½ teaspoon salt, and ¼ teaspoon freshly ground black pepper. Transfer the onions to a rimmed baking sheet that's been coated with cooking spray and spread out in a single layer. Spray the onions with cooking spray. Bake at 450°F for 10 to 15 minutes, until golden brown.

Vegetable Lasagna with Pesto Cream Sauce

PREP TIME: 20 to 25 minutes • COOK TIME: 45 to 50 minutes

1 tablespoon olive oil

4 cups diced, peeled eggplant

1 green bell pepper, seeded and diced

½ cup diced onion

2 garlic cloves, minced

1 teaspoon dried oregano

1 15-ounce container ricotta cheese

8 ounces shredded mozzarella cheese

2 tablespoons butter

2 tablespoons all-purpose flour

2 cups milk

½ cup prepared basil pesto

1 16-ounce package lasagna noodles (either regular or no-cook noodles)

The greatest time-saver I ever discovered was learning that I didn't have to cook lasagna noodles before using them. Not just the no-cook varieties, ALL varieties. That saves twenty minutes right there! As this lasagna cooks, the noodles absorb the amazing flavors of the eggplant, bell pepper, and prepared pesto.

1. Preheat the oven to 375°F.

2. Heat the oil in a large skillet over medium-high heat. Add the eggplant, bell pepper, onion, and garlic and cook for 5 minutes, or until the vegetables are soft. Add the oregano and cook for 1 minute, or until the oregano is fragrant. Remove from the heat and transfer to a large bowl. Add the ricotta and mozzarella cheeses and mix well.

3. Meanwhile, melt the butter in a medium saucepan over medium heat. Whisk in the flour and cook for 2 to 3 minutes, until the mixture is blended and smooth. Whisk in the milk and simmer for 3 minutes, or until the mixture thickens. Whisk in the pesto until blended.

4. Spoon a small amount (about ½ cup) of pesto cream sauce into the bottom of a lasagna pan, making an even layer. Top with a single layer of uncooked noodles and then spread half of the ricotta-vegetable mixture over the noodles. Top with a second layer of noodles. Pour 1 cup of the cream sauce over the top. Add the remaining ricotta-vegetable mixture and a final layer of noodles. Pour the remaining cream sauce over the top.

5. Cover with foil and bake for 30 minutes. Uncover and bake for 15 to 20 minutes more, until the top is golden brown.

Serves 4 to 6

Week 36

Chicken with Roasted Mushrooms and Pearl Onions

Grilled Shrimp and Pasta in Apple Vinaigrette
Quick Side Dish: Grilled Zucchini and Yellow Squash

Chicken Caesar Sandwich with Shaved Parmesan and Olive Tapenade

PREP LIST

* Cook extra chicken for the sandwiches when you prepare the chicken with mushrooms. (Refrigerate for up to 3 days or freeze for up to 3 months. Thaw overnight in the refrigerator or in the microwave on the defrost setting before using.)

* Cook the pasta for the shrimp dish. (Refrigerate for up to 3 days.)

* Make the vinaigrette for the shrimp dish. (Refrigerate for up to 3 days.)

* Make the olive tapenade for the sandwiches. (Refrigerate for up to 3 days or freeze for up to 3 months. Thaw overnight in the refrigerator before serving.)

Chicken with Roasted Mushrooms and Pearl Onions

PREP TIME: 10 to 15 minutes • COOK TIME: 25 to 30 minutes

Cooking spray

8 boneless skinless chicken breast halves (about 5 ounces each)

Salt and freshly ground black pepper

1 cup thinly sliced drained, oil-packed sun-dried tomatoes

1 pound whole cremini mushrooms, stems trimmed

8 ounces frozen pearl onions, thawed

1 tablespoon olive oil

1 teaspoon dried thyme

Roasting mushrooms and pearl onions brings out their earthy sweetness (while keeping your stovetop clean!) and takes the flavor of this dish to the next level. I like to serve this with quick-cooking barley that's been jazzed up with fresh herbs.

1. Preheat the oven to 400°F. Coat two large, rimmed baking sheets with cooking spray.

2. Season both sides of the chicken breast halves with salt and pepper. Arrange the chicken on one baking sheet and top 4 of the chicken breast halves with sun-dried tomato slices.

3. In a large bowl, combine the mushrooms, pearl onions, oil, and thyme. Add ½ teaspoon each salt and pepper and toss to combine. Transfer the vegetables to the second baking sheet and arrange in a single layer.

4. Roast the chicken and vegetables for 25 to 30 minutes, until the chicken is golden brown and cooked through and no longer pink on the inside and the vegetables are tender and browned.

5. Serve 4 of the chicken breast halves with all of the mushrooms and pearl onions. (Reserve the remaining 4 chicken breast halves for the sandwiches.)

Serves 4 (with leftovers for the sandwiches)

Morph to Another Meal ▶ ▶ ▶ Instead of using the extra chicken in the sandwich, use it in one of the recipes listed in the box on page 23.

Grilled Shrimp and Pasta in Apple Vinaigrette

PREP TIME: **15 to 20 minutes** • COOK TIME: **4 to 6 minutes**

12 ounces spiral pasta

1 cup diced roasted red bell peppers

Cooking spray

1¼ pounds peeled and deveined fresh large shrimp or thawed frozen large shrimp

Salt and freshly ground black pepper

½ cup apple cider or apple juice

2 tablespoons olive oil

2 tablespoons fresh lemon juice

2 tablespoons chopped fresh cilantro

2 teaspoons Dijon mustard

Lemon wedges, for serving (optional)

Smoky grilled shrimp, tender pasta, and roasted red peppers, tossed in a savory vinaigrette of apple cider, lemon juice, and cilantro—a unique and refreshing dish that's also great for parties!

1. Cook the pasta according to the package directions. Drain, transfer to a large bowl, fold in the roasted red peppers, and set aside.

2. Meanwhile, coat a stovetop grill pan or griddle with cooking spray and heat over medium-high heat. Season the shrimp all over with salt and pepper and place in the hot pan. Grill the shrimp for 2 to 3 minutes per side, until opaque and cooked through. Add the shrimp to the pasta mixture.

3. In a medium bowl, whisk together the cider, oil, lemon juice, cilantro, and Dijon mustard. Add the vinaigrette to the pasta mixture and toss to combine. Season to taste with salt and pepper. Serve with lemon wedges on the side if desired.

Serves 4

Morph to Another Meal ▶ ▶ ▶ Double the recipe for the shrimp portion and use the extra shrimp in Panzanella and Shrimp Salad (page 293).

Quick Side Dish: Grilled Zucchini and Yellow Squash

Slice 2 medium zucchini and 2 medium yellow squash lengthwise into long, ½-inch-thick slices. Brush both sides with garlic-flavored olive oil and season with salt and freshly ground black pepper. Grill for 2 minutes per side, or until golden brown.

Chicken Caesar Sandwich with Shaved Parmesan and Olive Tapenade

PREP TIME: 10 to 15 minutes

½ cup pitted kalamata olives

½ cup pimiento-stuffed Spanish olives

1 tablespoon drained capers

1 tablespoon olive oil, or more as necessary

1 tablespoon fresh flat-leaf parsley leaves

Salt and freshly ground black pepper

4 long sandwich rolls, toasted if desired

4 reserved cooked chicken breast halves, thinly sliced (or 4 cups thinly sliced cooked chicken)

1 cup thinly sliced cucumber, preferably seedless and unwaxed

1 4-inch chunk Parmesan cheese

We're a big Caesar salad family. We eat the garlicky, Parmesan-infused salad at least once each week. In this dish, I turn those classic flavors into a sandwich that's brimming with tasty extras like an olive-caper tapenade, chicken, and sliced cucumber.

1. In a food processor, combine both types of olives, the capers, oil, and parsley. Process until smooth and thick, adding more oil if necessary to create a thick paste. Season to taste with salt and pepper.

2. Spread the olive mixture onto the rolls and top with chicken and cucumber slices. Using a vegetable peeler, shave Parmesan into the sandwiches and serve.

Serves 4

Morph from Another Meal ▶ ▶ ▶ Instead of using chicken from the chicken with roasted mushrooms, make this dish with reserved cooked chicken from one of the recipes listed in the box on page 169.

Week 37

Singapore Sling Pork
Quick Side Dish: Unbaked Cornbread Dressing

Pork Fried Rice with Cashews and Raisins
Quick Dessert: Banana-Blueberry Fool with Honey-Roasted Peanuts

Arctic Char with Mushroom-Walnut Crust
Quick Side Dish: Oregano Roasted Tomatoes

PREP LIST

* Cook extra pork for the fried rice when you prepare the Singapore pork. (Refrigerate for up to 3 days or freeze for up to 3 months. Thaw overnight in the refrigerator or in the microwave on the defrost setting before using.)

* Cook the rice for the fried rice. (Refrigerate for up to 3 days.)

* Chop the carrots, scallions, garlic, and ginger for the fried rice. (Refrigerate for up to 3 days.)

* Make the mushroom crust for the fish. (Refrigerate for up to 3 days.)

Singapore Sling Pork

PREP TIME: 10 to 15 minutes • COOK TIME: 10 minutes

½ cup orange juice

½ cup pineapple juice

1 tablespoon fresh lime juice

2 teaspoons cornstarch

1 tablespoon peanut oil

6 boneless pork loin chops (about 5 ounces each)

Salt and freshly ground black pepper

1 cup drained canned pitted red cherries

¼ cup Cointreau, Triple Sec, or orange juice

I like to find alternate uses for classic drinks. Not that I don't love my cocktails, but when the flavors are so perfect together, they're very often perfect as a sauce or marinade! Pork works well with fruits, so it's a natural choice for a sauce that boasts orange juice, pineapple juice, cherries, and orange liqueur. (For a nonalcoholic version, substitute orange juice for the latter.)

1. In a medium bowl, whisk together the orange juice, pineapple juice, lime juice, and cornstarch. Set aside.

2. Heat the oil in a large, deep skillet over medium-high heat. Season both sides of the pork chops with salt and pepper and add to the hot pan. Cook for 1 to 2 minutes per side, until golden brown. Add the cherries and Cointreau and cook for 1 minute. Add the orange juice mixture and bring to a simmer. Simmer for 3 minutes, or until the sauce thickens and the pork is cooked through and still slightly pink in the center.

3. Serve 4 of the pork chops with all of the sauce spooned over the top. (Reserve the remaining 2 pork chops for the fried rice.)

Serves 4 (with leftovers for the fried rice)

Quick Side Dish: Unbaked Cornbread Dressing

In a large skillet over medium-high heat, cook 2 to 4 chopped bacon slices until crisp. Drain off all but 1 tablespoon fat. Add ½ cup each chopped onion and celery and cook for 2 minutes. Add 2 teaspoons dried sage and cook for 1 minute. Add 1 pound cubed prepared cornbread (6 cups) and 1 cup reduced-sodium chicken broth and cook for 2 minutes, tossing gently to break the cornbread into smaller pieces. Spread the cornbread mixture in a rimmed baking sheet in an even layer and place under the broiler. Broil for 2 to 3 minutes, until golden brown.

Pork Fried Rice with Cashews and Raisins

PREP TIME: 10 to 15 minutes • COOK TIME: 8 to 10 minutes

4 teaspoons peanut oil

2 large eggs, lightly beaten

½ cup diced carrots

½ cup chopped scallions (green and white parts)

3 garlic cloves, minced

1 tablespoon minced peeled fresh ginger

2 reserved cooked pork loin chops, diced (2 cups diced cooked pork)

3 cups cooked white rice

½ cup frozen green peas

½ cup raisins

3 tablespoons reduced-sodium soy sauce

1 tablespoon mirin (rice wine)

2 teaspoons toasted sesame oil

½ cup chopped cashews

Think of fried rice as a chance to clean out the fridge while enjoying an amazing meal. Grab ingredients from your vegetable drawer, your pantry, and your spice rack and you've got a family-friendly feast in just minutes. This dish is great with leftover chicken and shrimp, too.

1. Heat 2 teaspoons of the peanut oil in a large wok or skillet over medium-high heat. Add the eggs and cook, stirring frequently, for 3 minutes, or until cooked through. Remove the eggs from the pan and set aside.

2. In the same pan, heat the remaining 2 teaspoons peanut oil over medium-high heat. Add the carrots, scallions, garlic, and ginger and cook for 1 minute. Add the pork and cook, stirring, for 1 to 2 minutes, until golden brown on all sides. Add the rice, peas, raisins, soy sauce, mirin, and sesame oil and cook for 1 to 2 minutes to heat through. Fold in the cashews.

3. Spoon the mixture onto plates and top with the cooked egg.

Serves 4

Quick Dessert: Banana-Blueberry Fool with Honey-Roasted Peanuts

In a food processor, combine 2 cups cottage cheese, 3 tablespoons sugar, 2 teaspoons finely grated orange zest, and 1 teaspoon vanilla extract. Puree until smooth. Place a few banana slices and blueberries in the bottom of 4 tall glasses. Top with half of the cottage cheese mixture. Top with more banana slices and blueberries and then the remaining cottage cheese mixture. Garnish with honey-roasted peanuts just before serving.

Arctic Char with Mushroom-Walnut Crust

PREP TIME: **10 to 15 minutes** • COOK TIME: **10 to 15 minutes**

Cooking spray

2 teaspoons olive oil

¼ cup minced shallots

2 garlic cloves, minced

2 cups sliced shiitake mushrooms

1 teaspoon dried thyme

½ cup chopped walnuts

2 tablespoons chopped fresh flat-leaf parsley

4 Arctic char fillets (about 5 ounces each)

Salt and freshly ground black pepper

Arctic char is closely related to salmon and trout (which, by the way, make nice substitutions if you can't find Arctic char), and its rich flavor makes an excellent base for this savory crust—a unique blend of wild mushrooms, garlic, thyme, and walnuts. It's nutty, earthy, and fresh-tasting, all in one bite.

1. Preheat the oven to 400°F. Coat a rimmed baking sheet with cooking spray.

2. Heat the oil in a large skillet over medium-high heat. Add the shallots and garlic and cook for 1 minute. Add the mushrooms and cook for 3 to 5 minutes, until the mushrooms soften and release their juice. Add the thyme and cook for 1 minute, or until the thyme is fragrant. Remove from the heat and stir in the walnuts and parsley.

3. Arrange the Arctic char on the prepared baking sheet. Season the fish with salt and pepper. Spoon the mushroom mixture over the fish fillets and press down, making a thick crust.

4. Roast for 10 to 15 minutes, until the fish pulls apart when tested with a fork.

Serves 4

Quick Side Dish: Oregano Roasted Tomatoes

Slice 4 beefsteak tomatoes crosswise into ½-inch-thick slices. Transfer the tomato slices to a large, rimmed baking sheet, in a single layer, and drizzle with olive oil. Sprinkle with dried oregano, salt, and freshly ground black pepper and roast at 425°F for 10 to 15 minutes, until golden brown and tender.

Week 38

Peanut-Crusted Chicken with
Apple-Gorgonzola Relish
Quick Side Dish: String Beans with Pimiento-Stuffed Olives

Creamy Peanut Chicken Fettuccine
with Broccoli
Quick Side Dish: Sautéed Bell Peppers

Grilled Shrimp with Mandarin-
Horseradish Dipping Sauce
Quick Side Dish: Rice Pilaf with Tomatoes

PREP LIST

* Assemble the peanut-crusted chicken. (Refrigerate for up to 3 days or freeze for up to 3 months. Thaw overnight in the refrigerator before baking. I don't recommend thawing in the microwave. Because the apples will discolor after chopping, make the relish no more than 12 hours in advance.)

* Cook extra chicken for the fettuccine dish when you make the peanut-crusted chicken. (Refrigerate for up to 3 days or freeze for up to 3 months. Thaw overnight in the refrigerator or in the microwave on the defrost setting before using.)

* Cook the fettuccine and blanch the broccoli for the fettuccine dish. (Refrigerate for up to 3 days.)

* Make the dipping sauce for the shrimp dish. (Refrigerate for up to 3 hours.)

Peanut-Crusted Chicken with Apple-Gorgonzola Relish

PREP TIME: 10 to 15 minutes • COOK TIME: 25 to 30 minutes

Cooking spray

2 cups dry roasted unsalted peanuts

8 boneless skinless chicken breast halves (about 5 ounces each)

Salt and freshly ground black pepper

½ cup honey mustard

2 Granny Smith apples, cored and finely diced

⅓ cup crumbled blue cheese

2 tablespoons chopped fresh basil

2 tablespoons sherry vinegar

I love crusting mild-tasting foods with nuts (if you haven't already noticed!) because as nuts cook, they develop a deeper flavor and crunchy crust. This sweet chicken is balanced perfectly with a relish of tart apples, sweet blue cheese, and fresh basil.

1. Preheat the oven to 400°F. Coat a large, rimmed baking sheet with cooking spray.

2. Put the peanuts in a plastic bag and, using a heavy rolling pin or the bottom of a heavy skillet, crush into small pieces.

3. Season both sides of the chicken breast halves with salt and pepper. Brush both sides with honey mustard. Working in batches, add the chicken to the bag with the peanuts and press in the peanuts, coating both sides. Transfer the chicken to the prepared baking sheet and spray with cooking spray. Bake for 25 to 30 minutes, until the chicken is cooked through and no longer pink on the inside.

4. Meanwhile, to make the relish, in a medium bowl, combine the apples, blue cheese, basil, and vinegar. Toss to combine. Season to taste with salt and pepper.

5. Serve 4 chicken breast halves with all of the relish. Reserve the remaining 4 chicken breast halves for the fettuccine.

Serves 4 (with leftovers for the fettuccine)

Quick Side Dish: String Beans with Pimiento-Stuffed Olives

Heat 1 tablespoon olive oil in a large skillet over medium-high heat. Add 1 pound trimmed string beans, ½ cup drained, sliced pimiento-stuffed olives, 2 minced garlic cloves, and 1 tablespoon balsamic vinegar. Cook for 3 minutes, or until the string beans are crisp-tender. Season to taste with salt and freshly ground black pepper.

Creamy Peanut Chicken Fettuccine with Broccoli

PREP TIME: 15 to 20 minutes • **COOK TIME: 5 to 10 minutes**

12 ounces spinach or regular fettuccine

2 cups fresh broccoli florets

2 cups milk

3 tablespoons all-purpose flour

¼ cup grated Parmesan cheese, plus more for serving

Pinch of ground nutmeg

4 reserved cooked peanut-crusted chicken breast halves, cubed (or 4 cups cubed cooked chicken)

¼ cup chopped fresh flat-leaf parsley

Salt and freshly ground black pepper

Since the peanuts are already on the chicken, that's one less ingredient you need to add! This is a beautifully easy, incredibly tasty dish the whole family will adore.

1. Cook the fettuccine according to the package directions, adding the broccoli for the last 30 seconds of cooking. Drain and set aside.

2. In a large saucepan, whisk together the milk and flour. Set the pan over medium-high heat and bring to a simmer. Simmer for 3 minutes, or until the mixture thickens. Whisk in the Parmesan cheese and nutmeg and cook until the cheese melts. Add the fettuccine, broccoli, and chicken and cook for 1 minute to heat through.

3. Remove from the heat, fold in the parsley, and season to taste with salt and pepper. Serve with extra Parmesan cheese on the side.

Serves 4

Quick Side Dish: Sautéed Bell Peppers

Heat 1 tablespoon olive oil in a large skillet over medium-high heat. Add 2 sliced bell peppers (preferably 1 red and 1 yellow) and ½ cup sliced red onion and cook for 5 minutes, or until soft. Season to taste with salt and freshly ground black pepper.

Grilled Shrimp with Mandarin-Horseradish Dipping Sauce

PREP TIME: 10 to 15 minutes • COOK TIME: 5 minutes

Cooking spray

1½ pounds peeled and deveined fresh large or jumbo shrimp or thawed frozen large or jumbo shrimp

Salt and freshly ground black pepper

1 11-ounce can mandarin oranges in light syrup

¼ cup orange marmalade

¼ cup sour cream

1 tablespoon prepared horseradish

1 tablespoon chopped fresh cilantro

I'm passionate about shrimp and, because I love them so much, almost any preparation works for me. But grilled shrimp are my favorite, probably because grilling adds just enough flavor while keeping the flesh moist and sweet. I also adore horseradish, so I'm constantly inventing new uses for it: check out this unique blend of oranges, orange marmalade, sour cream, and horseradish. It's sweet, it's hot, and it's addictive!

1. Coat a stovetop grill pan or griddle with cooking spray and heat over medium-high heat. Season the shrimp all over with salt and pepper. Put the shrimp on the hot grill and cook for 2 minutes per side, or until opaque and cooked through.

2. Meanwhile, to make the dipping sauce, reserve 2 tablespoons syrup from the oranges then drain the oranges and put them and the reserved 2 tablespoons syrup in a blender. Add the marmalade, sour cream, horseradish, and cilantro. Puree until smooth. Season to taste with salt and pepper.

3. Serve the shrimp with the dipping sauce on the side.

Serves 4

Quick Side Dish: Rice Pilaf with Tomatoes

Heat 1 tablespoon olive oil in a medium saucepan over medium-high heat. Add 2 cups quick-cooking white rice, ½ cup minced white onion, and 2 minced garlic cloves. Cook for 3 to 5 minutes, until the rice is golden brown. Add one 14-ounce can diced tomatoes (undrained) and 1 cup reduced-sodium chicken broth or water. Bring to a boil. Cover, remove from the heat, and let stand for 5 minutes. Stir in ¼ cup chopped fresh basil and season to taste with salt and freshly ground black pepper.

Week 39

Walnut-Studded Pork with Cilantro-Orange Marmalade and Cheesy Risotto

Risotto Croquettes with Fontina and Basil Blender Sauce
Quick Side Dish: Spicy Sautéed String Beans

Turkey Sausage Sandwiches with Onions and Peppers on Onion Rolls
Quick Dessert: Pineapple-Banana Smoothies

PREP LIST

* Cook extra rice for the croquettes when you make the risotto. (Refrigerate for up to 3 days or freeze for up to 3 months. Thaw overnight in the refrigerator or in the microwave on the defrost setting before using.)

* Form the croquettes. (Refrigerate for up to 3 days or freeze for up to 3 months. Thaw overnight in the refrigerator before cooking. I don't recommend thawing in the microwave.)

* Make the blender sauce for the croquettes. (Refrigerate for up to 2 days.)

* Slice the onion and bell pepper for the sandwiches. (Refrigerate for up to 3 days.)

Walnut-Studded Pork with Cilantro-Orange Marmalade and Cheesy Risotto

PREP TIME: 15 to 20 minutes • COOK TIME: 25 minutes

Cooking spray

1 pork tenderloin (about 1¼ pounds)

Salt and freshly ground black pepper

½ cup walnut halves

½ cup orange marmalade

¼ cup chopped fresh cilantro

2 tablespoons sherry vinegar

2 tablespoons butter

2 cups short-grain rice (Arborio)

8 to 9 cups reduced-sodium chicken broth, at room temperature or warmed in the microwave

½ cup shredded Romano cheese

In this dish, I stuff walnuts into pork tenderloin before baking for a great nutty flavor. If you think risotto is too complicated or time-consuming, think again. With just a few simple ingredients, you'll have marvelous risotto in just twenty minutes.

1. Preheat the oven to 400°F. Coat a shallow roasting pan with cooking spray.

2. Season the pork all over with salt and pepper and put in the prepared pan. Using a sharp paring knife, make several 1-inch-long slits in the pork and insert a walnut half into each slit, allowing the walnut to peek out slightly.

3. In a small bowl, whisk together the marmalade, cilantro, and vinegar. Brush the mixture all over the pork. Roast the pork for 25 minutes, or until a meat thermometer inserted into the center reads 160°F. Let stand for 5 minutes before slicing crosswise into ½-inch-thick slices.

4. Meanwhile, melt the butter in a large Dutch oven or saucepan over medium heat. Add the rice and cook, stirring frequently, for 2 minutes, or until translucent. Add the chicken broth, ½ cup at a time, waiting until the liquid is absorbed until adding more. Continue cooking the risotto this way, stirring frequently, until the rice is tender, about 20 minutes.

5. Stir the Romano cheese into the rice and cook until the cheese melts. Season to taste with salt and pepper.

6. Serve the pork with half of the risotto. (Reserve the remaining risotto for the croquettes.)

Serves 4 (with leftovers for the croquettes)

Risotto Croquettes with Fontina and Basil Blender Sauce

PREP TIME: **15 minutes** • COOK TIME: **7 to 12 minutes**

2 cups reserved cooked risotto, chilled

2 tablespoons diced shallot

1 large egg, lightly beaten

1 teaspoon dried oregano

½ cup seasoned dry bread crumbs

1 tablespoon butter

1 tablespoon olive oil

4 slices Fontina cheese or ½ cup grated Fontina cheese

1 14-ounce can diced tomatoes

1 cup fresh basil leaves

2 garlic cloves, chopped

1 tablespoon balsamic vinegar

Salt and freshly ground black pepper

Croquettes are typically cylinder-shaped, made with potatoes, and deep-fried. But I use leftover risotto instead, add buttery-nutty Fontina cheese, and pan-fry rather than smothering them in oil. They're golden brown and amazing, especially with fresh tomato-basil sauce.

1. In a large bowl, mix together the risotto, shallot, egg, and oregano. Put the bread crumbs in a shallow dish. With wet hands, form the risotto mixture into 4 croquettes, each about 2 inches thick. Put the croquettes in the bread crumbs and turn to coat.

2. Heat the butter and oil together in a large, deep skillet over medium-high heat. Add the croquettes and cook for 3 to 5 minutes per side, until golden brown and cooked through. Top the croquettes with the cheese, tent with foil, and cook for 1 to 2 minutes more, until the cheese melts.

3. Meanwhile, to make the sauce, in a blender, combine the tomatoes, basil, garlic, and vinegar. Process until smooth. Season to taste with salt and pepper. If desired, heat the sauce in a small saucepan over medium heat.

4. Spoon the sauce (either hot or at room temperature) over the hot croquettes just before serving.

Serves 4

Quick Side Dish: Spicy Sautéed String Beans

Heat 2 teaspoons olive oil and 1 teaspoon hot chile oil together in a large saucepan over medium-high heat. Add 3 minced garlic cloves and cook for 1 minute. Add 8 ounces trimmed green beans, 8 ounces trimmed yellow wax beans, ½ cup reduced-sodium chicken broth or water, and ½ teaspoon crushed red pepper flakes and bring to a simmer. Cover and cook for 5 minutes, or until the beans are tender. Stir in 2 tablespoons chopped fresh flat-leaf parsley and season to taste with salt and freshly ground black pepper.

Turkey Sausage Sandwiches with Onions and Peppers on Onion Rolls

PREP TIME: 10 minutes • **COOK TIME: 11 minutes**

1 tablespoon olive oil

1 cup sliced yellow onion

1 large red bell pepper, seeded and sliced into thin strips

1 pound sweet or hot turkey sausage, cut into 2-inch pieces

½ cup red wine or reduced-sodium chicken broth

4 long onion rolls, or traditional long sandwich rolls, toasted if desired

1 4-inch chunk Parmesan cheese

Turkey sausage is great to have on hand for all types of dishes. You can find it sweet or hot, and it has fewer calories and grams of fat than traditional pork sausage. In this dish, I partner turkey sausage with sweet onions and bell peppers, Parmesan cheese, and onion rolls. If you can't find the rolls, substitute any variety of flavored roll (garlic, rosemary, "everything,"or whatever you like).

1. Heat the oil in a large skillet over medium-high heat. Add the onion and bell pepper and cook for 5 minutes, or until soft. Add the turkey and cook, stirring frequently, for 5 minutes, or until golden brown and cooked through. Add the wine and cook for 1 minute.

2. Spoon the sausage mixture into the rolls. Using a vegetable peeler, shave Parmesan cheese over the sausage before serving.

Serves 4

Quick Dessert: Pineapple-Banana Smoothies

In a blender, combine two 8-ounce cans crushed pineapple in juice, 2 bananas, 1 cup vanilla yogurt, and ½ cup ice cubes. Puree until smooth. Garnish with freshly grated nutmeg if desired.

Week 40

Pecan-Crusted Chicken with
Dried Cherry–Pear Relish

Grilled Salmon with Tequila-Orange
Vinaigrette
Quick Side Dish: Cucumber Boats with Artichokes and Bell Peppers

5-Ingredient Meatballs with
Chorizo Gravy
Quick Side Dish: Creamy Grits with Smoked Gouda

PREP LIST

* Make the vinaigrette for the salmon. (Refrigerate for up to 2 days.)

* Form the meatballs. (Refrigerate for up to 3 days or freeze for up to 3 months.)

Pecan-Crusted Chicken with Dried Cherry–Pear Relish

PREP TIME: 10 to 15 minutes • **COOK TIME: 25 to 30 minutes**

Cooking spray

1 cup pecan pieces

¼ cup seasoned dry bread crumbs

4 boneless skinless chicken breast halves (about 5 ounces each)

Salt and freshly ground black pepper

2 tablespoons Dijon mustard

2 ripe pears, cored and diced

¼ cup dried cherries or sweetened dried cranberries

¼ cup crumbled feta cheese

2 tablespoons chopped fresh flat-leaf parsley

2 teaspoons sherry vinegar

For this dish, I combined all the flavors you typically see on a cheese tray and turned them into a chicken dish! As the chicken cooks, the pecan crust becomes deeply flavored, making it the perfect base for a relish that's sweet from pears and cherries, salty from feta cheese, and mildly tart from sherry vinegar. Excellent (and impressive) for entertaining.

1. Preheat the oven to 400°F. Coat a shallow roasting pan with cooking spray.

2. Put the pecan pieces and bread crumbs in a plastic bag and seal the bag. Using a heavy rolling pin or the bottom of a heavy skillet, crush the nuts into fine crumbs.

3. Season both sides of the chicken breast halves with salt and pepper. Brush mustard all over both sides of the chicken. Add the chicken to the bag and turn to coat both sides with the crumbs.

4. Transfer the chicken to the prepared pan and spray it with cooking spray. Bake for 25 to 30 minutes, until the chicken is cooked through and no longer pink on the inside.

5. Meanwhile, to make the relish, in a medium bowl, combine the pears, cherries, feta cheese, parsley, and vinegar. Toss to combine and season with salt and pepper.

6. Serve the chicken with the relish spooned over the top.

Serves 4

Morph to Another Meal ▶ ▶ ▶ Double the recipe for the chicken portion of the meal and use the extra chicken in Creamy Peanut Chicken Fettuccine with Broccoli (page 221). Just switch the title from peanuts to pecans!

Grilled Salmon with Tequila-Orange Vinaigrette

PREP TIME: **10 minutes** • COOK TIME: **4 to 6 minutes**

Cooking spray

4 salmon fillets (about 5 ounces each)

Salt and freshly ground black pepper

½ **cup orange juice**

2 tablespoons olive oil

2 tablespoons tequila

2 teaspoons Dijon mustard

1 tablespoon chopped fresh cilantro

The inspiration for this tequila-laced fish recipe comes from one of my favorite Scottsdale restaurants, Café Carumba. They have a truly unique menu that leans toward Mexican and so they find amazingly wonderful uses for tequila!

1. Coat a stovetop grill pan, griddle, or large skillet with cooking spray and heat over medium-high heat. Season both sides of the salmon fillets with salt and pepper. Grill the salmon for 2 to 3 minutes per side, until the fish pulls apart when tested with a fork.

2. Meanwhile, to make the vinaigrette, in a small bowl, whisk together the orange juice, oil, tequila, mustard, and cilantro. Season to taste with salt and pepper.

3. Pour some vinaigrette over the salmon just before serving. Serve extra vinaigrette on the side if desired.

Serves 4

Morph to Another Meal ▶ ▶ ▶ Double the recipe for the salmon portion of the meal, and use the extra salmon in Creamy Salmon Chowder (page 253), Smoky Salmon Benedict (page 100), or Fish Soft Tacos with Black Beans (page 137).

Quick Side Dish: Cucumber Boats with Artichokes and Bell Peppers

In a medium bowl, combine two 12-ounce jars marinated artichoke hearts (drained), ½ cup chopped roasted red bell peppers, 1 chopped green bell pepper, and ¼ cup chopped white onion. Season to taste with salt and pepper, and toss to combine. Serve in hollowed-out cucumber halves.

5-Ingredient Meatballs with Chorizo Gravy

PREP TIME: 10 minutes • COOK TIME: 9 to 11 minutes

1¼ pounds lean ground beef

Salt and freshly ground black pepper

1 tablespoon vegetable oil

1 cup diced cooked chorizo or andouille sausage

1½ cups reduced-sodium beef broth

1 tablespoon cornstarch

2 tablespoons chopped fresh flat-leaf parsley (optional)

Chorizo's mildly spicy, intense flavor makes it a great addition to five-ingredient recipes: you get loads of flavor from just one source. Try the gravy with chicken, turkey, and pork, too. I like to serve this dish over rice or with the grits below.

1. In a large bowl, combine the beef, 1 teaspoon salt, and ½ teaspoon black pepper. Mix well and shape the mixture into 16 meatballs.

2. Heat the oil in a large, deep skillet over medium-high heat. Add the meatballs and cook for 5 minutes, or until browned on all sides. Add the chorizo and cook for 2 to 3 minutes, until golden brown.

3. In a small bowl, whisk together the beef broth and cornstarch. Add the mixture to the meatballs and bring to a simmer. Simmer for 2 to 3 minutes, until the meatballs are cooked through and the sauce thickens.

4. Remove from the heat and stir in the parsley if desired. Season to taste with salt and black pepper.

Serves 4

Quick Side Dish: Creamy Grits with Smoked Gouda

Combine in a large saucepan 1½ cups reduced-sodium chicken broth and 1 cup milk. Set the pan over medium-high heat and bring to a simmer. Gradually whisk in ¾ cup quick-cooking grits. Simmer for 5 minutes, stirring frequently. Stir in ¾ cup shredded smoked Gouda cheese and simmer for 2 to 3 minutes, until the cheese melts. Remove from the heat and season to taste with salt and freshly ground black pepper.

Week 41

Turkey Burgers with Pickle Mayo on Potato Rolls
Quick Side Dish: Sautéed Wild Mushrooms with Swiss Chard

Turkey Meatball Soup with Rice
Quick Side Dish: Green Pea Hummus with Pita

4-Ingredient Pork Chops in White Wine–Tarragon Broth
Quick Side Dish: Buttery Acorn Squash

PREP LIST

* Form the burgers and meatballs. (Refrigerate for up to 3 days or freeze for up to 3 months. Thaw overnight in the refrigerator or in the microwave on the defrost setting before cooking.)

* Cook the meatballs for the soup when you prepare the turkey burgers. (Refrigerate for up to 3 days or freeze for up to 3 months. No need to thaw meatballs before using them in the soup.)

* Make the pickle mayo for the burgers. (Refrigerate for up to 2 days.)

* Chop the onion, celery, and carrots for the soup. (Refrigerate for up to 3 days.)

Turkey Burgers with Pickle Mayo on Potato Rolls

PREP TIME: **15 minutes** • COOK TIME: **5 to 7 minutes**

Cooking spray

2 pounds ground turkey

2 teaspoons salt-free garlic and herb seasoning

½ teaspoon salt

¼ teaspoon freshly ground black pepper

¼ cup mayonnaise

2 tablespoons diced dill pickles

2 teaspoons Dijon mustard

4 potato hamburger rolls

½ cup thinly sliced red onion

This recipe is so simple it's almost embarrassing. The garlic and herb seasoning adds just enough flavor to the burgers to make them completely mouth-watering. (And by adding just the right amount of seasoning, we can use the extra turkey mixture to make a fabulous meatball soup later in the week!)

1. Coat a stovetop griddle or large skillet with cooking spray and heat over medium-high heat.

2. In a large bowl, combine the turkey, garlic and herb seasoning, salt, and pepper. Mix well. Shape two thirds of the mixture (about 1¼ pounds) into 4 burgers, each about 1 inch thick. Shape the remaining mixture into 1-inch meatballs. Add the burgers and meatballs to the hot pan and cook, turning the meatballs frequently, for 5 to 7 minutes, until the burgers and meatballs are cooked through.

3. Meanwhile, to make the pickle mayo, in a small bowl, combine the mayonnaise, pickles, and Dijon mustard.

4. Spread the pickle mayo on the bottom half of the rolls. Place the burgers on the rolls and top with onion slices. (Reserve the meatballs for the soup.)

Serves 4 (with leftovers for the soup)

Quick Side Dish: Sautéed Wild Mushrooms with Swiss Chard

Heat 1 tablespoon olive oil in a large skillet over medium-high heat. Add 2 to 3 minced garlic cloves and cook for 1 minute. Add 4 cups sliced shiitake mushrooms and cook for 3 minutes, or until the mushrooms soften and release their juice. Add 6 cups chopped Swiss chard leaves and 2 tablespoons dry sherry (or water), cover, and cook for 5 minutes, or until the Swiss chard wilts. Uncover and cook for 1 minute, or until the liquid evaporates. Season to taste with salt and freshly ground black pepper.

12 Fast Seafood Meals in the Can

Dinner is only a few minutes away with these simple meals made with canned seafood. Canned seafood is a quick cook's ally in the kitchen. No cooking is required and you reap the nutritional rewards seafood has to offer (protein, healthy fats, calcium). When you review the recipes below, you'll soon realize there's more to canned seafood than tuna salad! Since canned foods can be high in sodium, go easy on additional salt.

1. Tuna Wontons with Soy-Scallion Dipping Sauce: In a bowl, combine canned tuna, chopped scallions, and shredded carrots. Spoon the mixture onto the center of wonton wrappers. Fold over one side, making a triangle. With wet fingers, pinch the edges together to seal. Transfer the wontons to a large, rimmed baking sheet and spray them with cooking spray. Bake at 375°F for 10 to 12 minutes, until golden brown. Serve with a mixture of soy sauce and chopped scallions on the side for dunking.

2. Steamed Spicy Salmon Spring Rolls with Ponzu Sauce: In a bowl, combine canned salmon, shredded napa cabbage, thinly sliced red onion, prepared black bean sauce, and hot sauce. Spoon the mixture onto the center of prepared spring roll wrappers and roll up, folding in the edges. With wet fingers, seal the seam to the roll. Place the spring rolls side by side (but not touching) in the top of a bamboo steamer or in a colander over simmering water. Cover and steam for 5 to 10 minutes, until the wrappers are translucent. Serve with ponzu sauce on the side for dunking.

3. Crab Balls with Thai Peanut Sauce: In a bowl, combine canned crabmeat, beaten egg, mayonnaise, seasoned dry bread crumbs, and Old Bay seasoning. With your hands, shape the mixture into balls, each about the size of a golf ball. Transfer the balls to a rimmed baking sheet, and bake at 400°F for 15 minutes, or until golden brown and cooked through. In a bowl, whisk together peanut butter, chicken broth, soy sauce, sesame oil, and fresh lime juice. Serve the crab balls with the peanut sauce on the side for dunking.

4. Clam Chowder with Red Potatoes: In a stockpot, combine canned diced tomatoes (undrained), Clamato juice, chicken broth, cubed red potatoes, canned clams (undrained), diced celery, 2 bay leaves, and dried thyme. Set the pan over high heat and bring to a boil. Boil for 8 minutes, or until the potatoes are fork-tender. Remove the bay leaves and stir in chopped fresh flat-leaf parsley before serving.

5. Tuna Noodle Casserole with Hearts of Palm: In a bowl, combine cooked egg noodles, sour cream, mayonnaise, canned tuna, frozen green peas, sliced mushrooms, chopped hearts of palm, grated Parmesan cheese, and dried oregano. Transfer the mixture to a casserole dish, and top with a mixture of seasoned dry bread crumbs and grated Parmesan cheese. Bake at 350°F for 30 minutes, or until the filling is bubbling and the top is golden brown.

6. Parmesan Shrimp Bake: In a bowl, combine canned shrimp, cooked rice, mayonnaise, sliced water chestnuts, chopped pimientos, shredded cheddar cheese, grated Parmesan cheese, and dried oregano. Transfer the mixture to a buttered casserole dish, and top with more grated Parmesan cheese. Bake at 350°F for 30 minutes, until the filling is bubbling and the top is golden brown.

7. Crab-Stuffed Portobello Mushrooms with Swiss: In a bowl, combine canned crabmeat, mayonnaise, chopped scallions, minced roasted red peppers, and seasoned dry bread crumbs. Spoon the mixture into portobello mushroom caps. Transfer the stuffed mushrooms to a large, rimmed baking sheet, and top each mushroom with a slice of Swiss or Gruyère cheese. Bake at 350°F for 15 to 20 minutes, until the mushrooms are tender and the cheese is melted.

8. Shrimp Taquitos: In a bowl, combine chopped canned shrimp, sour cream, shredded cheddar cheese, chili powder, and ground cumin. Spoon the mixture onto the center of corn tortillas and roll up tightly (secure the rolls with wooden picks if needed). Cook the taquitos in olive oil in a large skillet over medium-high heat until golden brown. Serve with salsa on the side for dunking.

9. Roasted Red Pepper Soup with Crab: In a blender, puree one large jar of roasted red peppers (undrained) until smooth, making about 1 cup of pepper puree. Transfer the puree to a stockpot and add chicken broth, 2 bay leaves, garlic powder, and onion powder. Set the pan over medium heat and bring to a simmer. Simmer for 5 minutes. Remove the bay leaves, and stir in canned crabmeat before serving. Serve with lemon wedges on the side.

10. Salmon Rémoulade over Crostini: In a bowl, combine canned salmon, mayonnaise, and salt-free garlic and herb seasoning. Spoon the mixture over toasted bread (preferably a baguette-style loaf).

11. Seafood Gumbo: In a large saucepan, combine chicken or vegetable broth, canned diced tomatoes, canned salmon (or a combination of salmon and crab), diced andouille or chorizo sausage (optional), chopped onion, chopped green bell pepper, frozen sliced okra, and garlic powder. Set the pan over medium-high heat and bring to a simmer. Simmer for 5 to 10 minutes, until the okra is tender and the liquid has thickened slightly.

12. Southwest Tuna-Tortilla Roll-Ups: In a gowl, combine canned tuna, mayonnaise, canned diced green chiles or pickled jalapeños (drained), diced white onion, chopped fresh cilantro, chili powder, ground cumin, and garlic powder. Mix well and then spread onto flour tortillas. Roll up tightly and serve.

Turkey Meatball Soup with Rice

PREP TIME: 10 to 15 minutes • **COOK TIME: 15 minutes**

1 tablespoon olive oil

½ cup chopped yellow onion

2 celery stalks, chopped

2 carrots, chopped

1 teaspoon dried oregano

1 teaspoon dried thyme

2 bay leaves

Reserved cooked turkey meatballs (about 8 ounces meatballs)

4 cups reduced-sodium chicken broth

1 28-ounce can petite-diced tomatoes or regular diced tomatoes

1 cup quick-cooking white rice

½ cup frozen green peas

Salt and freshly ground black pepper

This is a fun and especially kid-friendly meal that's sure to become a weekly staple in your house. Plus, it freezes very well, so you might want to double the recipe and stash the extra in the freezer (for those late soccer-game nights!). You can also substitute shredded or cubed chicken for the meatballs and make the soup with leftovers from another meal.

1. Heat the oil in a Dutch oven or large pot over medium-high heat. Add the onion, celery, and carrots and cook for 5 minutes, or until the vegetables are soft. Add the oregano, thyme, and bay leaves and cook for 1 minute, until the herbs are fragrant.

2. Add the meatballs, chicken broth, and tomatoes, increase the heat to high, and bring to a boil. Add the rice and stir to combine. Reduce the heat to low, cover, and simmer for 5 minutes, or until the rice is tender. Add the peas and cook for 1 minute to heat through.

3. Remove from the heat, remove the bay leaves, and season to taste with salt and pepper.

Serves 4

Quick Side Dish: Green Pea Hummus with Pita

In a food processor, combine 2 cups thawed, frozen green peas, ¼ cup fresh flat-leaf parsley leaves, 3 tablespoons tahini (sesame paste), 2 tablespoons fresh lemon juice, 1 teaspoon each ground cumin and olive oil, and 2 chopped garlic cloves. Puree until smooth. Season to taste with salt. Serve with pita wedges on the side.

4-Ingredient Pork Chops in White Wine–Tarragon Broth

PREP TIME: 5 to 10 minutes • COOK TIME: 7 to 8 minutes

1 tablespoon olive oil

4 boneless pork loin chops (about 5 ounces each)

Salt and freshly ground black pepper

1 tablespoon dried tarragon

½ cup dry white wine or vermouth

1 cup reduced-sodium chicken broth

Pork chops are the perfect choice for dinner in a flash. A quick sear in a hot pan creates a golden-brown caramelized crust. As the wine cooks off, it leaves behind a sweet, fruity flavor that pairs nicely with licorice-scented tarragon. The meal is simple and divine at the same time.

1. Heat the oil in a large skillet over medium-high heat. Season both sides of the pork chops with salt and pepper. Rub the tarragon into both sides of the pork. Add the chops to the hot pan and cook for 2 minutes per side, until golden brown. Add the wine and cook for 1 minute. Add the broth and cook for 2 to 3 minutes, until the pork is cooked through and still slightly pink in the center.

Serves 4

Morph to Another Meal ▶ ▶ ▶ Double the recipe for the pork portion, and use the extra pork in Pork Fried Rice with Cashews and Raisins (page 216), Black Bean–Mandarin Salad with Sliced Pork and Cilantro (page 109), or Alsatian Tart (page 44).

Quick Side Dish: Buttery Acorn Squash

Halve and seed two acorn squash and place in a shallow, microwave-safe dish, flesh side up. Put 1 to 2 teaspoons butter into each half and season the flesh with salt and freshly ground black pepper. Add about ½ inch of water to the bottom of the dish and cover the dish with plastic wrap. Microwave on high for 5 to 7 minutes, until the squash is tender.

Week 42

Steak with Tarragon Brandy and Parsley-Parmesan Risotto

Asiago-Risotto Cakes with Wild Mushroom Sauce
Quick Side Dish: Roasted Carrots and Fennel

Crispy Polenta-Crusted Chicken
Quick Side Dish: Ranch Pasta Spirals

PREP LIST

* Cook extra risotto for the cakes when you prepare the steak dish. (Refrigerate for up to 3 days or freeze for up to 3 months. Thaw overnight in the refrigerator or in the microwave on the defrost setting before using.)

* Form the risotto cakes. (Refrigerate for up to 3 days or freeze for up to 3 months before cooking. Thaw overnight in the refrigerator before cooking. I don't recommend thawing in the microwave.)

* Assemble the chicken dish. (Refrigerate for up to 3 days or freeze for up to 3 months before baking. Thaw overnight in the refrigerator before baking. I don't recommend thawing in the microwave.)

Steak with Tarragon Brandy and Parsley-Parmesan Risotto

PREP TIME: **10 to 15 minutes** • COOK TIME: **25 minutes**

2 tablespoons butter

2 cups short-grain rice (Arborio)

10 cups reduced-sodium beef broth, at room temperature or warmed in the microwave

½ cup grated Parmesan cheese

½ cup chopped fresh flat-leaf parsley

Salt, freshly ground black pepper, and cracked black pepper

1 tablespoon olive oil

4 beef sirloin steaks (about 5 ounces each)

½ cup brandy or ½ cup apple juice mixed with ¼ teaspoon orange or vanilla extract

2 teaspoons cornstarch

1 teaspoon dried tarragon

Here's a meal that's impressive enough for your most finicky guests! A few intensely flavored ingredients (brandy, tarragon, cracked black pepper) liven up tender sirloin steaks nestled in cheesy risotto.

1. Melt the butter in a large Dutch oven or saucepan over medium heat. Add the rice and cook, stirring frequently, for 2 minutes, or until translucent. Add the beef broth, ½ cup at a time, waiting until the liquid is absorbed before adding the next ½ cup. Continue cooking the risotto this way, stirring frequently, until tender, about 20 minutes, reserving 1 cup of beef broth for the steaks. Stir in the Parmesan cheese and cook for 1 minute, or until the cheese melts. Remove from the heat, stir in the parsley, and season to taste with salt and ground pepper.

2. Meanwhile, heat the oil in a large, deep skillet over medium-high heat. Season both sides of the steaks with salt and cracked black pepper. Add the steaks to the hot pan and cook for 2 minutes per side, or until golden brown. Add the brandy and cook for 1 minute.

3. In a small bowl, whisk together the remaining 1 cup beef broth, the cornstarch, and the tarragon. Add the mixture to the steaks and bring to a simmer. Cook for 2 minutes, or until the sauce thickens and the steaks are medium-rare (or longer for medium-well).

4. Serve all of the steaks with half of the risotto. (Reserve the remaining risotto for the risotto cakes.)

Serves 4 (with leftovers for the risotto cakes)

Morph to Another Meal ▶ ▶ ▶ Double the recipe for the steak portion, and use the extra steak in one of the recipes listed in the box on page 115.

Asiago-Risotto Cakes with Wild Mushroom Sauce

PREP TIME: 15 minutes • COOK TIME: 15 to 17 minutes

1 ounce dried porcini or shiitake mushrooms

2 cups reserved cooked risotto, chilled

½ cup grated Asiago cheese

1 large egg, lightly beaten

2 tablespoons olive oil

2 cups mixed sliced wild mushrooms, such as shiitake, cremini, or portobello

1 teaspoon dried thyme

1 cup reduced-sodium chicken or beef broth

2 teaspoons cornstarch

2 tablespoons chopped fresh flat-leaf parsley

Salt and freshly ground black pepper

Asiago cheese has a mildly spicier flavor than Parmesan and Romano cheese. It marries perfectly with the deep flavor of mixed wild mushrooms.

1. Soak the dried mushrooms in 1 cup hot water for 15 minutes, or until tender.

2. Meanwhile, to make the risotto cakes, in a large bowl, mix together the risotto, Asiago cheese, and egg. With wet hands, shape the mixture into 4 cakes, each about 1 inch thick.

3. Heat 1 tablespoon of the oil in a large skillet over medium-high heat. Add the cakes and cook for 3 to 5 minutes per side, until golden brown and cooked through.

4. Heat the remaining oil in a separate large skillet over medium-high heat. Add the fresh mushrooms and cook for 3 minutes, or until soft. Add the thyme and cook for 1 minute.

5. Strain the dried mushrooms through a fine sieve, reserving the liquid, and dice the mushrooms. Add to the skillet. Add the liquid and bring to a simmer.

6. In a small bowl, whisk together the broth and cornstarch. Add to the mushrooms and simmer for 2 to 3 minutes, until thickened. Stir in the parsley and season with salt and pepper.

7. Serve the risotto cakes with the mushroom sauce on top.

Serves 4

Quick Side Dish: Roasted Carrots and Fennel

In a large bowl, combine 3 cups baby carrots, 1 thinly sliced fennel bulb, 2 tablespoons olive oil, and 1 teaspoon dried thyme. Toss to coat. Transfer the vegetables to a large, rimmed baking sheet, in a single layer, and season with salt and freshly ground black pepper. Sprinkle the top of the vegetables with ⅓ cup grated Pecorino or Parmesan cheese. Roast at 425°F for 20 minutes, or until golden brown and tender.

Crispy Polenta-Crusted Chicken

PREP TIME: 10 to 15 minutes • COOK TIME: 25 to 30 minutes

Cooking spray

4 boneless skinless chicken breast halves (about 5 ounces each)

Salt and freshly ground black pepper

½ cup all-purpose flour

2 large eggs, lightly beaten

1 teaspoon mustard powder

1 cup yellow cornmeal

¼ cup seasoned dry bread crumbs

You know that sensational crunch you get from the crust of a good pizza-shop pizza? Those crispy flecks are yellow cornmeal granules that adhere to the bottom of the pizza dough while it bakes. I wanted that same sensation and crunch on my chicken, and here it is! Sometimes I spoon pre-pared tomato sauce over this chicken, so feel free to add your favorite variety if desired.

1. Preheat the oven to 400°F. Coat a large baking sheet with cooking spray.

2. Season both sides of the chicken breast halves with salt and pepper.

3. Put the flour and eggs in separate shallow dishes. Whisk the mustard powder into the eggs. In a third shallow dish, combine the cornmeal and bread crumbs. Put the chicken breast halves in the flour and turn to coat both sides. Shake off the excess. Transfer the chicken to the egg mixture and turn to coat both sides. Shake off the excess. Finally, transfer the chicken to the corn-meal mixture and turn to coat both sides. Shake off the excess.

4. Arrange the chicken on the prepared baking sheet and spray with cooking spray. Bake for 25 to 30 minutes, until the chicken is golden brown and cooked through and no longer pink on the inside.

Serves 4

Quick Side Dish: Ranch Pasta Spirals

Cook 8 ounces spiral pasta according to the package directions. Drain and transfer to a large bowl. Add ⅓ to ½ cup bottled ranch dressing, 1 diced red bell pepper, ¼ cup chopped scallions (green and white parts), and 2 tablespoons drained capers and toss to combine. Season to taste with salt and freshly ground black pepper.

Week 43

Shanghai Chicken Strips with
Spicy Citrus-Ginger Glaze
and Wasabi–Blue Cheese Dip
Quick Side Dish: Red Potatoes with Butter and Parsley

Southwest Egg Rolls with Chipotle
Ranch Dip

Spinach Fettuccine with Gorgonzola
Alfredo
Quick Side Dish: Broccoli with Sun-Dried Tomatoes

PREP LIST

* Cook extra chicken for the egg rolls when you prepare the chicken strips. (Refrigerate for up to 3 days or freeze for up to 3 months. Thaw overnight in the refrigerator or in the microwave on the defrost setting before using.)

* Cook the fettuccine for the Alfredo dish. (Refrigerate for up to 3 days.)

* Assemble the egg rolls. (Refrigerate for up to 3 days or freeze for up to 3 months; thaw overnight in the refrigerator before baking. I don't recommend thawing in the microwave.)

* Make the chipotle ranch dip for the egg rolls. (Refrigerate for up to 3 days.)

Shanghai Chicken Strips with Spicy Citrus-Ginger Glaze and Wasabi–Blue Cheese Dip

PREP TIME: 10 minutes • COOK TIME: 25 to 30 minutes

Cooking spray

6 boneless skinless chicken breast halves (about 5 ounces each)

Salt and freshly ground black pepper

1 cup orange marmalade

1 tablespoon reduced-sodium soy sauce

2 teaspoons finely grated peeled fresh ginger

½ teaspoon chile oil

1 cup sour cream

¼ cup crumbled blue cheese

1 teaspoon wasabi paste

Celery stalks (optional)

This is my funky spin-off of Buffalo wings. First, I use skinless chicken breasts instead of wings. Then, I smother them in a spicy, orange-infused ginger glaze before baking them. For dunking, I create a sweet blue cheese dip that's spiked with pungent wasabi heat!

1. Preheat the oven to 400°F. Coat a large, rimmed baking sheet with cooking spray.

2. Arrange the chicken in a single layer on the prepared baking sheet and season with salt and pepper.

3. In a small bowl, whisk together the marmalade, soy sauce, ginger, and chile oil. Brush the mixture all over the chicken.

4. Bake for 25 to 30 minutes, until the chicken is cooked through and no longer pink on the inside.

5. Meanwhile, to make the dip, in a small bowl, combine the sour cream, blue cheese, and wasabi paste. Mix well.

6. Slice 4 chicken breast halves into thin strips and serve with all of the dip and with celery stalks if desired. (Reserve the remaining 2 chicken breast halves for the egg rolls.)

Serves 4 (with leftovers for the egg rolls)

Quick Side Dish: Red Potatoes with Butter and Parsley

Place 2 pounds quartered small to medium red potatoes in a large saucepan. Add enough water to cover, set the pan over high heat, and bring to a boil. Boil for 8 to 10 minutes, until the potatoes are fork-tender. Drain and return the potatoes to the pan with 2 tablespoons butter and ¼ cup chopped fresh flat-leaf parsley. Toss to coat. Season to taste with salt and freshly ground black pepper.

Southwest Egg Rolls with Chipotle Ranch Dip

PREP TIME: **10 to 15 minutes** • COOK TIME: **15 to 20 minutes**

Cooking spray

2 teaspoons vegetable oil

2 reserved chicken breast halves, diced (or 2 cups diced cooked chicken)

1 15-ounce can black beans, rinsed and drained

1 cup drained canned corn or fresh or thawed frozen corn

2 pickled jalapeño chile peppers, minced

1 cup shredded Monterey Jack cheese or pepper Jack cheese

2 tablespoons chopped fresh cilantro

4 8- to 10-inch flour tortillas

1 cup prepared ranch dressing

1 to 2 teaspoons minced chipotle chiles in adobo sauce, to taste

You know the flavors of the Southwest truly appeal to me when I use them in an egg roll! Check out my creation: flour tortillas stuffed with chicken, black beans, corn, jalapeño chile peppers, cheese, and cilantro. After you roll them up, dunk them in ranch dressing that's spiked with smoky heat from chipotle chiles.

1. Preheat the oven to 375°F. Coat a large, rimmed baking sheet with cooking spray.

2. Heat the oil in a large skillet over medium-high heat. Add the chicken, beans, corn, and jalapeño and cook for 3 minutes, or until hot. Remove from the heat and fold in the cheese and cilantro.

3. Spoon some of the chicken mixture onto the center of each tortilla. Roll up the tortillas halfway, fold in the sides, and then finish rolling them up. Transfer the egg rolls to the prepared baking sheet and spray them with cooking spray. Bake for 12 to 15 minutes, until golden brown.

4. Meanwhile, to make the dip, in a small bowl, whisk together the ranch dressing and chipotle chiles.

5. Serve the egg rolls hot with the dip on the side.

Serves 4

Morph from Another Meal ▶ ▶ ▶ Instead of using chicken from the chicken strips, make this dish with 2 cups of reserved, diced cooked chicken, such as from one of the recipes listed in the box on page 169.

Spinach Fettuccine with Gorgonzola Alfredo

PREP TIME: **5 to 10 minutes** • COOK TIME: **10 to 15 minutes**

1 pound spinach
fettuccine

2 tablespoons butter

2 tablespoons
all-purpose flour

2 cups milk

1 cup crumbled
Gorgonzola cheese or
any blue-veined cheese

¼ cup chopped fresh
flat-leaf parsley

Salt and freshly ground
black pepper

2 cups diced beefsteak
or plum tomato

I love blue cheese, so of course I found a use for it in a cheese sauce for pasta. Plus, I adore the flavor and color of spinach fettuccine and it makes the ideal base for this creamy, tangy sauce.

1. Cook the fettuccine according to the package directions. Drain and set aside.

2. Meanwhile, melt the butter in a large saucepan over medium heat. Whisk in the flour and cook for 2 to 3 minutes, until the mixture is blended and smooth. Whisk in the milk and simmer for 3 minutes, or until the mixture thickens. Stir in the Gorgonzola and cook for 1 to 2 minutes until the cheese melts. Add the fettuccine and parsley and stir to coat. Season to taste with salt and pepper.

3. Transfer the fettuccine mixture to individual shallow bowls and top with the diced tomato.

Serves 4

Quick Side Dish: Broccoli with Sun-Dried Tomatoes

Heat 1 tablespoon olive oil in a large skillet over medium-high heat. Add 2 minced garlic cloves and cook for 1 minute. Add 1 pound broccoli florets, ½ cup drained, diced oil-packed sun-dried tomatoes, ¼ cup water, and 1 tablespoon balsamic vinegar. Cover and cook for 2 minutes. Uncover and cook for 2 more minutes, until the broccoli is crisp-tender and the liquid evaporates. Season to taste with salt and freshly ground black pepper.

Week 44

Roasted Salmon with Citrus Mustard Sauce
Quick Side Dish: Creamy Egg Noodles with Peas

Creamy Salmon Chowder
Quick Side Dish: Rosemary-Walnut Biscuits

Quick-Fix Pasta e Fagioli
Quick Side Dish: Romaine Salad with Glazed Pecans and Tarragon-Grapefruit Vinaigrette

PREP LIST

* Cook extra salmon for the chowder when you prepare the roasted salmon. (Refrigerate for up to 2 days or freeze for up to 3 months. Thaw overnight in the refrigerator or in the microwave on the defrost setting before using.)

* Chop the onion, carrot, and celery for the chowder. (Refrigerate for up to 3 days.)

* Cook the pasta for the pasta e fagioli. (Refrigerate for up to 3 days.)

* Chop the onion for the pasta e fagioli. (Refrigerate for up to 3 days.)

Roasted Salmon with Citrus Mustard Sauce

PREP TIME: **10 minutes** • COOK TIME: **12 to 15 minutes**

Cooking spray

6 salmon fillets (about 5 ounces each)

Salt and lemon pepper or freshly ground black pepper

¾ cup orange juice

2 tablespoons fresh lemon juice

2 teaspoons Dijon mustard

2 teaspoons cornstarch

2 teaspoons chopped fresh chives

Salmon seems to get paired with lemon frequently, and I definitely don't have a problem with that. But I like to jazz up my lemon mixture with orange juice and tangy Dijon mustard. I also add a little cornstarch so the sauce thickens as it cooks.

1. Preheat the oven to 400°F. Coat a large, rimmed baking sheet with cooking spray.

2. Season both sides of the salmon fillets with salt and lemon pepper and place on the prepared baking sheet. Roast for 12 to 15 minutes, until the fish pulls apart when tested with a fork.

3. Meanwhile, to make the sauce, in a small nonreactive saucepan, whisk together the orange juice, lemon juice, Dijon mustard, and cornstarch. Whisk until the cornstarch dissolves. Set the pan over medium heat and bring to a simmer. Simmer for 5 minutes, or until the sauce thickens. Remove from the heat and stir in the chives.

4. Serve 4 of the salmon fillets with all of the sauce spooned over the top. (Reserve the remaining 2 salmon fillets for the chowder.)

Serves 4 (with leftovers for the chowder)

Quick Side Dish: Creamy Egg Noodles with Peas

Cook 12 ounces egg noodles according to the package directions. Drain and transfer to a large bowl. While the noodles are still warm, stir in 1 cup sour cream, 1 cup thawed frozen green peas, and 1 tablespoon chopped fresh thyme. Toss to combine and season to taste with salt and freshly ground black pepper.

Creamy Salmon Chowder

PREP TIME: 15 minutes • COOK TIME: 25 to 30 minutes

4 strips bacon (regular or turkey bacon)

½ cup chopped onion

½ cup chopped carrot

2 celery stalks, chopped

1½ teaspoons Old Bay seasoning

4 small red potatoes, cubed

3 cups reduced-sodium chicken broth

3 tablespoons all-purpose flour

3 cups milk

2 reserved cooked salmon fillets (or 2 cups raw or cooked fish pieces, such as cod, haddock, or halibut)

1 11-ounce can corn, drained, or fresh or thawed frozen corn

2 tablespoons chopped fresh flat-leaf parsley

Salt and freshly ground black pepper

Turning extra seafood into chowder is an excellent way to use up leftovers—both the fish and the vegetables in your crisper drawer. This creamy version also contains smoky bacon, red potatoes, and corn, making it a New England–style dish. Top with chowder crackers, if you like.

1. In a large Dutch oven or pot over medium-high heat, cook the bacon until crisp. Remove the bacon from the pan, drain on paper towels, and crumble into small pieces. Set aside.

2. Drain all but 2 teaspoons of the bacon fat from the pot. Set back over medium-high heat and add the onion, carrot, and celery. Cook for 3 minutes, or until the vegetables are soft. Add the Old Bay seasoning and stir to coat. Add the potatoes and broth, increase the heat to high, and bring to a boil. Reduce the heat to medium and simmer for 6 to 8 minutes, until the potatoes are fork-tender.

3. Whisk the flour into the milk until blended. Add the milk mixture to the pot and return to a simmer. Add the fish and corn and simmer for 3 to 5 minutes, until the chowder thickens. Remove from the heat, stir in the parsley, and season to taste with salt and pepper.

4. Ladle the chowder into bowls and top with the bacon pieces.

Serves 4

Quick Side Dish: Rosemary-Walnut Biscuits

Open one 7.5-ounce can refrigerated buttermilk biscuits and knead into one ball. Knead in ¾ cup finely chopped walnuts and 1 tablespoon chopped fresh rosemary. Divide the dough into 10 pieces and shape each piece back into a biscuit (first roll into a ball and then press down). Transfer the biscuits to a large baking sheet and brush the surface of the biscuits with olive oil. Bake at 375°F for 15 minutes, or until golden brown.

Quick-Fix Pasta e Fagioli

PREP TIME: 10 to 15 minutes • COOK TIME: 14 to 16 minutes

8 ounces ditalini or small shell-shaped pasta

2 teaspoons olive oil

½ cup chopped onion

8 ounces ground beef

1 teaspoon dried oregano

1 15-ounce can white beans, rinsed and drained

1 15-ounce can pink beans, rinsed and drained

2 cups reduced-sodium beef broth

1 8-ounce can tomato sauce

1 to 2 teaspoons hot sauce, to taste

2 tablespoons chopped fresh basil

Salt and freshly ground black pepper

¼ cup grated Parmesan cheese

I used to love this dish as a kid. In fact, I still make it when I need a comforting meal fast. It's a hearty blend of beans and pasta, simmered in a mildly spicy tomato sauce. I also add a little ground beef to "beef it up." I like to serve this with additional hot sauce on the side for those who need it!

1. Cook the pasta according to package directions. Drain and set aside.

2. Meanwhile, heat the oil in a large saucepan over medium-high heat. Add the onion and cook for 3 minutes, or until soft. Add the beef and cook for 3 to 5 minutes, until browned, breaking up the meat as it cooks. Add the oregano and cook for 1 minute, or until the oregano is fragrant. Add both types of beans, the broth, tomato sauce, and hot sauce and bring to a simmer. Simmer for 5 minutes.

3. Stir in the pasta and cook for 2 minutes to heat through. Remove from the heat and stir in the basil. Season to taste with salt and pepper.

4. Ladle the mixture into bowls and top with Parmesan cheese.

Serves 4 to 6

Quick Side Dish: Romaine Salad with Glazed Pecans and Tarragon-Grapefruit Vinaigrette

Top 6 cups chopped romaine lettuce with 1 cup sugar-glazed pecans or toasted plain pecan halves and 2 diced McIntosh or Granny Smith apples. In a small bowl, whisk together ½ cup grapefruit juice, 2 tablespoons olive oil, 1 tablespoon chopped fresh tarragon, and 2 teaspoons Dijon mustard. Season to taste with salt and freshly ground black pepper. Drizzle the vinaigrette over the salad just before serving.

Week 45

Pan-Seared Scallops with Spinach-Mushroom Sauté
Quick Side Dish: White Bean and Broccoli Salad

Pasta Paella with Saffron Broth
Quick Dessert: Aunt Mary's Yogurt Pie

Pork Chops with Lemon-Scallion Tartar Sauce
Quick Side Dish: Chutney Rice

PREP LIST

* Cook extra scallops for the pasta paella when you prepare the pan-seared scallops. (Refrigerate for up to 2 days or freeze for up to 3 months. Thaw overnight in the refrigerator before using. I don't recommend thawing in the microwave.)

* Cook the penne for the pasta paella. (Refrigerate for up to 3 days.)

* Make the tartar sauce for the pork chops. (Refrigerate for up to 2 days.)

Pan-Seared Scallops with Spinach-Mushroom Sauté

PREP TIME: 10 to 15 minutes • COOK TIME: **11 to 13 minutes**

1 tablespoon olive oil

2 pounds sea scallops, patted dry

Salt and freshly ground black pepper

2 garlic cloves, minced

2 cups sliced shiitake mushrooms

1 teaspoon dried oregano

1 teaspoon dried thyme

1 10-ounce package baby spinach leaves

¼ cup vermouth or dry white wine or reduced-sodium chicken broth

Pan-searing scallops is a great way to cook them quickly to keep them succulent while creating a golden brown crust. I love pairing this delicately sweet seafood with wild shiitake mushrooms and tender baby spinach for a complete and satisfying meal.

1. Heat the oil in a large skillet over medium-high heat. Season both sides of the scallops with salt and pepper and add to the hot pan. Sear for 1 minute per side, or until golden brown. Remove the scallops from the pan and set aside.

2. To the same pan over medium-high heat, add the garlic. Cook for 1 minute. Add the mushrooms and cook for 3 to 5 minutes, until the mushrooms soften and release their juice. Add the oregano and thyme and cook for 1 minute, or until the herbs are fragrant. Add the spinach and vermouth and cook for 30 seconds, or until the spinach leaves just begin to wilt.

3. Return the scallops to pan, nestled into the spinach and mushrooms, and cook for 3 more minutes, or until the scallops are opaque and cooked through. Serve all but 1 cup of the scallops (4 to 6 scallops) with all of the mushrooms and spinach. (Reserve the remaining scallops for the pasta paella.)

Serves 4 (with leftovers for the pasta paella)

Quick Side Dish: White Bean and Broccoli Salad

In a large bowl, whisk together ⅓ cup plain yogurt, 2 tablespoons red wine vinegar, and 1 teaspoon chopped fresh thyme or rosemary. Add two 15-ounce cans (rinsed and drained) cannellini beans, 2 cups fresh broccoli florets, and ¼ cup minced red onion. Toss to coat. Season to taste with salt and freshly ground black pepper.

Pasta Paella with Saffron Broth

PREP TIME: 15 to 20 minutes • **COOK TIME: 9 to 12 minutes**

12 ounces penne pasta

1 tablespoon olive oil

½ cup chopped onion

3 garlic cloves, minced

1 teaspoon saffron threads

1 teaspoon ground turmeric

2 bay leaves

1 28-ounce can diced tomatoes

1½ cups reduced-sodium chicken broth

4 to 6 reserved cooked scallops, quartered

2 pounds littleneck clams (12 to 16), washed

8 ounces peeled and deveined fresh medium to large shrimp or thawed frozen medium to large shrimp

1 halibut fillet (about 5 ounces), cut into 2-inch pieces

Salt and freshly ground black pepper

¼ cup chopped fresh basil

Paella is a bountiful dish that's typically made with rice. Since I'm always trying to tweak things, I often make my paella with pasta. Just like rice, the pasta absorbs the intense flavors of garlic, saffron, and turmeric. In this dish, I add scallops, clams, shrimp, and halibut, but feel free to add your favorite seafood, such as cod or flounder. You can also add spicy sausage (such as chorizo or andouille) and cubed chicken. Have a party in the pan if you want!

1. Cook the pasta according to the package directions. Drain and set aside.

2. Meanwhile, heat the oil in a large skillet or paella pan over medium-high heat. Add the onion and garlic and cook for 3 minutes, or until soft. Add the saffron, turmeric, and bay leaves and cook for 1 minute, or until the spices are fragrant.

3. Add the tomatoes and broth and bring to a simmer. Add the scallops, clams, shrimp, and halibut, cover, and cook for 5 to 8 minutes, until the clam shells open (discard any that do not eventually open). Remove from the heat and remove the bay leaves. Season the sauce with salt and pepper.

3. Transfer the pasta to a serving platter. Pour the seafood mixture on top and garnish with the basil.

Serves 4

Quick Dessert: Aunt Mary's Yogurt Pie

In a medium bowl, whisk together 1 cup strawberry yogurt, 2 cups whipped cream or one 8-ounce container non-dairy whipped topping, and ½ cup seedless strawberry preserves. Mix well and spoon the mixture into one prepared graham cracker crust. Refrigerate until ready to serve. Garnish with fresh strawberries if desired.

Pork Chops with Lemon-Scallion Tartar Sauce

PREP TIME: **10 minutes** • COOK TIME: **6 minutes**

1 tablespoon olive oil

4 boneless pork loin chops (about 5 ounces each)

Salt and freshly ground black pepper

2 teaspoons salt-free all-purpose seasoning

½ cup mayonnaise

2 scallions, minced (green and white parts)

2 teaspoons fresh lemon juice

1 teaspoon finely grated lemon zest

Check out the preparation and cooking time for this dish! No doubt it'll be your go-to for crazy week-nights. The best part is, the seared pork chops are moist and delicious and the lemon-scallion tartar sauce puts them over the top. Nobody will believe it took just sixteen minutes.

1. Heat the oil in a large skillet over medium-high heat. Season both sides of the pork chops with salt, pepper, and the all-purpose seasoning. Add the pork to the hot pan and cook for 3 minutes per side, or until golden brown and tender and still slightly pink in the center.

2. Meanwhile, to make the tartar sauce, in a small bowl, whisk together the mayonnaise, scallions, lemon juice, and lemon zest. Season to taste with salt and pepper.

3. Serve the pork with the tartar sauce spooned over the top.

Serves 4

Morph to Another Meal ▶ ▶ ▶ Double the recipe for the pork portion, and use the extra pork in Pork Fried Rice with Cashews and Raisins (page 216), Black Bean–Mandarin Salad with Sliced Pork and Cilantro (page 109), or Alsatian Tart (page 44).

Quick Side Dish: Chutney Rice

In a medium saucepan, combine 2 cups reduced-sodium chicken broth, 2 cups quick-cooking rice, and ½ cup prepared mango chutney. Set the pan over high heat and bring to a boil. Cover, remove from heat, and let stand for 5 minutes. Stir in ¼ cup chopped fresh cilantro and season to taste with salt and freshly ground black pepper.

Week 46

Aunt Mary's Stuffed Eggplant
Quick Side Dish: Fennel-Mint Salad

Parmesan Chicken Burgers
Quick Side Dish: Spinach Salad with Bacon and Egg

Layered Enchilada with Roasted Garlic Béchamel
Quick Side Dish: Spaghetti Squash with Butter and Sage
Quick Dessert: Cappuccino Parfaits

PREP LIST

* Roast the garlic for the enchilada alongside the eggplant.
(Refrigerate for up to 3 days.)

* Assemble the stuffed eggplant. (Refrigerate for up to
2 days or freeze for up to 3 months. Thaw overnight in the
refrigerator before baking. I don't recommend thawing in
the microwave.)

* Sauté the mushrooms for the enchilada. (Refrigerate for
up to 3 days.)

* Assemble the enchilada. (Refrigerate for up to 3 days or
freeze for up to 3 months. Thaw overnight in the refrigerator before baking. I don't recommend thawing in the
microwave.)

* Form the burgers. (Refrigerate for up to 3 days or freeze
for up to 3 months. Thaw overnight in the refrigerator or in
the microwave on the defrost setting before cooking.)

Aunt Mary's Stuffed Eggplant

PREP TIME: 10 to 15 minutes • **COOK TIME: 30 to 35 minutes**

Cooking spray

2 medium eggplants

1 large egg, lightly beaten

½ cup plus 2 tablespoons grated Parmesan cheese

½ cup seasoned dry bread crumbs

2 teaspoons olive oil

1 teaspoon garlic powder

1 teaspoon onion powder

8 garlic cloves, peeled

My aunt Mary sent me this recipe, one my dad's mother used to make for the family regularly. I think your family, too, will love this flavorful dish, loaded with Parmesan cheese, crunchy bread crumbs, and savory seasonings.

1. Preheat the oven to 375°F. Coat a shallow roasting pan with cooking spray.

2. Halve the eggplants lengthwise and prick the flesh all over with a fork. Place the eggplant halves, flesh side up, in a microwave-safe baking dish and cover with plastic wrap. Microwave on high for 4 minutes, or until the flesh is tender.

3. When cool enough to handle, scoop out each eggplant half, leaving ¼ inch of flesh with the skin, being careful not to break the skin. Transfer the flesh to a large bowl and add the egg, ½ cup of the cheese, the bread crumbs, olive oil, garlic powder, and onion powder. Mix well and then stuff the mixture back into the eggplant shells. Sprinkle the remaining 2 tablespoons Parmesan cheese over the top.

4. Transfer the stuffed eggplant halves to the prepared roasting pan and bake for 25 to 30 minutes, until a light crust forms on top. Serve hot.

5. To roast the garlic for the enchilada, wrap the 8 peeled garlic cloves in foil and roast at 375°F for 20 minutes (alongside the stuffed eggplant), until the cloves are golden brown and tender.

Serves 4 (with roasted garlic for the enchilada)

Quick Side Dish: Fennel-Mint Salad

In a medium bowl, combine 3 cups sliced fennel, 2 tablespoons chopped fresh mint, 1 tablespoon sherry vinegar, 2 teaspoons olive oil, salt, and freshly ground black pepper.

Parmesan Chicken Burgers

PREP TIME: 10 minutes • COOK TIME: 7 minutes

Cooking spray

1 pound ground chicken

⅓ cup grated Parmesan cheese

⅓ cup seasoned dry bread crumbs

1 teaspoon dried minced garlic

1 teaspoon dried oregano

½ teaspoon salt

¼ teaspoon freshly ground black pepper

1 cup shredded mozzarella cheese

4 hamburger buns, toasted if desired

Sliced beefsteak tomato (optional)

Fresh basil leaves (optional)

Ground chicken is a great alternative to beef in terms of cutting calories and fat, but sometimes it can also mean a cut in flavor. Not true with these burgers; I jack them up with Parmesan cheese, seasonings, and garlic before nestling them under melted mozzarella cheese.

1. Coat a stovetop grill pan, griddle, or large skillet with cooking spray and heat over medium-high heat.

2. In a large bowl, combine the ground chicken, Parmesan cheese, bread crumbs, garlic, oregano, salt and pepper. Mix well and shape into 4 patties, each about 1 inch thick.

3. Cook the burgers for 3 minutes per side, or until cooked through. Top with the mozzarella cheese, tent with foil, and cook for 1 minute, or until the cheese melts. Serve on the hamburger buns with tomato slices and fresh basil leaves if desired.

Serves 4

Quick Side Dish: Spinach Salad with Bacon and Egg

Top 6 cups baby spinach leaves with ½ cup crumbled cooked bacon (regular or turkey bacon), ½ cup thinly sliced red onion, and 4 hard-cooked eggs that have been quartered. In a small bowl, whisk together 3 tablespoons white balsamic vinegar, 2 tablespoons olive oil, and 1 teaspoon Dijon mustard. Season to taste with salt and freshly ground black pepper. Drizzle the dressing over the salad just before serving.

Layered Enchilada with Roasted Garlic Béchamel

PREP TIME: 15 to 20 minutes • COOK TIME: 30 to 35 minutes

Cooking spray

1 tablespoon olive oil

2 cups sliced mushrooms (any combination and/or variety)

1 teaspoon dried oregano

1 15-ounce container ricotta cheese

¼ cup fresh goat cheese

1 cup diced roasted red bell peppers

1 10-ounce package frozen chopped spinach, thawed and well drained

2 tablespoons chopped fresh cilantro

2 tablespoons butter

2 tablespoons all-purpose flour

1 cup milk

8 reserved roasted garlic cloves, smashed with a fork

½ teaspoon onion powder

Enchiladas are typically rolled tortillas that are smothered with sauce and cheese. They also require a little bit of work to assemble. That's why I decided to make an enchilada that's similar to a lasagna, using layers of tortillas, a cheesy vegetable filling, and a garlicky cream sauce.

1. Preheat the oven to 400°F. Coat a shallow baking dish with cooking spray.

2. Heat the oil in a large skillet over medium-high heat. Add the mushrooms and cook for 5 minutes, or until they release their juice. Add the oregano and cook for 1 minute, or until the oregano is fragrant.

3. Transfer the mushrooms to a large bowl and add the ricotta, goat cheese, red peppers, spinach, and cilantro. Mix well and set aside.

4. To make the béchamel, melt the butter in a small saucepan over medium heat. Whisk in the flour and cook for 2 to 3 minutes, until the mixture is blended and smooth. Whisk in the milk, garlic, and onion powder and simmer for 3 minutes, or until the mixture thickens. Season to taste with salt and pepper.

Salt and freshly ground black pepper

8 8- to 10-inch flour tortillas, quartered

1 cup prepared salsa

5. Arrange half of the tortilla pieces in the bottom of the prepared baking dish, making an even layer and covering the entire surface. Top with all of the ricotta mixture. Top with the remaining tortilla pieces. Pour the béchamel on top. Bake for 20 minutes, or until the filling is bubbly and the top is golden brown. Serve with the salsa spooned over the top.

Serves 4

Quick Side Dish: Spaghetti Squash with Butter and Sage

Halve one spaghetti squash (2½ to 3 pounds) and remove the seeds. Place the halves flesh side up in a microwave-safe baking dish. Add ½ inch of water to the baking dish and cover with plastic wrap. Microwave on high for 5 minutes, or until the skin and flesh are soft when pressed. Using a fork, scrape and separate the strands of squash from the shell and transfer the flesh to a large bowl. In a small saucepan, combine 3 tablespoons butter and 3 tablespoons chopped fresh sage. Set the pan over medium heat and cook until the butter is melted and golden brown. Add the butter to the squash and toss to coat. Fold in ½ cup grated Parmesan cheese and season to taste with salt and freshly ground black pepper.

Quick Dessert: Cappuccino Parfaits

In a food processor, combine one 15-ounce container ricotta cheese, ⅓ cup sugar, and 2 teaspoons espresso powder. Puree until smooth. Spoon a few tablespoons of crushed biscotti, amaretti, or Stella D'oro cookies into 4 tall glasses. Top with a layer of ricotta mixture (use only half of the ricotta mixture). Top with another layer of cookies and the rest of the ricotta. Place a whole cookie on top of each and serve.

12 Fast Meals with Canned Beans

Rich in fiber, vitamins, and minerals, canned beans are an excellent pantry staple. Because they're precooked, there's no need for the long soaking and cooking times typical of dried beans. Beans not only fortify a dish, they add a wonderful "meatiness," making any meal more substantial and satisfying. Canned beans are often high in sodium, so feel free to rinse the drained beans in water before using them in the following recipes, and go easy on additional salt.

1. Chickpea Salad with Tomato, Avocado, Scallions, and Goat Cheese: In a bowl, combine canned chickpeas (drained), chopped tomato and scallions, diced avocado, sliced black olives, crumbled fresh goat cheese, ground cumin, white wine vinegar, and extra-virgin olive oil.

2. Smoky Hummus Pita Pockets with Grilled Mushrooms and Fontina: To make hummus, combine canned chickpeas (drained), tahini (sesame paste), lemon juice, minced garlic, liquid smoke, and chicken broth in a blender, and blend until the mixture forms a thick paste (adding more chicken broth if necessary). Grill portobello mushroom caps on a grill pan or griddle until tender. Top the mushroom caps with sliced Fontina cheese and cook for 1 minute, or until the cheese melts. Spread the hummus into pita pockets, and fill the pockets with the sliced grilled mushrooms and fresh watercress or baby spinach leaves.

3. Navy Bean Salad with Bacon and Tomato-Basil Vinaigrette: To make the vinaigrette, combine diced tomatoes (fresh or canned and undrained), fresh basil leaves, chopped garlic, red wine vinegar, and extra-virgin olive oil in a blender. Puree until smooth. In a bowl, combine canned navy beans (drained), diced cooked bacon, chopped white onion, and chopped fresh flat-leaf parsley. Add the vinaigrette and toss to combine.

4. Tuscan White Beans with Olives and Sage: In a bowl, combine canned white beans (drained), a variety of pitted olives, chopped fresh sage, fresh lemon juice, and extra-virgin olive oil.

5. Hot and Sour Tomato Soup with White Beans: In a stockpot, combine tomato juice, canned pureed tomatoes, canned white or cannellini beans (drained), fresh lemon juice, hot sauce, and a little sugar. Set the pan over medium heat, and simmer for 10 minutes. Stir in chopped fresh basil before serving.

6. Mixed Bean and Mandarin Salad with Mint: In a bowl, combine a variety of canned beans (drained), canned mandarin oranges (drained), chopped fresh mint, and ground cumin.

7. Chickpeas and Spinach in Spicy Curry Broth: In a large saucepan, combine canned chickpeas (drained), baby spinach leaves, chicken broth, 2 bay leaves, and hot curry powder (or regular curry powder and hot sauce). Set the pan over medium heat, and simmer for 10 minutes. Remove the bay leaves and stir in chopped fresh cilantro before serving.

8. Vegetarian Chili with Couscous:
In a stockpot, combine a variety of canned beans (drained), canned tomato puree, vegetable broth, minced jalapeño pepper, chili powder, ground cumin, and some couscous. Set the pan over high heat and bring to a boil. Reduce the heat to low and simmer for 5 minutes, or until the couscous is tender (adding more broth if necessary). Stir in chopped fresh flat-leaf parsley before serving. Serve with a dollop of sour cream and a sprinkling of shredded cheddar cheese on top if desired.

9. Black Bean–Corn Salad with Chipotle Chiles: In a bowl, combine canned black beans (drained), canned or thawed frozen corn, diced pimentos, minced chipotle chiles in adobo sauce, chopped fresh cilantro, and fresh lime juice.

10. Creamy White Bean Pesto: In a blender, combine canned white or cannellini beans (drained), fresh basil leaves, chopped garlic, fresh lemon juice, extra-virgin olive oil, grated Parmesan cheese, and toasted pine nuts. Puree until smooth, adding chicken or vegetable broth if needed to make a thinner consistency. Serve over grilled chicken or fish or with crackers, toasted pita triangles, or crostini.

11. Italian Three Bean Salad: In a bowl, combine canned white beans (drained), canned kidney or red beans (drained), canned or frozen and thawed green beans (drained), diced white onion, red wine vinegar, and a little good-quality olive oil. Toss to combine. For the best results, refrigerate for at least 1 hour before serving (and up to 24 hours).

12. Moroccan Couscous with Beans and Raisins: In a small saucepan, bring $1\frac{1}{4}$ cups water or chicken broth to a boil. Add 1 cup couscous, 1 cup canned black or pink beans (drained), $\frac{1}{3}$ cup dark or golden raisins, and 1 teaspoon ground cumin. Remove from the heat, cover, and let stand for 5 minutes. Fluff with a fork and season to taste with salt and black pepper.

Week 47

Raspberry-Dijon Baked Ham
Quick Side Dish: Rice Dressing with Cranberries and Pecans

"Ham Sandwich" Penne with Pumpernickel-Parmesan Bread Crumbs
Quick Side Dish: Mixed Greens with Grapefruit and Cashews

Five-Cheese Pizza with Sun-Dried Tomatoes
Quick Dessert: Ginger-Berry Compote over Angel Food Cake

PREP LIST

* Cook extra ham for the penne dish when you prepare the baked ham. (Refrigerate for up to 3 days or freeze for up to 3 months. Thaw overnight in the refrigerator or in the microwave on the defrost setting before using.)

* Cook the penne for the pasta dish. (Refrigerate for up to 3 days.)

* Assemble the pizza. (Refrigerate for up to 3 days or freeze for up to 3 months. No need to thaw before baking, just add 5 to10 minutes to the cooking time.)

Raspberry-Dijon Baked Ham

PREP TIME: **5 to 10 minutes** • COOK TIME: **1 hour**

Cooking spray

1 4-pound boneless baked ham

½ cup seedless raspberry preserves

¼ cup orange juice

2 tablespoons Dijon mustard

Ham is a true crowd-pleaser and the leftovers make fabulous future meals. I love pairing salty ham with sweet ingredients like raspberry preserves and orange juice. The flavors complement each other perfectly, and because there are so few of them, this dish is a snap to put together.

1. Preheat the oven to 350ºF. Coat a shallow roasting pan with cooking spray. Put the ham in the pan.

2. In a small bowl, whisk together the preserves, orange juice, and Dijon mustard. Brush the mixture all over the ham.

3. Bake for 1 hour, or until a meat thermometer inserted into the center reads 140ºF (approximately 15 minutes per pound). Let stand for 5 minutes before slicing into ¼-inch-thick slices.

4. Serve three quarters of the ham for this meal. (Reserve the remaining ham for the penne.)

Serves 4 to 6 (with leftovers for the penne dish)

Quick Side Dish: Rice Dressing with Cranberries and Pecans

Melt 1 tablespoon butter in a medium saucepan over medium-high heat. Add ½ cup chopped onion and 2 minced garlic cloves and cook for 2 minutes. Add 2 cups quick-cooking white rice and cook for 3 to 5 minutes, until the rice is golden brown. Add 2 cups reduced-sodium chicken broth and bring to a boil. Cover, remove from the heat, and let stand for 5 minutes. Stir in ½ cup each toasted pecan pieces and dried cranberries and ¼ cup chopped fresh flat-leaf parsley. Season to taste with salt and freshly ground black pepper.

"Ham Sandwich" Penne with Pumpernickel-Parmesan Bread Crumbs

PREP TIME: **10 to 15 minutes** • COOK TIME: **15 minutes**

1 pound penne pasta

2 slices dark pumpernickel bread, toasted and cooled

2 tablespoons grated Parmesan cheese

1½ cups heavy cream

2 tablespoons honey mustard

2 cups diced reserved baked ham

1 cup cubed Swiss cheese

2 cups baby spinach leaves

Salt and freshly ground black pepper

Imagine all the fantastic ingredients you nestle into a mile-high sandwich (ham, cheese, greens, mustard), only tossed with tender pasta instead. What a delicious way to utilize leftover ham!

1. Cook the pasta according to the package directions. Drain and set aside.

2. Meanwhile, to make the bread crumbs, put the toasted pumpernickel bread and Parmesan cheese in a plastic bag and seal the bag. Using a heavy rolling pin or the bottom of a heavy skillet, crush the bread into fine crumbs. Set aside.

3. In a large saucepan, whisk together the cream and honey mustard. Set the pan over medium-high heat and bring to a simmer. Add the cooked pasta, ham, Swiss cheese, and spinach leaves and cook for 1 minute to heat through (the cheese will just begin to melt). Remove from the heat and season to taste with salt and pepper.

4. Spoon the pasta mixture into individual shallow bowls and top with the pumpernickel crumb mixture.

Serves 4

Quick Side Dish: Mixed Greens with Grapefruit and Cashews

Top 6 cups mixed greens with 1 to 2 cups ruby red grapefruit segments and ½ cup dry-roasted, salted cashews. In a small bowl, whisk together 2 tablespoons each red wine vinegar and olive oil and 1 tablespoon each grainy Dijon mustard and honey. Season to taste with salt and freshly ground black pepper. Drizzle the dressing over the salad just before serving.

Five-Cheese Pizza with Sun-Dried Tomatoes

PREP TIME: 10 to 15 minutes • **COOK TIME: 12 to 15 minutes**

1 pound fresh or thawed frozen pizza or bread dough

1 8-ounce container ricotta cheese

1 cup shredded mozzarella cheese

½ cup shredded provolone cheese

½ cup crumbled blue cheese

¼ cup grated Parmesan cheese

½ cup thinly sliced drained oil-packed sun-dried tomatoes

1 teaspoon dried oregano

As if three or four aren't enough! Nope, I couldn't stop with the old standbys (mozzarella, ricotta, Parmesan). The addition of provolone and blue cheese—and sweet sun-dried tomatoes—makes this a pizza your family will be talking about for eons! Plus, because it's fast, you have more time to spend with them!

1. Preheat the oven to 450°F.

2. Roll the dough out on a large baking sheet into a 12 x 15-inch rectangle. Using a spatula, spread the ricotta all over the dough, to within 1 inch of the edges. Top the ricotta with the mozzarella, provolone, blue, and Parmesan cheeses. Top with the sun-dried tomatoes and then sprinkle the oregano over everything. Bake for 12 to 15 minutes, until the crust is golden brown and the cheese is bubbly.

Serves 4 to 6

Quick Dessert: Ginger-Berry Compote over Angel Food Cake

In a medium saucepan, combine one 8-ounce bag frozen raspberries; one 8-ounce bag frozen blueberries; 2 tablespoons confectioners' sugar; 1 teaspoon finely grated lemon, lime, or orange zest; and 1 teaspoon minced candied ginger. Set the pan over medium heat and bring to a simmer. Simmer for 5 to 7 minutes, until the fruits soften. Cool slightly before serving over slices of store-bought angel food cake. The compote may be served warm, at room temperature, or chilled. Also, you can make the compote in advance and store it in the refrigerator for up to 3 days. Pull it out and reheat it before serving or take it to a party as a hostess gift.

Week 48

Turkey Tenderloin with Hearts of Palm Stuffing
Quick Side Dish: Potato Gratin with Smoked Fontina

Garlic-Ginger Salmon with Tangerine Sauce

Roast Beef Ravioli with Creamy Blue Cheese Sauce
Quick Dessert: Jen's Vanilla-Ricotta Dollop

PREP LIST

* Make the stuffing for the turkey. (Refrigerate for up to 3 days.)

* Assemble the optional side dish gratin for the turkey. (Refrigerate for up to 2 days before baking.)

* Make the garlic-ginger topping for the salmon. (Refrigerate for up to 3 days.)

* Form the ravioli. (Refrigerate for up to 2 days or freeze for up to 3 months. Thaw overnight in the refrigerator before cooking. I don't recommend thawing in the microwave.)

Turkey Tenderloin with Hearts of Palm Stuffing

PREP TIME: 20 to 25 minutes • COOK TIME: **30 to 40 minutes**

Cooking spray

2 cups cubed white or whole-wheat bread, preferably slightly stale

1 14.5-ounce can hearts of palm, drained and chopped

⅓ cup sweetened dried cranberries

2 tablespoons grated Parmesan cheese

2 tablespoons chopped fresh flat-leaf parsley

1 teaspoon dried thyme

Salt and freshly ground black pepper

½ cup reduced-sodium chicken broth, or more as necessary

1 turkey tenderloin (1 to 1¼ pounds)

Turkey tenderloin is moist and mild so I like to jazz up the flavor with unusual ingredient pairings. This stuffing blends salty hearts of palm with sweet cranberries, nutty Parmesan cheese, and fresh parsley.

1. Preheat the oven to 400°F. Coat a shallow roasting pan with cooking spray.

2. In a large bowl, mix the bread, hearts of palm, cranberries, Parmesan cheese, parsley, thyme, ½ teaspoon salt, and ¼ teaspoon black pepper. Add the chicken broth and mix until the stuffing sticks together, adding more broth as necessary.

3. Cut the turkey tenderloin almost in half crosswise, as if butterflying it. Open up the turkey and spoon the stuffing on half. Close it and secure with wooden picks.

4. Transfer the turkey to the prepared pan and season the top with salt and pepper. Roast for 30 to 40 minutes, until an instant-read thermometer inserted into the thickest part of the meat as well as the stuffing reaches 160°F. Let stand for 5 minutes before slicing crosswise into 2-inch-thick slices.

Serves 4

Quick Side Dish: Potato Gratin with Smoked Fontina

Place 2 pounds thinly sliced medium Yukon Gold potatoes in a large saucepan. Add enough water to cover, set the pan over high heat, and bring to a boil. Boil for 8 minutes, or until the potatoes are fork-tender. Arrange one third of the potato slices in the bottom of a buttered shallow baking dish. Season with salt and freshly ground black pepper and top with ⅔ cup shredded smoked Fontina or smoked mozzarella cheese. Top with another third of the potatoes, salt and pepper, and ⅔ cup shredded cheese. Top with the remaining potatoes and ⅔ cup cheese. In a small bowl, whisk together 1½ cups milk, 1 teaspoon dried thyme, and ⅛ teaspoon ground nutmeg. Pour the mixture over the potatoes. Cover with foil and bake at 375°F for 25 minutes. Uncover and bake for 25 to 30 more minutes, until the filling is bubbly and the top is golden brown. Let stand for 10 minutes before slicing.

Garlic-Ginger Salmon with Tangerine Sauce

PREP TIME: **10 to 15 minutes** • COOK TIME: **12 to 15 minutes**

Cooking spray

4 salmon fillets (about 5 ounces each)

Salt and freshly ground black pepper

1 tablespoon olive oil

1 tablespoon chopped fresh cilantro

1 tablespoon minced peeled fresh ginger

2 garlic cloves, minced

1 cup tangerine juice

2 teaspoons cornstarch

1 teaspoon dried coriander

1 tablespoon butter

Light and refreshing, this dish is the perfect reprieve from the filling meals and decadent desserts typical of holiday gatherings. You'll love this unique flavor combination of tangerine juice, garlic, ginger, and coriander. It's an excellent sauce for salmon, as well as for other types of seafood and shellfish. You can certainly substitute orange juice for the tangerine and get a similar result.

1. Preheat the oven to 400°F. Coat a shallow roasting pan with cooking spray.

2. Season the salmon fillets all over with salt and pepper and place in the prepared pan.

3. With a mortar and pestle or in a food processor, combine the oil, cilantro, ginger, and garlic. Mash or process until blended. Spread the mixture all over the top of the salmon.

4. Roast the salmon for 12 to 15 minutes, until the fish pulls apart when tested with a fork.

5. Meanwhile, in a small saucepan, whisk together the tangerine juice, cornstarch, and coriander. Set the pan over medium heat and bring to a simmer. Add the butter and simmer for 3 to 5 minutes, until the sauce thickens.

6. Drizzle the sauce over the salmon just before serving.

Serves 4

Roast Beef Ravioli with Creamy Blue Cheese Sauce

PREP TIME: 15 to 20 minutes • COOK TIME: 8 to 10 minutes

4 ounces thinly sliced roast beef, diced

½ cup ricotta cheese

½ teaspoon dried sage

48 wonton wrappers

2 tablespoons butter

2 tablespoons all-purpose flour

2½ cups milk

⅔ cup crumbled blue cheese

Salt and freshly ground black pepper

¼ cup chopped fresh flat-leaf parsley

Sounds crazy, but this is so delicious! Roast beef is mixed with ricotta cheese and floral sage and then stuffed inside wonton wrappers, making ravioli. The ravioli become tender as they simmer in a blue cheese–spiked cream sauce. This is a fabulous make-ahead dish to have on hand make for guests during the holidays.

1. In a medium bowl, combine the roast beef, ricotta, and sage. Mix well to combine.

2. Arrange 24 wonton wrappers on a flat surface. Spoon a small amount (about 1 heaping teaspoon) of roast beef mixture onto each wonton. Top each with a second wonton. Using wet fingers (dip fingers in water), wet the edges of the bottom wontons and press the tops into the bottoms, sealing the edges.

3. Melt the butter in a large saucepan over medium heat. Whisk in the flour and cook for 2 to 3 minutes, until the mixture is blended and smooth. Whisk in the milk and bring to a simmer. Add the blue cheese and simmer for 1 minute. Gently add the ravioli and simmer for 5 minutes, or until the wontons are tender.

4. Remove from the heat and season to taste with salt and pepper. Transfer the ravioli and sauce to shallow bowls and top with the parsley.

Serves 4

Quick Dessert: Jen's Vanilla-Ricotta Dollop

In a medium bowl, whisk together 1 cup ricotta cheese, 2 tablespoons confectioners' sugar, and 1 teaspoon vanilla extract. Spoon the mixture over fresh strawberry and kiwi slices or slices of pound cake or angel food cake.

Week 49

Chicken Melts with Creamy Spinach
Pesto
Quick Side Dish: Orzo with Basil and Scallions

5-Ingredient Flank Steak with
Sun-Dried Tomato–Caper Tapenade
Quick Side Dish: Roasted Curried Cauliflower

Pork Stew with Poblano Chiles
and Hominy
Quick Side Dish: Parmesan-Buttermilk Biscuits

PREP LIST

* Make the pesto. (Refrigerate for up to 3 days or freeze for up to 3 months. Thaw overnight in the refrigerator or in the microwave on the defrost setting before serving.)

* Make the tapenade for the steak. (Refrigerate for up to 2 days or freeze for up to 3 months. Thaw overnight in the refrigerator before serving.)

* Chop the onion and poblano chile for the stew. (Refrigerate for up to 3 days.)

* Prepare the stew. (Refrigerate for 3 days or freeze for up to 3 months.)

Chicken Melts with Creamy Spinach Pesto

PREP TIME: 10 to 15 minutes • COOK TIME: 25 to 30 minutes

Cooking spray

4 boneless skinless chicken breast halves (about 5 ounces each)

Salt and freshly ground black pepper

2 plum tomatoes, sliced into ¼-inch-thick rounds

8 ounces mozzarella cheese, sliced into ¼-inch-thick slices

3 tablespoons pine nuts

1 10-ounce package frozen chopped spinach, thawed and well drained

⅓ cup mayonnaise

3 garlic cloves, chopped

3 tablespoons grated Parmesan cheese

Golden-brown chicken, nestled under caramelized tomato and melted mozzarella cheese and then topped with a vibrant, garlicky, nutty spinach pesto. Need I say more?

1. Preheat the oven to 400°F. Coat a rimmed baking sheet with cooking spray.

2. Season both sides of the chicken breast halves with salt and pepper and place on the prepared baking sheet. Roast for 20 minutes.

3. Remove the chicken from the oven and top with the tomato and mozzarella cheese slices. Return to the oven and bake for 5 to 10 more minutes, until the chicken is cooked through and no longer pink on the inside and the cheese melts.

4. Meanwhile, to make the pesto, put the pine nuts in a small dry skillet and set the pan over medium heat. Cook, shaking the pan frequently, for 3 minutes, or until golden brown. Transfer the nuts to a blender and add the spinach, mayonnaise, garlic, and Parmesan cheese. Process until smooth. Season to taste with salt and pepper.

5. Serve the chicken with the pesto spooned over the top.

Serves 4

Quick Side Dish: Orzo with Basil and Scallions

Cook 8 ounces orzo pasta according to the package directions. Drain and transfer to a large bowl. Stir in ½ cup chopped scallions (green and white parts), ¼ cup chopped fresh basil, 2 tablespoons olive oil, and 1 tablespoon red wine vinegar. Toss to combine and season to taste with salt and freshly ground black pepper.

5-Ingredient Flank Steak with Sun-Dried Tomato–Caper Tapenade

PREP TIME: **10 to 15 minutes** • COOK TIME: **10 minutes**

Cooking spray

1 flank or skirt steak (1 to 1¼ pounds)

Salt and freshly ground black pepper

Dried minced onion

1 cup drained oil-packed sun-dried tomatoes, with 1 tablespoon oil from the jar

2 tablespoons drained capers

2 tablespoons chopped fresh basil

I've said it before and I'll say it again, when you use only a few ingredients, those ingredients need to be powerful. In this case, perfectly grilled steak is topped with a stellar chunky puree of sweet sun-dried tomatoes, tangy capers, and fresh basil.

1. Coat a stovetop grill pan or griddle with cooking spray and heat over medium-high heat. Season both sides of the steak with salt, pepper, and minced onion. Grill the steak for 5 minutes per side for medium-rare. Remove the steak from the pan and let stand for 5 minutes.

2. Meanwhile, to make the tapenade, in a blender, combine the sun-dried tomatoes, their oil, and the capers. Process until almost smooth. Transfer to a bowl and stir in the basil. Season to taste with salt and pepper.

3. Slice the steak crosswise, against the grain, into thin strips. Top the steak with the tapenade just before serving.

Serves 4

Morph to Another Meal ▶ ▶ ▶ Double the recipe for the steak, and use the extra steak in one of the recipes listed in the box on page 115.

Quick Side Dish: Roasted Curried Cauliflower

In a large bowl, whisk together 3 tablespoons olive oil and 2 teaspoons curry powder. Add 6 cups cauliflower florets (from 1 head) and toss to coat. Transfer the cauliflower to a large, rimmed baking sheet, in a single layer, and season with salt and freshly ground black pepper. Roast at 450°F for 20 minutes, or until golden brown.

Pork Stew with Poblano Chiles and Hominy

PREP TIME: 10 to 15 minutes • COOK TIME: 15 minutes

1 tablespoon
vegetable oil

½ cup chopped onion

1 medium or two small
poblano chiles, seeded
and diced

2 garlic cloves, minced

1 pork loin (about
1 pound), cut into 2-inch
cubes

1 teaspoon chili powder

1 teaspoon ground
cumin

1 12-ounce beer or
1½ cups reduced-sodium
chicken broth

1 14-ounce can diced
tomatoes

1 15-ounce can hominy,
drained

¼ cup chopped fresh
cilantro

Salt and freshly ground
black pepper

This stew dishes up sweet heat: sweet from sugary, soft hominy (also called pozole; it's whole corn without the outer hull) and hot from poblano chiles. Both are simmered in a Southwest-style stew that features chili powder, cumin, tomatoes, garlic, and cilantro.

1. Heat the oil in a large saucepan over medium-high heat. Add the onion, poblano chile, and garlic and cook for 3 minutes, or until soft. Add the pork and cook for 5 minutes, or until golden brown on all sides. Add the chili powder and cumin and cook for about 1 minute, until the spices are fragrant.

2. Add the beer and cook for 1 minute. Add the tomatoes and hominy and bring to a simmer. Simmer for 5 minutes, or until the pork is cooked through and still slightly pink in the center.

3. Remove from the heat and stir in the cilantro. Season to taste with salt and pepper.

Serves 4

Quick Side Dish: Parmesan-Buttermilk Biscuits

Separate one 7.5-ounce can refrigerated buttermilk biscuits into 10 biscuits. Brush each biscuit with olive oil and then roll in grated Parmesan cheese. Transfer the biscuits to a baking sheet and bake at 375°F for 15 minutes, or until golden brown.

Week 50

Tandoori Chicken with Flash-Fried Chickpeas
Quick Side Dish: Baked Stuffed Tomatoes with Pesto

Chicken Pilaf with Porcini Mushrooms and Almonds
Quick Side Dish: Roasted Brussels Sprouts

Thai Sea Bass with Coconut Cream Sauce

PREP LIST

* Cook extra chicken for the pilaf when you prepare the tandoori chicken. (Refrigerate for up to 3 days or freeze for up to 3 months. Thaw overnight in the refrigerator or in the microwave on the defrost setting before using.)

* Combine the lime juice mixture and/or sauce ingredients for the fish. (Refrigerate for up to 3 days.)

* Make the coconut cream sauce for the fish. (Refrigerate for up to 3 days. Reheat in a small saucepan over medium heat.)

Tandoori Chicken with Flash-Fried Chickpeas

PREP TIME: 10 to 15 minutes • COOK TIME: 25 to 30 minutes

Cooking spray

6 boneless skinless chicken breast halves (about 5 ounces each)

Salt and freshly ground black pepper

½ cup plain yogurt

2 tablespoons fresh lemon juice

1 tablespoon minced peeled fresh ginger

2 garlic cloves, minced

1 tablespoon chili powder

2 teaspoons curry powder or garam masala

1½ teaspoons ground cumin

1 tablespoon olive oil

1 15-ounce can chickpeas, rinsed and drained

1 tablespoon chopped fresh cilantro

This fresh, creamy sauce and marinade for chicken blends lemon, ginger, garlic, chili powder, curry powder, and cumin. A powerful experience on your palate. Quickly searing the chickpeas in a little oil before serving brings out their natural nuttiness.

1. Preheat the oven to 400°F. Coat a shallow roasting pan with cooking spray.

2. Season the chicken breast halves all over with salt and pepper and place in the prepared pan. In a medium bowl, whisk together the yogurt, lemon juice, ginger, garlic, chili powder, curry powder, and cumin. Spoon the yogurt mixture all over the chicken in the pan.

3. Roast for 25 to 30 minutes, until the chicken is cooked through and no longer pink on the inside.

4. Meanwhile, heat the oil in a large skillet over medium-high heat. Add the chickpeas and cook, stirring frequently, for 3 to 5 minutes, until golden brown. Remove from the heat and stir in the cilantro. Season to taste with salt and pepper.

5. Serve 4 of the chicken breast halves with all of the chickpeas. (Reserve the remaining 2 chicken breast halves for the pilaf.)

Serves 4 (with leftovers for the pilaf)

Quick Side Dish: Baked Stuffed Tomatoes with Pesto

Core 4 beefsteak tomatoes and scoop out the inner flesh, leaving a ½-inch outer shell. In a medium bowl, combine ⅓ cup seasoned dry bread crumbs, ¼ cup prepared basil pesto, and 2 teaspoons olive oil. Mix well and spoon the mixture into the hollowed tomatoes. Transfer the tomatoes to a shallow baking dish and sprinkle the tops with grated Parmesan cheese. Bake at 375°F for 20 minutes, or until the tomatoes are tender and the tops are golden brown.

Chicken Pilaf with Porcini Mushrooms and Almonds

PREP TIME: 15 minutes • **COOK TIME: 24 to 28 minutes**

1 ounce dried porcini mushrooms

1 cup hot water

2 teaspoons olive oil

½ cup slivered almonds

½ cup chopped scallions (green and white parts)

3 garlic cloves, minced

1 cup basmati or regular white rice (not quick-cooking)

2 teaspoons chopped fresh thyme, or 1 teaspoon dried

1¼ cups reduced-sodium chicken broth

2 reserved cooked chicken breast halves, cubed (or 2 cups cubed cooked chicken)

¼ cup chopped fresh flat-leaf parsley

Salt and freshly ground black pepper

Take rice pilaf out of the side-dish category and make it a main dish! The deep, wild flavor of dried porcini mushrooms is fantastic with the fresh scallions, toasted almonds, and fresh herbs in this recipe.

1. Soak the mushrooms in the hot water for 10 minutes. Drain the mushrooms through a fine sieve, reserving the liquid.

2. Meanwhile, heat the oil in a large, deep skillet over medium-high heat. Add the almonds, scallions, and garlic and cook for 3 minutes, or until the almonds are golden brown. Add the rice and thyme and cook, stirring frequently, for 3 to 5 minutes, until the rice is golden brown.

3. Chop the mushrooms into small pieces and add to the pan with the mushroom liquid and chicken broth. Bring to a simmer. Reduce the heat to low, cover, and cook for 15 minutes.

4. Stir in the chicken and cook for 3 to 5 more minutes, until the rice is tender. Remove from the heat and stir in the parsley. Season to taste with salt and pepper.

Serves 4

Quick Side Dish: Roasted Brussels Sprouts

In a large bowl, combine 2 to 3 cups small fresh or frozen Brussels sprouts and ¼ cup diced shallots. In a small bowl, whisk together 3 tablespoons olive oil, 2 tablespoons balsamic vinegar, 1 tablespoon honey, and ½ teaspoon each salt and freshly ground black pepper. Add the mixture to the Brussels sprouts and toss to coat. Transfer to a rimmed baking sheet and roast at 400°F for 15 to 20 minutes, until golden brown and tender.

Thai Sea Bass with Coconut Cream Sauce

PREP TIME: 10 to 15 minutes • **COOK TIME: 12 to 15 minutes**

Cooking spray

4 sea bass fillets (about 5 ounces each)

Salt and freshly ground black pepper

3 tablespoons fresh lime juice

1 tablespoon fish sauce

1 tablespoon peanut oil

2 small Thai chiles, jalapeños, or serranos, minced

1 teaspoon peeled and grated fresh ginger

1 teaspoon sugar

1 cup unsweetened coconut milk

2 tablespoons peanut butter

1 tablespoon reduced-sodium soy sauce

½ teaspoon finely grated lime zest

2 tablespoons chopped fresh cilantro

There are two levels of flavor going on here. The first starts with the fish, lime juice, fish sauce, Thai chiles, and ginger. Once the fish cooks, it meets the second level, a sauce of coconut milk, peanut butter, soy sauce, and cilantro. Truly amazing.

1. Preheat the oven to 400°F. Coat a shallow roasting pan with cooking spray.

2. Season both sides of the fish fillets with salt and pepper and place in the prepared pan. In a small bowl, whisk together the lime juice, fish sauce, peanut oil, chiles, ginger, and sugar. Spoon the mixture over the fish.

3. Roast the fish for 12 to 15 minutes, until it pulls apart when tested with a fork.

4. Meanwhile, to make the sauce, in a small saucepan, whisk together the coconut milk, peanut butter, soy sauce, and lime zest. Set the pan over medium heat and bring to a simmer. Simmer for 3 to 5 minutes, until the sauce thickens. Remove from the heat and stir in the cilantro. Season to taste with salt and pepper.

5. Spoon the sauce over the fish just before serving.

Serves 4

Week 51

Marsala, Brown Sugar, and Pineapple Glazed Ham
Quick Side Dish: Whipped Sweet Potatoes
Quick Dessert: Chocolate-Pecan Meringue Cookies

Creamy Linguine with Ham, Goat Cheese, and Basil
Quick Side Dish: Orange-Jicama Salad with Dried Cherries

Panzanella and Shrimp Salad
Quick Dessert: Fluffy Chocolate Dip

PREP LIST

* Cook extra ham for the pasta dish when you prepare the glazed ham. (Refrigerate for up to 3 days or freeze for up to 3 months. Thaw overnight in the refrigerator or in the microwave on the defrost setting before using.)

* Cook the linguine for the pasta dish. (Refrigerate for up to 3 days.)

* Chop the shallots for the pasta dish. (Refrigerate for up to 3 days.)

* Cut the baguette and vegetables for the salad. (Store the bread in an airtight container at room temperature for up to 3 days; refrigerate the vegetables for up to 3 days.)

* Make the optional cookies for dessert. (Store in an airtight container at room temperature for up to 5 days.)

Marsala, Brown Sugar, and Pineapple Glazed Ham

PREP TIME: **15 minutes** • COOK TIME: **1½ hours**

Cooking spray

1 cup Marsala or Madeira wine (or 1 cup pineapple or orange juice with ½ teaspoon vanilla extract)

½ cup pineapple juice

¼ cup light brown sugar

1 tablespoon ground coriander

¼ teaspoon ground allspice

1 bone-in fully cooked ham (5 to 7 pounds), with thin fat layer

15 to 20 1-inch pieces cubed pineapple

15 to 20 whole cloves

Ham is perfect for holiday meals not just because it's traditional but because it stretches into future meals with ease. The sweet taste of Marsala wine and brown sugar balance out the tartness of pineapple juice and coriander and the peppery quality of allspice. I like to serve this ham with steamed green vegetables, such as spinach, broccoli, asparagus, or green beans. Adding toasted nuts to the greens makes it a celebration on the plate. Although the recipe starts with a fully-cooked ham to cut down on baking time, this dish still requires 1½ hours of cooking. That's the perfect amount of time to finish decorating or wrapping those gifts.

1. Preheat the oven to 350°F. Coat a roasting pan with cooking spray.

2. In a small nonreactive saucepan, combine the Marsala, pineapple juice, brown sugar, coriander, and allspice. Set the pan over medium-high heat and bring to a boil. Reduce the heat to medium and simmer for 5 minutes, or until the sauce reduces to ⅔ cup. Remove from the heat.

3. Trim the rind and much of the fat from the ham if necessary, leaving a ⅛- to ¼-inch layer of fat. Using a sharp knife, score the outside of the ham in a diamond pattern, in 2-inch intervals. Put a piece of pineapple in the center of each diamond and secure with a wooden pick. Stick 1 clove in the center of each pineapple piece.

4. Put the ham in the prepared pan and brush ¼ cup of the Marsala mixture over the ham. Bake for 1½ hours, basting every 30 minutes with the remaining Marsala mixture, until a thermometer inserted into the center of the ham reads 140°F. Let stand for 10 minutes before slicing into thin pieces. (Reserve 2 cups diced ham for the pasta dish.)

Serves 4 to 6 (with leftovers for the pasta dish)

Quick Side Dish: Whipped Sweet Potatoes

Put 2 pounds peeled sweet potatoes cut into 2-inch cubes in a large saucepan. Add enough water to cover, set the pan over high heat, and bring to a boil. Boil for 8 minutes, or until the potatoes are fork-tender. Drain and transfer the potatoes to a food processor or stand mixer. While the potatoes are still hot, add ⅓ cup orange juice, 3 tablespoons butter, and ¼ teaspoon ground cinnamon. Process or mix until blended and smooth. Season to taste with salt and freshly ground black pepper.

Quick Dessert: Chocolate-Pecan Meringue Cookies

In a large bowl with an electric mixer, beat 4 large egg whites with ¼ teaspoon each cream of tartar, salt, and vanilla extract until soft peaks form. Gradually beat in 1 cup sugar and beat for 2 to 3 minutes until stiff peaks form. Fold in ½ cup mini semisweet chocolate morsels and ⅓ cup chopped pecans. Drop the meringue mixture by rounded tablespoons, about 1 inch apart, onto parchment-lined baking sheets. Bake at 225°F for 2 hours, or until the cookies are dry. Cool completely on the baking sheets.

Creamy Linguine with Ham, Goat Cheese, and Basil

PREP TIME: 15 minutes • COOK TIME: 15 minutes

1 pound linguine

1 tablespoon olive oil

½ cup chopped shallots

2 garlic cloves, minced

2 cups reserved diced cooked ham or 2 cups diced baked ham

1 teaspoon dried oregano

1 teaspoon dried thyme

2 cups milk

2 tablespoons all-purpose flour

1 cup crumbled goat cheese (regular or herbed)

¼ cup chopped fresh basil

Salt and freshly ground black pepper

Use leftover ham to create an entirely new meal for friends and family that is just right for the holiday season. Linguine is tossed with a sensational goat cheese–spiked cream sauce, shallots, garlic, ham, and herbs for a dish that is as beautiful as it is tasty.

1. Cook the linguine according to the package directions. Drain and set aside.

2. Meanwhile, heat the oil in a large saucepan over medium-high heat. Add the shallots and garlic and cook for 3 minutes, or until soft. Add the ham, oregano, and thyme and cook, stirring frequently, for 2 minutes, or until the ham is golden brown and the herbs are fragrant.

3. In a small bowl, whisk together the milk and flour until the flour dissolves. Add the mixture to the pan and bring to a simmer. Simmer for 3 minutes, or until the sauce thickens. Add the linguine and cook for 1 minute to heat through.

4. Remove from the heat and fold in the goat cheese and basil. Season to taste with salt and pepper.

Serves 4

Quick Side Dish: Orange-Jicama Salad with Dried Cherries

In a large bowl, combine 3 peeled and sliced navel oranges, 1 peeled and sliced jicama (matchsticks would be perfect), and ½ cup each thinly sliced red onion and dried cherries. In a small bowl, whisk together ¼ cup cherry preserves, 3 tablespoons fresh lemon juice, 2 tablespoons olive oil, and 2 teaspoons Dijon mustard. Add the dressing to the orange-jicama mixture and toss to coat. Season to taste with salt and freshly ground black pepper.

Panzanella and Shrimp Salad

PREP TIME: **15 to 20 minutes** • COOK TIME: **5 minutes**

1 sourdough baguette, stale, cut into 2-inch cubes (about 6 cups)

1 pound cooked, peeled, deveined medium shrimp

2 cups diced tomato

½ cup minced red onion

½ cup halved pimiento-stuffed olives

1 celery stalk, chopped

¼ cup chopped fresh flat-leaf parsley

2 tablespoons drained capers

2 tablespoons grated Parmesan cheese

½ cup reduced-sodium chicken broth

¼ cup olive oil

2 tablespoons red wine vinegar

2 teaspoons Dijon mustard

Salt and freshly ground black pepper

This is a fabulous dish during the holidays because it's light and flavorful. Let's face it, we all crave a lighter meal during the more gluttonous months! Panzanella is a salad made from stale bread that often includes tomatoes, onion, olive oil, and vinegar. As a "leftovers" salad, it fits into my kitchen strategy perfectly! I also add lots of other flavorful ingredients, including shrimp, olives, capers, and Parmesan cheese.

Note: For the best results, let the salad stand for at least 30 minutes (and up to 12 hours) before serving.

1. Preheat the oven to 400°F.

2. Arrange the bread cubes on a large, rimmed baking sheet in a single layer (use 2 baking sheets if necessary to prevent crowding). Bake for 5 minutes, or until golden brown.

3. Transfer the toasted bread cubes to a large bowl and add the shrimp, tomato, onion, olives, celery, parsley, capers, and Parmesan cheese. Toss to combine.

4. In a small bowl, whisk together the chicken broth, oil, vinegar, and Dijon mustard. Pour the dressing over the bread mixture and toss to combine. Season to taste with salt and pepper.

Serves 4

Quick Dessert: Fluffy Chocolate Dip

In a microwave-safe bowl, combine ½ cup unsweetened cocoa powder, ⅓ cup milk, and 1 tablespoon butter. Cover and microwave on high for 1 minute. Whisk in 2 tablespoons rum. Fold in 1½ cups whipped cream or non-dairy whipped topping. Serve with sugar cookies and fresh fruit (such as banana slices, pear wedges, fresh cherries, and strawberries) for dunking.

Week 52

OPTIONAL HOLIDAY WEEK

Steak with Cognac Cream and Baked
Brie Tartlets with Pear Relish

BBQ Steak Kebabs over Avocado
Puree

Smoked Turkey Cigars with Grated
Onion and Swiss

Quick Side Dish: Creamy Maple-Mustard Dip
Quick Dessert: Lemon-Poached Pears with Fudge Sauce

PREP LIST

* Cook extra steak for the kebabs when you prepare the steak with Cognac cream. (Refrigerate for up to 3 days or freeze for up to 3 months. Thaw overnight in the refrigerator or in the microwave on the defrost setting before using.)

* Assemble the Brie tartlets. (Refrigerate for up to 2 days before baking.)

* Chop the onion for the kebabs. (Refrigerate for up to 3 days.)

* Make the avocado puree for the kebabs. (Refrigerate for up to 24 hours.)

* Assemble the turkey cigars. (Refrigerate for up to 2 days.)

Steak with Cognac Cream and Baked Brie Tartlets with Pear Relish

PREP TIME: 10 to 15 minutes • COOK TIME: 12 to 15 minutes

1 9-inch refrigerated pie crust, divided into 12 equal pieces

8 ounces Brie cheese

Cooking spray

8 sirloin steaks (about 5 ounces each)

Salt and freshly ground black pepper

1 cup heavy cream

2 tablespoons Cognac or apricot nectar

2 ripe pears, cored and diced

2 tablespoons minced white or red onion

2 tablespoons currants

1 tablespoon sherry vinegar

Elegant enough for a New Year's celebration, these grilled steaks topped with a Cognac-spiked cream sauce are phenomenally good and a breeze to prepare. On the side, I nestle creamy Brie cheese in little tart shells before baking and topping with a sweet and tangy blend of pears, onion, currants, and sherry vinegar. If you plan to use this as a holiday meal, wow the crowd and add a mixed green salad topped with pomegranate seeds and your favorite vinaigrette.

1. Preheat the oven to 375°F.

2. Shape each pie crust piece into a ball and press into a 12-cup mini muffin pan, allowing crust to come up the sides about halfway. Spoon an equal amount of Brie into each tart shell. Bake for 12 to 15 minutes, until the Brie melts and the crust is golden brown.

3. Meanwhile, coat a stovetop grill pan or griddle with cooking spray and heat over medium-high heat. Season the steaks with salt and pepper. Grill for 5 minutes per side for medium-rare. Remove from the pan and let stand for 5 minutes.

4. Combine the cream and Cognac in a small saucepan and set over medium heat. Bring to a simmer, reduce the heat to low, and simmer for 5 minutes.

5. To make the relish, in a medium bowl, mix the pears, onion, currants, and sherry vinegar. Season with salt and pepper.

6. Spoon the relish over the tartlets just before serving. Serve 4 of the steaks with all of the cream sauce spooned over the tops and all of the tartlets. (Reserve the remaining 4 steaks for the kebabs.)

Serves 4 (with leftovers for the kebabs)

BBQ Steak Kebabs over Avocado Puree

PREP TIME: 15 minutes • COOK TIME: 5 minutes

2 tablespoons grainy mustard

1 tablespoon reduced-sodium soy sauce

2 teaspoons Worcestershire sauce

2 teaspoons olive oil

1 teaspoon garlic powder

1 teaspoon dried thyme

4 reserved cooked steaks, cut into 2-inch cubes (or 4 cups cooked cubed steak or chicken)

Cooking spray

1 red onion, cut into 2-inch pieces

4 ears corn, cut into 2-inch wheels

2 ripe avocados, pitted, peeled, and coarsely chopped

2 garlic cloves, chopped

1 tablespoon fresh lime juice

1 tablespoon fresh cilantro leaves

Salt and freshly ground black pepper

Perfect for casual entertaining, this meal meets the needs of most diners, even those with New Year's resolutions. The coating for these kebabs is super-tasty thanks to a blend of grainy mustard, soy sauce, Worcestershire sauce, garlic, and thyme. I love to put wheels of corn on the cob on kebabs because they add flavor and color and are something you don't see every day. The puree is a colorful and savory combination of ripe avocado, garlic, lime juice, and cilantro. It also makes an excellent dip for corn chips!

Note: When using wooden skewers, soak them in water for at least 20 minutes prior to using to prevent burning.

1. In a medium bowl, whisk together the mustard, soy sauce, Worcestershire sauce, oil, garlic powder, and thyme. Add the steak and toss to coat.

2. Coat a stovetop grill pan or griddle with cooking spray and heat over medium-high heat.

3. Skewer alternating pieces of steak, onion, and corn onto metal or wooden skewers. Grill the skewers, turning frequently, for 5 minutes, or until the corn is tender.

4. Meanwhile, in a food processor, combine the avocado, garlic, lime juice, and cilantro. Puree until smooth. Season to taste with salt and pepper.

5. Spoon the puree onto plates and top with the skewers.

Serves 4

Smoked Turkey Cigars with Grated Onion and Swiss

PREP TIME: 15 minutes • **COOK TIME: 12 to 15 minutes**

Cooking spray

1 sheet frozen puff pastry, thawed according to the package directions

1½ tablespoons Dijon or honey mustard

1¼ cups shredded Swiss cheese

12 ounces sliced smoked turkey

1 small white onion, grated

1 teaspoon dried oregano

The ideal family-friendly, finger-licking dish for guests! I call these "cigars" because I cram my favorite sandwich fillings into puff pastry before rolling it up and baking. These are fun to make and dunk. I typically serve the cigars with ranch dip, honey mustard, or the dip below.

1. Preheat the oven to 375°F. Coat a large, rimmed baking sheet with cooking spray.

2. Unfold the pastry on a flat surface and roll into a 16 x 12-inch rectangle. Spread the mustard all over the pastry, to within ½ inch of the edges. Top the mustard with the cheese, turkey slices, and grated onion. Sprinkle the oregano over everything.

3. Starting at one of the long sides, roll up the pastry like a jelly roll, making a log. Using a sharp knife, cut the log crosswise into 4 equal pieces or "cigars." Transfer the cigars to the prepared baking sheet and bake for 12 to 15 minutes, until golden brown.

Serves 4

Quick Side Dish: Creamy Maple-Mustard Dip

In a medium bowl, whisk together 1 cup sour cream and 2 tablespoons each Dijon mustard and 100% pure maple syrup. Serve alongside the cigars with crudités (baby carrots, celery and zucchini sticks, cherry tomatoes, and sliced cucumber) for dunking.

Quick Dessert: Lemon-Poached Pears with Fudge Sauce

In a large saucepan, combine 3 cups water, 1 cup sugar, and 2 tablespoons fresh lemon juice. Set the pan over high heat and bring to a boil. Add 4 to 6 small peeled ripe pears (with stems), reduce the heat to low, cover, and simmer for 20 minutes, or until the pears are fork-tender. Serve with warmed fudge sauce spooned over the top and garnish with fresh mint leaves if desired.

Acknowledgments

I would like to thank some very important people for helping with the evolution of this project, key players who turned my heartfelt recipes into a fabulous cookbook.

Bonnie Tandy Leblang, my agent, manager, and friend, thank you for your tireless effort and management of my career (and oftentimes my life!). You should know—just hearing your voice adds a sparkle to my day. I'm lucky to know you.

Debra Goldstein, my literary agent, thank you for enduring the paperwork marathon required to put this deal together. As usual, you kept your cool (and sanity) every step of the way.

Rica Allannic, my editor, thank you for enhancing my book and for using a voice that was so close to mine; the editing process was a complete breeze. Ashley Phillips, thanks for running a fine-tooth comb through the manuscript and making it easy for readers ro create fantastic meals without fretting.

Ben Fink, thank you for the beautiful photography seen on the cover and on the inside pages of this mouth-watering book. Thanks, too, to his assistant, Jeff Kavanagh, and studio manager, Jeffrey Jones. Alberto Machuca, thanks for the remarkable job you do with hair and makeup (is that really me?). To Jamie Kimm, the amazing food stylist who turned my recipes into works of art, and his assistant, Sara Abrams—I can almost smell the food. And also to Barb Fritz, for finding the perfect props to showcase the finished dishes, and her assistant, Vanessa Boer.

Food Network, thanks for helping me get my message out to busy people searching for delicious weeknight-meal solutions. It's my goal and complete pleasure to provide family-friendly meals that folks can feel good about serving to those they care about.

Jen Montgomery, thanks for being my buddy and for your always-inspirational words of wisdom during our "treadmill chats."

Amy Taheri, Shelley Teall, Lorna Nirenberg, and Sabrina Carlson, thanks for listening to my stories (and sharing yours!) every day at the elementary school while we wait for our kids.

Darrin, my husband, thank you for another year of patience and recipe testing! And, most important, thank you Kyle and Luke, my awesome little boys. Thanks for tasting, testing, and helping to make my recipes fun to create and yummy to eat. Your presence in my kitchen, and my world, makes my life complete.

Index